FINDING

HOPE AND

strength

IN GOD

Endorsements

Amilliah Kenya's words are much like pebbles in your shoe, you can try to dismiss them but sooner or later you will have to deal with them. *Finding Hope and Strength in God* does not center on you but points directly at the character of God, and that will inspire you to rise above yourself and fix your eyes on His presence.

Jason Lawson
Youth Pastor and Author of *The Potter's Hands: A 366-Day Journey to Knowing God*
www.jasonlawsonbooks.com

In her book *Finding Hope and Strength in God*, author Amilliah Kenya underscores an important Biblical truth. "Sometimes, God calls you to something that is greater than yourself." While powerful, this concept is challenging to implement without guidance on how to do so. This beautifully crafted devotional offers Christians practical ways to step forward in their walk of faith.

From topical, daily reflections, to Scriptures that illuminate each passage, readers will be encouraged to dig deeper into the Word, find their God-inspired purpose, and grow their relationship with Jesus. The short but thoughtful entries offer a momentary pause to begin each day with a fresh breath of God's promises.

Chris Corradino
Author of *Finding Joy In Every Season: 60 Men's Devotionals for Winning with Jesus*
www.pentopraise.com

With a voice of tenderness and compassion that's infused with strength, Amilliah Kenya invites you to embark on a year-long journey to a deeper knowledge of the Lord. As you walk through *Finding Hope and Strength in God*, you will find comfort when you're grieving, godly guidance when you're questioning, conviction when it is required, and wise counsel every single day of your year. Tackling some of our most intimate and challenging questions, Amilliah thoroughly covers a new topic each month. She dives deep and speaks to the heart on such vital issues as trusting our Good Shepherd and partnering with the Lord to see Him turn what the enemy meant for evil for our good. Slow down for just a few moments each day and give yourself the gift of this devotional pathway to an enhanced walk with your Lord.

Ami Looper
Author of *Constant Companion: Your Practical Path to Real Interaction with God*
www.amiloper.com

FINDING HOPE AND *strength* IN GOD

AMILLIAH KENYA

Ambassador International
GREENVILLE, SOUTH CAROLINA & BELFAST, NORTHERN IRELAND

www.ambassador-international.com

Finding Hope and Strength in God

ISBN: 978-1-64960-418-7, paperback
eISBN: 978-1-64960-466-8

Cover Design by Hannah Linder Designs
Interior Typesetting by Dentelle Design
Edited by Avrie Roberts

Scripture taken from the King James Version of the Bible. Public Domain.

AMBASSADOR INTERNATIONAL
Emerald House
411 University Ridge, Suite B14
Greenville, SC 29601
United States
www.ambassador-international.com

AMBASSADOR BOOKS
The Mount
2 Woodstock Link
Belfast, BT6 8DD
Northern Ireland, United Kingdom
www.ambassadormedia.co.uk

The colophon is a trademark of Ambassador, a Christian publishing company.

Dedicated to my family—The Charles Kenya Family

God has taken us through a long, exciting and adventurous journey together. These are the lessons He taught while holding our hands.

In times of fear and uncertainty, we learned the secret of finding our hope and strength in Him. Not one of His good promises has failed to come through.

God is good. He is faithful. God is dependable.

Table of Contents

January
TRUSTING THE CHARACTER AND
SOVEREIGNTY OF GOD 9

February
TRUSTING THE SHEPHERD 41

March
FINDING HOPE AND STRENGTH IN THE
CHARACTER OF GOD 71

April
CHRISTIAN GROWTH 103

May
GROWING IN SPIRITUAL MATURITY 134

June
CHRISTIAN RELIABILITY 166

July
FINDING SPIRITUAL STRENGTH IN
THE PROMISES OF GOD 197

August
TRUSTING THE CHARACTER OF GOD 229

September
GROWING IN SPIRITUAL WARFARE 261

October
GROWING WITH GOD. 292

November
LIVING BY THE PRINCIPLES OF GOD'S WORD. 324

December
LIVING A FULFILLED CHRISTIAN LIFE
OF FRUITFULNESS. 355

January
TRUSTING THE CHARACTER AND SOVEREIGNTY OF GOD

God is not thrusting you into a new year to walk and endure alone. He has gone ahead of you, and nothing will happen that He does not already know because He cares for you. Trust His character as you start this new year.

GOD IS HERE FOR YOU.

As we begin this new year, our excitement will soon be replaced with reality as we are confronted with different aspects of life. Among the many concerns and questions our hearts must face include:

- What kind of year will this be?
- How different will it be from the past one?
- What must we do to succeed in this new year?
- How will we deal with challenges, and even enemies?

Regardless of the memories of the previous year, it is good to know God has good plans for all who put their trust in Him. He is not wringing His hands and wondering how to take care of you. He is your Shepherd. He will be with you every moment and every day of this new year. He will take care of you, and He will meet your needs.

God understands how challenges of life may make you weak and weary. He will hold your hand and lead you to quiet waters that will refresh your spirit and replenish your strength. In moments of fear and despair, not only will He restore your soul, but He will also be present to comfort and walk with you.

God will take care of your enemies. He will surround you with His presence. Meditate on Psalm 23.

> The Lord is my shepherd; I shall not want.
>
> He maketh me to lie down in green pastures: he leadeth me beside the still waters.
>
> He restoreth my soul: he leadeth me in the paths of righteousness for his name's sake.
>
> Yea, though I walk through the valley of the shadow of death, I will fear no evil: for thou art with me; thy rod and thy staff they comfort me.
>
> Thou preparest a table before me in the presence of mine enemies: thou anointest my head with oil; my cup runneth over.
>
> Surely goodness and mercy shall follow me all the days of my life: and I will dwell in the house of the LORD FOR EVER.

READ PSALM 37:3–7.

GOD IS IN CHARGE.

God has power to direct your life in unfathomable ways this year. "Let not your heart be troubled" (John 14:1) as you look to the days ahead with anticipation. Life begins with God, and He has power over all His creation.

In Genesis 1:1–4, God introduces us to Himself and the power of His hands, saying, "In the beginning God created the heaven and the earth. And the earth was without form, and void; and darkness was upon the face of the deep. And the Spirit of God moved upon the face of the waters. And God said, Let there be light: and there was light. And God saw the light, that it was good: and God divided the light from the darkness."

You are not born to fate. You are created in the image of God. God takes care of His creation. Regardless of the means through which you came to the world, know that God is your Creator, and He only creates what is good and needed. God has power to turn things around for your good. The God Who turned the formless world filled with darkness to have light and to give life still has the same thrill for all His creation.

It is God's desire that:

- You have an honorable position.
- You go through life blessed and fulfilled.
- Your specific needs are met.
- Your physical and emotional needs are met.

Trust this powerful God to speak peace and hope in hopeless situations. Allow Him to mold you into a vessel of honor that will display His glory and splendor. Let God's Spirit be at work in your life this year. When God is in charge, life is never the same.

READ 1 PETER 2:9–10.

January 3

BE IN TOUCH WITH GOD.

When our vehicles and other important, useful equipment malfunction, we take them to their specific dealers or manufacturers for repair and maintenance. For man, our Creator is God. He understands how He made us. He knows what constitutes us and what we can handle in life.

As the new year begins, purpose to be in touch with God. Life becomes unbearable when you are far away from Him. You cannot handle all your stresses and troubles without His help.

Look at His timely counsel from Psalm 32:8-10 as you seek ways in which to succeed and prosper in this new year: "I will instruct thee and teach thee in the way which thou shalt go: I will guide thee with mine eye. Be ye not as the horse, or as the mule, which have no understanding: whose mouth must be held in with bit and bridle, lest they come near unto thee. Many sorrows shall be to the wicked: but he that trusteth in the Lord, mercy shall compass him about."

Take time and listen to God this year. Purpose to seek His counsel and wait on His direction. Share your heart with Him as you would do with a close friend. Allow Him to govern every aspect of your life. Life is different when God is by your side. Fear will not characterize your life when He speaks to your daily situations. Be in touch with God and live a fulfilled life this year.

READ EPHESIANS 2:10.

GOD CARES FOR YOU.

There is a sad notion that grips the hearts of God's children, especially in moments of difficulty where we feel that God does not care. In those tough times, we see God as a distant Being Who does not hold our best interests at heart. This is contrary to the plans and the intentions God has for His beloved children.

Right from creation, God has man's best interests at heart. He made us special from all creation. He made you in His own image and breathed in your nostrils the breath of life before you became a living soul (Genesis 2:7).

Not only did God want man alive, but He also made plans for him to go through life comfortably, according to Genesis 2:8–9, which says, "And the LORD God planted a garden eastward in Eden; and there he put the man whom he had formed. And out of the ground made the LORD God to grow every tree that is pleasant to the sight, and good for food; the tree of life also in the midst of the garden, and the tree of knowledge of good and evil."

God has not stopped caring for His children. God watches over you. He meets your needs and places you in favorable places where your life can be nourished and fulfilled. God is not leaving you to chance for the rest of this year. Do not face this year alone without God. Get close to Him and enjoy His care.

READ PSALM 115:10–18.

GOD HAS GIVEN US AN EXAMPLE TO FOLLOW.

God created the world and everything therein in one week. On the first day, He created and separated light from darkness. Second, He created the skies that divided the waters above and below the heavens. God further gathered the waters in one place on the third day and allowed seas, dry land, grass, and plants to appear. The sun, moon, and stars were created on the fourth day. In the days that followed, God made all living creatures. He finalized His work by creating man in His own image. God saw that everything He had created was very good. On the seventh day, God ended His work and rested.

Here are a few things we can learn and copy from God to help us go through life with purpose this year:

- Plan out your work and designate realistic time for it. This will help you manage your time wisely. As you can see, God is a God of order. His work in creation was not haphazard.

- Work intentionally and with purpose. Keep your focus and complete your work in the required time. This will give you a sense of purpose while taking away the sense of being overwhelmed by the work.

- Rest. God stepped back to look at what He had created and saw it was very good. He rested as He was filled with a sense of fulfillment. Learn from God and rest. To run all day, all week, and all year without catching your breath is to endanger your life and to subject yourself to stress and burnout.

- Map out what you want to accomplish in the days, weeks, and months ahead. Pace yourself and work diligently.

READ ECCLESIASTES 3:1–8.

OVERCOME FEAR; LOVE GOD.

Many of us are afraid of God. Even though we seek and desire a close relationship with Him, we often find ourselves distant and not sure how to relate to Him. It is easy to pursue and maintain close relationships with friends and family members, save God. I believe this is attributed to the strongly held notion that God is a Disciplinarian Who does not put up with any nonsense.

Unfortunately, this deep fear denies us the confidence with which to face life, resulting from a close relationship with God, our Father. God desires a close walk with you. Look at His quest for you in 2 Corinthians 6:16: "And what agreement hath the temple of God with idols? for ye are the temple of the living God; as God hath said, I will dwell in them, and walk in them; and I will be their God, and they shall be my people."

In Ezekiel 37:27 and Jeremiah 32:38, God reveals that His intention is to have His dwelling in you, to be with you, and to be your God.

You cannot face the eventualities of life on your own. Overcome your fear and take intentional steps toward God this year. Cultivate a relationship of talking to Him through prayer and listening responsively through His Word. Relate to Him at a personal level out of deep love and obedience and enjoy a vibrant and meaningful relationship with Him. Life will take on new meaning. Your daily encounters with Him will be memorable and enriching.

READ PSALM 125:1–2.

LEARN FROM YESTERDAY AND GROW.

God had great intentions for Adam and Eve as He created and placed them in the wonderful Garden of Eden. This place of rare beauty was filled with pleasant trees, animals, rivers, gold, and precious stones for God's children to enjoy. However, Satan, the deceiver, stepped onto the scene, beguiled Eve, and caused them to disobey God.

For the first time, Adam and Eve realized they were naked. They sewed fig leaves to cover their nakedness, but they could no longer face God with confidence or look forward to walking and fellowshipping with Him as before. They hid from God (see Genesis 3).

All of us make mistakes. Nevertheless, when we learn from our mistakes, we can proceed with confidence to not only avoid similar mistakes but to grow and flourish in life.

Take a moment to reflect on the past year. What were your strengths? What mistakes did you make and how did they affect your relationship with God? Do not run or hide from God. Confess your faults and seek His forgiveness. Do not dwell on the wrongs of last year.

Get back into fellowship with Him and learn and grow from past mistakes. God is not done with you; otherwise, He would not be seeking you out—you have a place in God. "If we confess our sins, he is faithful and just to forgive us our sins, and to cleanse us from all unrighteousness" (1 John 1:9).

READ JEREMIAH 18:1–6.

BECOME A KEEPER.

You belong to your family by God's Sovereign and Divine choice. God knows where each one of us should be born, who should be our neighbors, and who we should interact with on our paths of life. This is because God sees eternity from the beginning. He looks at your life span at a glance.

God blessed Adam and Eve with two sons who were very different. Abel kept flocks while Cain tilled grounds. Abel offered sacrifices to God from the firstborns of his animals. God was pleased. Cain became angry because God did not look favorably to the harvest he offered, and in anger, Cain killed his brother.

God confronted Cain and asked, "Where is Abel thy brother?" Cain put on an "I don't care" attitude and claimed not to know the whereabouts of his brother. "Am I my brother's keeper?" he asked (Genesis 4:9). Unfortunately, the voice of his brother's blood kept crying out to God from the ground.

God has appointed brothers and sisters into your keeping—whether biological or not. God has placed people of different abilities, giftings, and capabilities in your life. He wants you to be their keeper. This is a responsibility God often uses to determine and affect many aspects of our lives as He calls us to eternal accountability. Look at the people God has placed in your life. See those you may have looked down upon, neglected, or denied care. Who has been placed in your life for you to love? Follow God and become a keeper.

READ GENESIS 4.

GOD HAS GOOD PLANS FOR YOU.

Christians live in a world filled with evil and sinful people. We are surrounded with immense wickedness on every side as we face their hurtful schemes. Instead of God taking His children away from such chaos, He leaves us here to be a light and a witness until our time on earth is done.

Noah, God's choice servant, lived in such unprecedented times. Despite the rampant immorality of his day, "Noah found grace in the eyes of the Lord" (Genesis 6:8). God had good plans for the man who strove to live a righteous life amid unimaginable sinfulness. He knows what surrounds you today, and He is not blind to your daily fights against evil.

God has the power to:

- Defeat every wicked scheme
- Avert evil
- Keep you safe
- Safeguard your heart
- Give you resilience amid looming conspiracies
- Lift you above the cheap ventures of Satan
- Grant you victory and help you stand and live for Him

God formed you with these days and circumstances in mind. You would not be living in this century if God did not create you with the resilience and ability to shine and win.

Regardless of where you find yourself today or what surrounds you, remember, God has good plans for you. He does not leave His children to fate or to the mercies of their enemies.

"For I know the thoughts that I think toward you, saith the LORD, thoughts of peace, and not of evil, to give you an expected end" (Jeremiah 29:11).

READ PSALM 32:8–10.

GOD REMEMBERS HIS BELOVED.

God is mindful of His children. He is just, and there is no unfairness in Him. When you look at your journey with God, you can ascertain that God favors His children and looks out for them in tough times. God takes special interest in you. I am sure you have personal testimonies of God's working behind the scenes on your behalf and helping you in special ways.

When God chose to use the flood to destroy the world in biblical times, He remembered Noah and his family (Genesis 8). When He destroyed Sodom and Gomorrah with fire, He remembered Lot and his family (Genesis 19). He spared them.

Tough times often carry a heavy cloud that overshadows God, causing us to doubt His love and care. Don't let such moments deny you the joy and excitement of loving and following God.

Look at God's charge to Noah at a fateful time in life: "Bring forth with thee every living thing that is with thee, of all flesh, both of fowl, and of cattle, and of every creeping thing that creepeth upon the earth; that they may breed abundantly in the earth, and be fruitful, and multiply upon the earth. And Noah went forth, and his sons, and his wife, and his sons' wives with him" (Genesis 8:17–18).

Even after the flood, God remembered Noah. God blessed Noah and his sons and promised to make them abundantly fruitful, that they would be feared in all the earth. God handed the care and keeping of earth and its treasures to Noah and his family and established a covenant with them (see Genesis 9).

God is watching over you. He will remember you, together with your children and family. God is a shield to all who trust and take refuge in Him (Psalm 18:30).

READ HEBREWS 6:10.

HOW'S YOUR DESCENT?

Have you ever wondered why God chose to populate us by our families? There is no single person who does not belong to a family. God could have created individuals and designed us to live as loners, but He didn't. God values relationships. God has patterned us to thrive in strong relationships. There is no question that man enjoys places where he is valued, taken care of, and appreciated. Families who cherish their members and share heartfelt moments of true joy and fellowship hold strong regardless of what they face in life.

This familial theme caught my attention as I read through the life of Abraham. Abram, Nahor, and Haran were brothers born to their father, Terah. This common family was subject to normal family challenges. Haran died at an early age. When Abram married Sarai, it became evident that his wife could not bear children. However, when challenges warranted that they move to another land, Terah did something that we can still learn from in this century. "And Terah took Abram his son, and Lot the son of Haran his son's son, and Sarai his daughter in law, his son Abram's wife; and they went forth with them from Ur of the Chaldees, to go into the land of Canaan; and they came unto Haran, and dwelt there" (Genesis 11:31).

Terah held his family together. He moved with his sons, their wives, and their children.

Ask God to help you hold your family together, regardless of its members or the challenges they face. Individualism may be popular today, but it hurts the family unit and those God has entrusted to you. May God help you move, walk, work, grow, and fellowship with your family.

READ PSALM 127:1–5.

WALK IN YOUR CALLING.

When God created Adam and Eve, He placed them in the great garden of Eden, but He did not leave them without a charge. Their work was to dress and take care of it (see Genesis 2:15).

I believe that God has a purpose for every person He creates. Of course, purposes can be different, but God never creates anyone just because.

God calls His children to different works. In one family, God may call each child to a different job. Most times, we do not choose our works. However, God, Who is Sovereign, fashions us for His work ahead of time. It is for this reason we can side with the Bible confidently as we say, "For we are his workmanship, created in Christ Jesus unto good works, which God hath before ordained that we should walk in them" (Ephesians 2:10).

Sometimes, God calls you to something that is greater than yourself. He did this for Abram in Genesis 12 when He called Abram out of his home and made a big promise to him.

God promised to make a great name and nation out of Abram. He would bless all the families of the earth through this single man.

God has not stopped calling men and women to big courses in life. God still calls people from one nation to another to do His great works. He asks people to pioneer works that will profit mankind. He is directing and opening the eyes of His children to the needs of the world.

Pray that God will speak and direct you to what He has for you. Do not be afraid to step into your calling, however big. Remember, the God Who calls you into His service will equip you for the work. Fulfillment in life comes from accomplishing God's purposes. Seek to walk in your calling, regardless of how big or small it may seem.

READ JOHN 15:16.

GOD BLESSES THROUGH CHANGE.

The God Who created you knows the details of your journey on earth. He understands when you need change in your life and where you can best grow and serve Him.

When Abram was seventy-five years old and settled in the land and place where his father Terah took him, God appeared and interrupted his stay. God's message to Abram was interesting. It had room for joy and excitement, yet there were reasons for wonder and anxiety, too.

> Now the Lord had said unto Abram, Get thee out of thy country, and from thy kindred, and from thy father's house, unto a land that I will shew thee: And I will make of thee a great nation, and I will bless thee, and make thy name great; and thou shalt be a blessing: And I will bless them that bless thee, and curse him that curseth thee: and in thee shall all families of the earth be blessed. (Genesis 12:1–3)

Who moves from his home in old age to seek new settlements? How do you build new friendships or do life all over again? As we all know, Abram believed and obeyed God. God stood by His Word and established His servant to be the father of all nations. Let us learn some important facts from Abram's account to help us in life.

- It is easy to resist change when you do not know the mind of God. God uses change to bless and to meet the needs of many people. Look at change from God's viewpoint.
- God's blessings in your life are not limited to one specific place. God will bless you wherever He leads you.
- God has the power to change your current situations regardless of how long you have lived in them.
- Change does not need to be in major issues or from one place to another. Daily changes in life have power to yield lifetime benefits.

READ ROMANS 11:33–36.

AGE IS NOT A FACTOR.

God calls and uses people of different ages to accomplish His work and purposes on earth. Since we are finite beings, our lives are constrained by time. We determine what we can and cannot do depending on our age and the time available. However, this is not how God assigns His work on earth. Your age should not be the excuse for refraining from God's work. Remember, God knows and understands your age before He calls you to any assignment.

Do not sit back and look helplessly at things you can do just because you have allowed your age to stand in the way. Age is not an issue with God:

- You can hear and obey God's call at any age. Samuel was a young child when He first heard and obeyed God (see 1 Samuel 3). Abram was an old man when he first encountered and followed God (see Genesis 12).
- You can follow God diligently and wholeheartedly at any age. Josiah was eight years old when he became the king of Judah. He reigned for thirty-one years, and God tells us in 2 Kings 22:2 that "[Josiah] did that which was right in the sight of the Lord, and walked in all the way of David his father, and turned not aside to the right hand or to the left." Another faithful servant, Anna, a prophetess and a widow, served God with prayer and fasting day and night even at eighty-four years of age (see Luke 2:36–38).
- God is counting on you to serve Him in this generation. Do not focus on your age. Listen, follow, and obey.

God will work through you if you let Him. "For thus saith the high and lofty One that inhabiteth eternity, whose name is Holy; I dwell in the high and holy place, with him also that is of a contrite and humble spirit, to revive the spirit of the humble, and to revive the heart of the contrite ones" (Isaiah 57:15).

READ ISAIAH 55:8–9.

January 5

YOUR PROTECTION IS A PRIORITY TO GOD.

No one enjoys protection in this world like God's children. This does not mean Christians do not get hurt or find themselves in danger. That would be contrary to what you already know or may have even witnessed. However, God orchestrates events in the lives of His children and does not leave us helpless to the evil schemes of our enemies.

We live among enough vile people who would end our lives at any time if it were left to them. This should not keep you afraid and anxious. Do not let your joy and fullness of life be curtailed with treachery. Nothing will come your way except what God permits.

Look at God's promise of care and protection for you as detailed in Isaiah 41:10–13:

> Fear thou not; for I am with thee: be not dismayed; for I am thy God: I will strengthen thee; yea, I will help thee; yea, I will uphold thee with the right hand of my righteousness. Behold, all they that were incensed against thee shall be ashamed and confounded: they shall be as nothing; and they that strive with thee shall perish. Thou shalt seek them, and shalt not find them, even them that contended with thee: they that war against thee shall be as nothing, and as a thing of nought. For I the LORD thy God will hold thy right hand, saying unto thee, Fear not; I will help thee.

God is looking out for you today. He is aware of what surrounds or faces you, and He will deal with those who cause your heart to fear and tremble. God will deal with those who think and scheme evil against you. He has the power to cover and let you walk unseen or unarmed through the troops of the enemy. Your protection is a priority to God.

READ PSALM 121:8.

UNDESERVED CURSES DO NOT HOLD.

God made a promise to His servant and friend, Abram, in Genesis 12:3, saying, "And I will bless them that bless thee, and curse him that curseth thee." God made this promise before sending Abram to the unknown—a place he had never been nor knew where it was. God knew what awaited this man. He understood the dangers of passing through unfamiliar territories and interacting with diverse groups of people. The all-knowing God foresaw Abram making and encountering both friends and enemies in his daily walk.

A life of uncertainty, great friendships, and enmity is not foreign to Christians. God will fill your life with true friends with whom to share lifetime memories as you walk and serve Him. Nevertheless, you will also have a share of those who will not care about you. Your life is not free from those who will curse and hurl abuses at you audibly or silently.

- You must learn to walk past such curses as you look to God and trust His promise.
- Do not believe the fate and the misfortunes they pronounce in your life. They are like clouds without rain (Proverbs 25:14), full of threats and intimidations that are powerless and fruitless.
- Do not allow your heart to be troubled. Walk confidently with God in peace.

Those who did not care for Abram did not affect God's promises in any way. Undeserved curses do not hold. Look at God's promise in Proverbs 26:2. There is a greater power that governs and protects your life. Curses, witches, sorcerers, enemies, and even the devil are subject to this authority. Your God is an all-powerful God.

READ PSALM 23:5.

January 17

PROBLEMS DON'T ALWAYS DENOTE THE ABSENCE OF GOD.

There is an enduring trend that associates problems in life with the absence of God. This belief keeps Christians searching and beating up their hearts while living defeated lives fearing that God is no longer pleased with them. Not all problems denote the absence of God.

God visited Abram and asked him to leave his country for an unknown land. God's promises to Abram were heartwarming and exceptional. They included wonderful inheritance and the acquiring of enormous wealth in addition to fame and honor. This was not what Abram experienced as he walked in God's perfect will, obeying and following the command of the Almighty.

There was a deadly famine in the land when Abram arrived. He moved down into Egypt to escape the hunger. Little did he know what awaited him. God tells us that the inhabitants of the land were perplexed when they saw how beautiful Sarai, Abram's wife, was. The women and princes who saw her recommended her to Pharaoh for a wife. Pharaoh could not resist it either (see Genesis 12).

Let us learn from this account together the following:

- Problems do not always signify the absence of God. God always stands with His children.
- You can face numerous challenges even when you are in the center of God's perfect will. Do not doubt His Word and position when faced with storms of life. He will stand with you.
- Always hold onto what God spoke to your heart through His Word until you hear from Him again as you face challenges in life.
- God will make it clear when problems are for punishment. Your heart will be convicted and know when you offend God.

READ PSALM 119:165.

God always keeps His word.

Are you struggling with God's promises that do not seem to align with the circumstances of your life? When God speaks to us, He does not always give us the timeline in which things will take place. This is tough for finite human beings who operate within daily boundaries of time. Our inability to see and understand the future does not make it easier.

As you reflect on Abram's journey with God, you will see that God kept His word. Abram dwelled in the land of Canaan, and God blessed him just as He had promised (Genesis 13:1–6).

Before you change your mind on God, here are a few things to remember:

- God has never lied. He will come through with His promises as He declared them.
- Hold onto God's Word. It will stand the test of time and remain true and victorious. Do not doubt what you heard from Him during times of prevailing difficulties and uncertainty.
- Follow God diligently until you attain His promise. Avoid the temptation of consulting and following people who were not part of this promise. They will make your heart doubt God and seek options that will deny you God's best choices for your life.
- "God is not a man, that he should lie; neither the son of man, that he should repent: hath he said, and shall he not do it? or hath he spoken, and shall he not make it good?" (Numbers 23:19).

Read Titus 1:2 and Hebrews 6:18–19.

DEALING WITH STRIFE

It is easy to team with members of your family to stand against an intruder or an enemy. You can resist combative and angry individuals when members of your household are on your side. However, how do you deal with envy, enmity, and strife when it is within your own family?

Abram, God's choice servant, faced such discord with his nephew, Lot. When Haran, Abram's brother, and Terah, Abram's father, died, Lot lived and traveled with Abram. Lot benefited from the numerous blessings God promised Abram. He, too, had flocks, herds, and riches. When the land could no longer support the abundant riches of the two men, their servants engaged in disagreements that affected the good family relationships that had endured through tough times.

Abram addressed the conflict and gave his nephew a choice on which section of the land to dwell with his flocks, herds, and servants. Let us learn from Abram's situation as we deal with strife in our homes.

- Abram had every right to evict and teach Lot some sobering life lessons and remind him of how he wouldn't own a thing without his help, but he didn't.

- Abram did not reiterate or fuel the strife. Instead, he dwelt in wisdom and still gave Lot the land of his choice.

- If you must part ways, let it not be in anger and war. Find ways to make peace and keep an open door.

- At the end of the day, family relationships are more important than your wealth and possessions.

- Be wise. Family strife against you will not stop God's blessings in your life if you remain true to the source of blessings.

READ GENESIS 13.

CHOICES HAVE CONSEQUENCES.

As a follow-up on Abram and Lot, let us look at the choices made and the consequences that followed as recorded in Genesis 13.

Abram did not want to get in a war with his nephew. To resolve their differences, he said, "Is not the whole land before thee? separate thyself, I pray thee, from me: if thou wilt take the left hand, then I will go to the right; or if thou depart to the right hand, then I will go to the left" (Genesis 13:9).

Lot chose the best of the land without any regard that it all belonged to his uncle. One might have expected him to politely wait on Abram for a decision. Lot chose the well-watered plains and lived in the cities near Sodom and Gomorrah. Abram had no choice but to live in the remaining section of the land in Canaan.

However, look at what followed this decision:

- God appeared to Abram after Lot departed and promised to increase and give him all the land north, south, east, and west of where he lived.
- It was after the separation that God promised to give Abram offspring like the dust of the earth; numerous without number.
- Abram walked closer to God, lived in Hebron, and built an altar to the Lord.
- Lot found himself in the warring and sinful chaos of Sodom and Gomorrah. As the kings of the land waged war, they captured Lot, took his goods, and departed. Abram had to assemble an army in his own house to rescue Lot (see Genesis 14).
- Lot lost everything when God finally destroyed Sodom and Gomorrah. Even his wife did not make it out of the wicked cities.

Be careful when you must make choices in life. Choices have consequences. Seek God's counsel and do what is true to your heart as a child of God. Ask God for knowledge and wisdom.

READ PROVERBS 2:6.

BEWARE OF ENTANGLEMENT

It is easy to fall prey to people's schemes unknowingly. This is because it is hard to see and read one's motives or intentions. However, God warns us, "The heart is deceitful above all things, and desperately wicked: who can know it?" (Jeremiah 17:9). It is hard to pick out malice when actions are camouflaged with attractive offers or compliments.

Man can use praise to blind your eyes while using your work as a stepping-stone for his career advancement. What looks like a gift may turn out to be a bribe intended to keep you silent in the future or take sides for things for which you wouldn't stand.

God gives an interesting account in Genesis 14 regarding such incidences. The king of Sodom met Abram as he returned from war with a strange offer. "Give me the persons, and take the goods to thyself" (Genesis 14:21).

Abram was smarter than that. How could he make a treaty with a wicked man after all the promises God had given him? Abram replied, "That I will not take from a thread even to a shoelatchet, and that I will not take any thing that is thine, lest thou shouldest say, I have made Abram rich" (Genesis 14:23).

- Imagine the hold the king would have had on Abram for the riches accorded to him by God.
- Be wise. Not everyone who seems genuine has your best interest at heart. Do not be entangled. Do not sell yourself and your God-given honor, freedom, and blessings for cheap compromise.
- Beware of the offers presented before you. Seek God's counsel before you look back on them with regret.
- Purpose to be a person of honor, respect, and integrity.

PROVERBS 3:5–7.

GOD SPARES HIS CHILDREN.

God looks out for His children in unprecedented times. From creation until now, the world has faced days of lawlessness. Rebellion is engraved in the heart of man, and only the blood of the Lord Jesus Christ can cleanse and purify one from within.

Lot, Abram's nephew, found himself amid exceedingly wicked and vile men in Sodom (Genesis 13:13). God could not find ten righteous people in the entire land to cause Him to withhold judgment. When God sent His angels to survey the land as He prepared to destroy it with fire, the inhabitants extended their abominable acts to them. Both young and old men stormed Lot's house and demanded to have sex with them (Genesis 19:1–8).

It is true there are moments when Christians find themselves in the same danger as evil men and women. However, God looks out for His children. He rescues and saves us on numerous occasions without always revealing it.

Abram implored God regarding the destruction of Sodom and Gomorrah, saying, "Wilt thou also destroy the righteous with the wicked? . . . Shall not the Judge of all the earth do right?" (Genesis 18:23, 25).

The angels God sent to determine the wickedness of Sodom and execute His punishment were the very ones God used to rescue Lot and his family. Yes, Lot was a righteous man who made bad choices that vexed his righteous soul with the sins of those who surrounded him (see 2 Peter 2:7–8).

- Do not be tempted to yield to the seductions of evil men and women. God looks out for His children. Stand for God, and He will stand for you.
- God understands what surrounds you. He deals with wickedness in a timely manner.
- Come out from the wicked and take your place on the Lord's side.

READ PSALM 1:6.

GOD IS NOT BLIND TO YOUR DEEP-SEATED NEED.

Life is a perplexing puzzle that is only understood by God. What you see on the outside does not tell the entire story of a man or woman, and neither does it reveal the deep-seated needs of the heart. A smile does not always signify a heart at rest and free from cares. The abundance of substance may obscure the lack of more valuable things than riches in an individual's life. Outward beauty, adornment, or spiffiness rarely divulge the inner chaos or disorders of the heart and mind.

Look at Abram's life as we apply this concept. God blessed His friend, Abram, with an abundance of flocks, wealth, servants, and honor. Imagine a man who could mount an army of over three hundred men born and trained in his own house to fight and win against four kings together with their armies (see Genesis 14:14).

However, all these could not suffice the need that threatened the stability and continuity of Abram's dynasty. As Abram got intimate with God, he could not hide the plight that gnawed at him daily. His heart's cry rose above God's voice of blessings, saying, "What wilt thou give me, seeing I go childless, and the steward of my house is this Eliezer of Damascus? And Abram said, Behold, to me thou hast given no seed: and, lo, one born in my house is mine heir" (Genesis 15:1–3).

What is the deep ache of your heart? Have you talked to God about it? God is not blind to your pain. Do not camouflage it any longer. Pour out your heart to Him.

God honored Abram's heartfelt request and promised to not only give him a son, but also as many children as the sand of the sea. "[Abram] believed in the LORD; and he counted it to him for righteousness" (Genesis 15:6).

READ JEREMIAH 32:27.

REMEMBER AND TRUST AGAIN.

In the Bible days, it was not unusual to find older men walking with staffs that had numerous markings on them. The markings represented major events and happenings they had to remember.

Most of us have a robust short-term memory. We focus on current situations as they shape and affect our lives. There is something about this kind of memory that deletes or forgets the happenings of yesterday, regardless of how memorable and pleasant they were. This memory is heightened amid pain and anguish until it suppresses the voice of God and the memory of His workings in our lives.

- Remember, the same God Who helped in you in the years past has not changed, and neither has His power dwindled or weakened.
- The God Who stood with you in the dark hours of your life is the same One Who is standing for you today.
- The God Who performed miracles and brought you out of tough times is standing in the same place for you today.
- When your short-term memory begins to supersede your long-term memory, make deliberate effort to look back at the workings of God in your life.

At a time when Abram focused on the momentary troubles of his time and the deep desire for a child, God reminded him of the stability of His Divine and eternal character. He is God. "And he said unto him, I am the LORD that brought thee out of Ur of the Chaldees, to give thee this land to inherit it" (Genesis 15:7).

God orchestrated the events that led to the promises. Only God could fulfill those promises in Abram's life.

There is no need to fret. God is working behind the scenes, and He will see to it that all His promises for your life are fulfilled. So, remember what He has done and trust Him for what is ahead.

READ PSALM 136.

YOUR FUTURE IS KNOWN TO GOD.

Do you ever desire to know what your tomorrow will look like? I wonder what we would do or how we would handle life if God gave us foreknowledge of our lives a month at a time. The fact that God does not give us a premonition does not make Him blind or ignorant about our upcoming days. God knows the good, the evil, the dangers, and even the pleasures that await us in our later days.

The God Who blessed Abram knew the changes and challenges that awaited his future descendants. God revealed troubling facts to His friend.

> And he said unto Abram, Know of a surety that thy seed shall be a stranger in a land that is not theirs, and shall serve them; and they shall afflict them four hundred years; And also that nation, whom they shall serve, will I judge: and afterward shall they come out with great substance. And thou shalt go to thy fathers in peace; thou shalt be buried in a good old age. But in the fourth generation they shall come hither again: for the iniquity of the Amorites is not yet full. (Genesis 15:13–16)

Walk courageously with God and allow Him to hold your hand as you stride into the future. Fretting about tomorrow will not change anything. Commit the fears and concerns to God and trust Him to do what is right. He has power to avert evil or to shield you from its harm.

Should God choose to reveal what lies ahead, remember, it is not to hurt but to prepare you. God always has your best interests at heart. Yes, your future is known to Him.

READ DEUTERONOMY 31:8 AND ISAIAH 55:8–9.

God challenges us to wait.

What do you do when God seems to run behind schedule, forget what He promised, and keeps quiet? Have you found your back pressed against the wall as you held onto God's Word and promises?

It is often hard to face family members, colleagues, and friends when your actions are viewed as foolishness just because you are waiting on God. What do you do when the world urges you to act or when peer pressure does not make it any easier?

Abram and Sarai faced such a predicament. God promised to give Abram an heir and innumerable children (Genesis 15:4–5). Nonetheless, God did not specify the timeline in which He would accomplish this.

Sarai did not know how long to wait before holding a child in her arms, given that she was old. Sarai decided to help God. She talked to her husband and made plans for Abram to sleep with her housemaid and to become a wife who could bear them children. This was contrary to the plans God had for Abram and Sarai.

Let me share some helpful thoughts from this account.

- One of the greatest challenges of our Christian walk is waiting on God in moments of uncertainty and want. Speak to your heart and wait. The God Who spoke to your heart will not lie.
- Delay does not mean denial. Wait when you cannot hear God.
- God's timeline is different from ours, but it is the best. Remember, He sees the beginning from the end.
- Waiting is hard. It takes courage and commitment.
- It is better to do without it than to panic and take ungodly actions.
- You will end up settling for God's second-best options if you do not wait on Him.

Hagar, Sarai's slave girl, conceived and gave birth to a baby boy, Ishmael. What Sarai envisioned bringing joy and contentment became the source of strife and pain, not just in her own family but in many parts of the world.

Read Isaiah 40:31.

TRUST THE GOD WHO SEES.

Hagar, Sarai's maid, found herself in situations beyond her comprehension after conceiving Abram's child. Sarai, who orchestrated and planned the unpleasant unfolding of events, failed to reconcile her intentions and the outcomes. Hagar rejoiced at the conception of a child and had no regard for Sarai. She despised her mistress for her barrenness. How could the two women share a man and a house in such a state?

Sarai put aside her kindness and gentleness and decided to mistreat her maid. The punishments were so tough that Hagar opted to run away. Suddenly, she was in the wilderness without a single person knowing where she was. "And the angel of the Lord found her by a fountain of water in the wilderness, by the fountain in the way to Shur. And he said, Hagar, Sarai's maid, whence camest thou? and whither wilt thou go? And she said, I flee from the face of my mistress Sarai" (Genesis 16:7–8).

God understood that Hagar was a victim of circumstances. He did not wink at her sin in despising her mistress, but He stood with her. After instructing her to go back to Sarai, He proclaimed great blessings and words of hope, saying, "I will multiply thy seed exceedingly, that it shall not be numbered for multitude" (Genesis 16:10).

- Have you found yourself a victim of other people's selfish plans and unwise schemes?
- Are you suffering the consequences of other people's mistakes?
- God is not blind to your plight. The God Who saved Hagar from the dark wilderness and its dangers still looks out for you.
- You will not go under because of the mistakes made by other people. You may suffer their consequences, but God has good plans for you, too.
- God's eyes are on you. He is looking out for you. He has not forgotten, and neither will He forsake you.

Find strength, hope, and comfort from God's promise in Psalm 46:7–10.

READ PSALM 33:10–11.

FROM WHERE ARE YOU COMING, AND WHERE ARE YOU GOING?

Dark times are a reality that drive us to places and situations we never envisioned for our lives. What do you do when all you have lived for or known is taken away in a moment?

How do you proceed when you find yourself alone and away from those you loved and served and whose company you enjoyed? How do you react when the only place you knew or owned has neither a welcoming gesture nor an open door for your return?

Hagar found herself in such a dilemma after running away from Sarai. When you think about it, she must have been a loyal and wonderful maid to be given charge over such a mistress. Furthermore, she did not solicit to be Abram's concubine. However, she found herself with child following her act of obedience to Sarai. God went ahead of Hagar into the wilderness. When she thought all was over, God's great and overshadowing hand was right there beside her (Genesis 16:7–13).

Are you running today? From what are you running? Where are you going?

Are you headed to a place of uncertainty, with no plans and not sure what to expect? Even when you cannot explain your challenges to anyone, remember, God sees all things and knows and understands everything. You do not have to go through this alone. The God Who cared for Hagar has His holy hand guiding and looking out for you. Look at His Word for you today:

> Whither shall I go from thy spirit? or whither shall I flee from thy presence? If I ascend up into heaven, thou art there: if I make my bed in hell, behold, thou art there. If I take the wings of the morning, and dwell in the uttermost parts of the sea; Even there shall thy hand lead me, and thy right hand shall hold me. If I say, Surely the darkness shall cover me; even the night shall be light about me. Yea, the darkness hideth not from thee; but the night shineth as the day: the darkness and the light are both alike to thee (Psalm 139:7–12).

READ HEBREWS 6:10.

January 29

GOD REPLACES FEAR WITH HOPE.

Change happens to all of us. There are many good changes that keep us hoping and rejoicing; then there are those that turn our worlds upside down. These are changes that leave us empty and desolate. They deprive us of what was pleasant and familiar, leaving us vulnerable and anxious. Some changes create voids, engrave memories, and leave scars so deep that you cannot wipe them away.

God does not leave us desolate or in despair in such times of intense fear. Otherwise, He would act contrary to His Word in Isaiah 42:3, which says, "A bruised reed shall he not break, and the smoking flax shall he not quench."

I would like you to think back to the time of resurrection. As Mary Magdalene stood alone by the grave weeping bitterly, Christ appeared to her, saying, "Woman, why weepest thou?" When Mary did not recognize the voice that reached out to her for the second time, the Lord Jesus said, "Mary." Suddenly, the lonely and dark place became serene and a place of Divine visitation. All fear gave way to faith, hope, and courage (see John 20:13–16).

This is the same God Who reached out to Hagar in her time of bewilderment. "Hagar, Sarai's maid," He called.

God sent Mary away with a special message of hope and joy to the disciples. Hagar departed from the wilderness back to Abram's house with joy and a message of hope and courage. Both women returned to tough situations. Christ ascended to Heaven for what Mary and His disciples must have thought was the last time. Hagar returned to the cold and iron hand of her mistress. Nonetheless, their fears were gone. They faced each day with hope and courage.

This is your day of visitation. It is your turn. God does not want you to live in fear and despair. Commit everything to Him. Be honest, like Mary and Hagar, and tell Him what is troubling you. Take him at His Word and face life with hope and courage. "Fear thou not; for I am with thee: be not dismayed; for I am thy God: I will strengthen thee; yea, I will help thee; yea, I will uphold thee with the right hand of my righteousness" (Isaiah 41:10).

READ ISAIAH 43:1.

GOD DETERMINED YOUR BIRTH.

We all show up in the world through different ways. All of us are birthed, true, but varied circumstances determined our conception. Some were at will, while others were out of misfortunes. Some were celebrated, but others were abhorred.

The stories that surround our conception and births can affect us in monumental ways when we give them fertile ground to grow. Such narratives can make you feel wanted, celebrated, and loved—or lonely, unfortunate, and second-class. All these are manmade scales. God does not see first and last classes, wanted or illegitimate children when He looks at us. All births are from God, and He celebrates us. He creates us for a purpose.

When Hagar conceived, God ensured Ishmael's safe delivery. Ishmael was born in God's will like you and me. His birth did not take God by surprise, and neither did yours. It was God Who revealed the gender of the child to Hagar. God chose a name for the little fellow! He even proclaimed blessings on the boy. Through Ishmael, God promised to give Hagar uncountable children (see Genesis 16:10–13).

It is important for us to understand these truths:

- No one is illegitimate in the eyes of God.
- God loves you regardless of the circumstances that dictated your birth.
- God wanted you, and that is the only reason He allowed you to be born.
- You are valued in the eyes of God. You have a legitimate place by Him in life. God has good plans for you.

"For we are his workmanship, created in Christ Jesus unto good works, which God hath before ordained that we should walk in them" (Ephesians 2:10).

READ PSALM 139:14–17.

TRUST THE GOD OF IMPOSSIBILITIES.

God has a very high sense of humor. It is not easy to understand His workings either. God can pick individuals from a family or a group and cause them to succeed in surpassing ways that were unpredictable.

God can take a student and cause him or her to supersede others whose prospects of success were higher or even looked obvious. God can use the most unlikely people to bring change, hope, and prosperity in ways you least expected. God can work through entangled situations in your life in ways you could never fathom. He can put your feet on paths you only dreamed about and use you to accomplish what you only imagined.

When Abram was ninety-nine years old, God appeared to him with what looked like an out-of-mind offer. "I am the Almighty God; walk before me, and be thou perfect. And I will make my covenant between me and thee, and will multiply thee exceedingly" (Genesis 17:1–2).

I would like you to put yourself in Abram's shoes for a moment. The old man was at a point where having children was nothing less than a dream. Things changed when Abram encountered the all-powerful God, with whom "all things are possible" (Matthew 19:26). God gave the aged man the son of promise when he was one hundred years old.

- Are you faced with a tough situation beyond your comprehension? Share it with the God of impossibilities.
- Do your circumstances demand a miracle if they must change? You are in the right place. Give them to God, Who sees no impracticability.
- Do you lack a godfather or mentor to hold your hand and help you navigate through difficult situations? God is your Portion. He will help.

Find rest and hope in the God of impossibilities today as He speaks to your heart through Isaiah 43:18–19: "Remember ye not the former things, neither consider the things of old. Behold, I will do a new thing; now it shall spring forth; shall ye not know it? I will even make a way in the wilderness, and rivers in the desert."

READ 1 SAMUEL 2:6–8.

February

TRUSTING THE SHEPHERD

Sheep cannot predict what their day will look like. They depend on their shepherd to plan and take them through the day.

God does the same for His children. You do not know what this month holds, but the Shepherd does. He will hold your hand and lead you.

Let us learn to trust the Shepherd this month.

KNOW THE SHEPHERD.

Not many of us are comfortable walking in dark hours of the night alone and empty-handed. During such times, our steps are quick but gingered. Our senses are heightened, and we are cautious with our actions. Our experience and actions will be different if we were accompanied by high-ranked security personnel and the dark corners flooded with lights. Suddenly, our fear will be replaced with courage. Our feeble and fearful steps will turn into affirmatory strides of bravery, confidence, and power.

Darkness surrounds us in this world, and there is danger on every side. Many times, our steps are shaky and our hearts uncertain. We quietly wish for secure company, a flooding of lights, and the assurance that all will be well.

For the child of God, this should not characterize our daily lives. God is true. He is not a myth. He is our Shepherd. We are better protected in His presence than anywhere else in this world. There is no safer place to be than to go through the day hand in hand with God. There will be no dark corners where He will not accompany you. There is no danger He cannot ward off with His great and powerful hand.

Give your fears and uncertainty to God. Rest your heart in the unfailing promise of His Word for His children today.

> Whither shall I go from thy spirit? or whither shall I flee from thy presence?
>
> If I ascend up into heaven, thou art there: if I make my bed in hell, behold, thou art there.
>
> If I take the wings of the morning, and dwell in the uttermost parts of the sea;
>
> Even there shall thy hand lead me, and thy right hand shall hold me.
>
> If I say, Surely the darkness shall cover me; even the night shall be light about me.
>
> Yea, the darkness hideth not from thee; but the night shineth as the day: the darkness and the light are both alike to thee. (Psalm 139:7–12)

JOHN 10:11–15.

February 2

The Lord is our Shepherd.

The LORD is my shepherd; I shall not want.

He maketh me to lie down in green pastures: he leadeth me beside the still waters.

He restoreth my soul: he leadeth me in the paths of righteousness for his name's sake.

Yea, though I walk through the valley of the shadow of death, I will fear no evil: for thou art with me; thy rod and thy staff they comfort me.

Thou preparest a table before me in the presence of mine enemies: thou anointest my head with oil; my cup runneth over.

Surely goodness and mercy shall follow me all the days of my life: and I will dwell in the house of the LORD forever. (Psalm 23)

Why does God call Himself a Shepherd? What do shepherds do? Who needs a shepherd?

You belong to God. You did not choose God; instead, He chose you when your heart was not thinking about Him (see John 15:16). You are His responsibility. The way a shepherd takes full responsibility for his herd, so the Lord takes charge of you.

The Lord will take care of you regardless of what surrounds you today. Yes, life may be full of challenges and the future uncertain, but do not focus on that. There is no day you are not in the sight of the Shepherd. Nothing will take Him by surprise. Instead, He will surprise you with the good plans He has for you. The Lord is your Shepherd. He will walk with you today. He will hold you by the hand and help you.

Read Deuteronomy 31:8.

SHEEP CANNOT SURVIVE
WITHOUT A SHEPHERD.

Of all the animals in the world, God likens Christians to sheep. Have you ever wondered why He did not liken us to dogs or lions? It is interesting that God uses dogs to refer to the unchanging behavior in persons who do not know Him. They return to their sins just as a dog can return to its vomit (Proverbs 26:11).

God uses a lion to portray strength, boldness, determination, and the unending passion of pursuing and subduing a prey. Evidently, God does not embolden His children with these characteristics. Instead, He equates us most commonly to the tender, dependent, and helpless traits of sheep.

It is easy to find dogs and lions unattended going about their business without any care. This is not true with sheep. Sheep need a shepherd. Without one, sheep are vulnerable and easy prey for their enemies. Unlike dogs or lions, sheep are defenseless.

God is your Shepherd. He understands you and takes full responsibility for you. Stay close to the Shepherd. The greatest safeguard for a defenseless sheep is to stay close to the shepherd. To stay afar off is to sharpen the appetite of your enemies and to fall in their cages. You will not make it without the Shepherd. You have an enemy who hopes to find you away from the Shepherd so he can devour you. The Shepherd will satisfy you. There is no want for those who stay close to the Shepherd. He knows what is best for you.

READ ISAIAH 41:10–13.

February 4

THE SHEPHERD TAKES CARE OF HIS SHEEP.

How do you take care of an animal you love? What about a beloved child? Can you tell when they are hungry, distressed, or sick? Yes, but you do not stop at that. You get busy looking out for their welfare. You involve those who can help them, and you spend time and other resources on them.

God does not leave His children to chance. He takes care of His children better than the best parents in this world. Just like a shepherd knows what is good for his sheep, so the Lord knows His children and understands their needs. He is neither blind nor overtaken by their circumstances. He knows what is best for His children.

The Lord will take care of you today. God knows when you are weak and weary. That is why He leads you beside the still waters—that your soul may be refreshed and nourished (Psalm 23:2).

God knows when your nerves are torn apart and when you are on the verge of despair. It is for such reasons that He comforts and soothes you. It is in such seasons He calls with tenderness, saying, "Come unto me, all ye that labour and are heavy laden, and I will give you rest. Take my yoke upon you, and learn of me; for I am meek and lowly in heart: and ye shall find rest unto your souls. For my yoke is easy, and my burden is light" (Matthew 11:28-30).

God knows when your heart is fearful. It is not in vain that He speaks to you today, saying, "Let not your heart be troubled" (John 14:1) and "I will never leave thee, nor forsake thee" (Hebrews 13:5).

"What time I am afraid, I will trust in thee" (Psalm 56:3).

READ DEUTERONOMY 31:6.

February 5
TRUST THE CHARACTER OF THE SHEPHERD.

One of the greatest challenges of our Christian journey is trusting the God we cannot see. Is it true that God is real and He cares for those whose hearts trust in Him? Is God trustworthy? Can He stand strong with His children in difficult times for them to know, with deep assurance, that He cares? Does God think about us by chance, or are we a priority to Him?

These are tough questions, especially when times are difficult and the circumstances of your life are uncertain. They are tougher when you cannot feel Him, yet He is your only help. When your heart is broken and tears are drenching the collar and sleeve of your clothes, you long to hear and see God in tangible ways.

However, despite the limitations of our senses and spiritual discernment, God is always with you. As the Good Shepherd, He does not lead His sheep down a dark and lonely path without being close.

The Shepherd knows you. No one can compare to God in taking care of His flock. The Shepherd knows when you are weak and weary. He will hold your hand and lead you beside quiet waters. When you get exhausted from the fights you face in your spiritual walk, the Shepherd will ensure that you are refreshed. As you get bruised because of the difficult terrain you must walk, He will sooth you. He will carry you. He will nourish you. He will comfort you. Should you find it hard to walk, press on, or fight, the Shepherd will carry you. God loves you. God is concerned with what befalls you.

> Hear my voice, O God, in my prayer: preserve my life from fear of the enemy. Hide me from the secret counsel of the wicked; from the insurrection of the workers of iniquity: Who whet their tongue like a sword, and bend their bows to shoot their arrows, even bitter words (Psalm 64:1–3).

READ JOSHUA 1:9.

Depend on the Character of the Shepherd.

The Shepherd understands you very well. Suffering is real. Life is characterized by pain and troubling situations. Nights can be long and lonely. It is true that your faith can be threatened, and your strength can grow weak and weary on occasions. The Shepherd understands and cares deeply for you in those moments. God will stand with you. He will help you. Look at the Shepherd's promise in 1 Peter 5:10: "But the God of all grace, who hath called us unto his eternal glory by Christ Jesus, after that ye have suffered a while, make you perfect, stablish, strengthen, settle you."

It is not in vain that God looks at you today and reminds you of those precious words in Psalm 46:10–11, saying, "Be still, and know that I am God: I will be exalted among the heathen, I will be exalted in the earth. The Lord of hosts is with us; the God of Jacob is our refuge. Selah."

The Shepherd will come through for you. He knows how long the nights will be. He will not make them any longer. He will not keep you longer than needed in your current situations. Through the surging and the roaring of the storms, the Shepherd will be there. When the sun seems to take forever to shine, He will be there. When the tall mountains of life quake and prove too high to climb, He will be with you.

The Shepherd will make wars to cease. You will come through stronger and victorious because He will stay by your side. He will carry you should you need it.

Read Psalm 46.

February 7

THE SHEPHERD KNOWS HOW MUCH YOU CAN HANDLE.

When a shepherd gets little lambs, he sets his heart on a journey to feed, groom, and grow them into sheep that will fulfill desired purposes. This process takes time and patience on the part of the lambs and the shepherd. Sheering time is not pleasant for the sheep. Their daily routines are interrupted, just like their comfort. They are stripped of their warm coverings to face and adjust to weather conditions.

God does the same for His children. We come to Him tender and delicate, and He must work in us and with us to meet His intended purposes.

Every Christian is molded in God's crucible. This involves purifying, chiseling, and pruning. God does this with love and tender care as He shapes and conforms while still holding our best interests at heart.

Your shaping depends on what kind of a vessel you are before God. Sometimes, this calls for an increase in the temperature. Other times, it demands that you stay on God's molding wheel a little longer. The Shepherd knows how much you can handle. He will not keep you on the wheel longer than necessary. He will not hurt you either. The Shepherd is right there with you. He will refresh, soothe, and comfort you, even as you go through the painful process of being shaped by His mighty hand for His purposes.

Remember, you are clay in the hands of a mighty Potter. "But now, O LORD, thou art our father; we are the clay, and thou our potter; and we all are the work of thy hand" (Isaiah 64:8).

God is the Good Shepherd. Regardless of how much it hurts, He is working it all for your good. "I am the good shepherd: the good shepherd giveth his life for the sheep" (John 10:11).

READ JEREMIAH 18:1–6.

THE SHEPHERD IS TOUCHED
BY WHAT AFFECTS YOU.

God took full responsibility to lead His chosen people from their land of bondage, Egypt, to Canaan, the Promised Land. Psalm 78:52 records, "He made his own people to go forth like sheep, and guided them in the wilderness like a flock."

The journey was long and treacherous as the wilderness was filled with uncertainties. Nevertheless, like a good Shepherd, not only did God know the terrain of the roads, but He also understood His people too. He knew what they could endure and what would challenge them. In moments of great danger, He made a special highway in the Red Sea for His children. In times of deep hunger, He rained food from heaven to feed millions of people. True to His Word, "He fed them according to the integrity of his heart; and guided them by the skillfulness of his hands" (Psalm 78:72).

While facing tough times, it is often hard to see the end. It is not easy to comprehend the outcome either. As you squirm in the heat of battle, your heart may wonder, "How long . . . why, Lord?" In those dark moments of life, you doubt your own strength and your ability to make it.

God has good news for you. Take courage; fear not! God understands your circumstances. He will not leave you alone in your times of great need. "My grace is sufficient for thee: for my strength is made perfect in weakness" (2 Corinthians 12:9). You will not go under; instead, you will emerge a victor in God. God will give you the ability to go through it. Yes, the Shepherd is touched by the feelings of your infirmities, and He will help you.

"Yea, though I walk through the valley of the shadow of death, I will fear no evil: for thou art with me; thy rod and thy staff they comfort me" (Psalm 23:4).

READ 1 PETER 5:7.

February 9
CHOOSE TO FOLLOW THE SHEPHERD.

Sheep are very interesting animals. Unlike most animals (and even human beings) who desire to follow their own way, sheep must be led. You can drop off dogs and cats many miles from your home, but they will find their way back with ease. This is not true for sheep. Once lost, you might as well forget the hope of finding them unless you seek them. However, sheep follow their shepherd better than other animals. They follow at will without coercion, threat, or discipline.

Sheep are defenseless animals. They can neither bark, growl, or bite like dogs and cats. It is no wonder they stay close to the shepherd; they must be protected. The easiest way for sheep to remain safe is to stay close to the shepherd. Born-again Christians are not different from sheep. "For ye were as sheep going astray; but are now returned unto the Shepherd and Bishop of your souls" (1 Peter 2:25).

The easiest way to stay out of trouble is to follow the Shepherd. Do not follow at a distance; instead, follow very closely. The Shepherd knows your needs. He understands you. He knows when you are hungry and in need of grazing in green pastures. He knows when you are thirsty and in need of a drink.

The Shepherd knows when you are tired and in need of rest beside quiet waters. The Shepherd also knows when you are weak, weary, wounded, and too feeble to walk on your own. It is in those moments that He carries, comforts, and nurses you back to health.

Those who follow closely are well-nourished and spiritually healthy. To not follow the Shepherd is to be lonely. It is to have an overload of burdens. It is to wilt, but ultimately, it is to fail.

> He leadeth me beside the still waters. He restoreth my soul: he leadeth me in the paths of righteousness for his name's sake (Psalm 23:2b–3).

READ HEBREWS 13:6.

CHOOSE TO LISTEN TO THE SHEPHERD.

You will hear many voices speaking to you today. Among them will be the distinctive voice of the Shepherd. How will you differentiate those voices?

Sheep can tell the voice of their shepherd from that of a stranger. They will not follow a stranger; instead, they will run away out of fear. Likewise, God's child must know from whom to run away and to what to listen.

God's voice is powerful. It cannot be likened to the seductive and lying voices of peers and the enemy. When He speaks, there will be peace, calmness and direction (see Luke 8:24–25). God's voice brings change. It heals, restores, builds, grows, steadies, comforts, warms, and gives strength, courage, and hope. His voice takes away fear (see Psalm 29:3–9).

God will speak to you at a personal level with certainty. Regardless of where and when He speaks, He will single you out and speak to your heart. God knows all His sheep, and He speaks to each one by name.

In a time of great distress, He called out to Mary by name as she stood by the graveside (John 20:11-18). In moments of temptation, He singled out Peter and addressed him by name (Luke 22:31). While in doubt, He spoke to Thomas by name (John 20:24).

Listen to the Shepherd today. The Shepherd knows what is best for you. Those who enjoy green pastures and find rest for their souls listen to the Shepherd. "My sheep hear my voice, and I know them, and they follow me" (John 10:27).

God's Word is God's voice in your life today. Tune in and find out what the Shepherd is saying. It is in His Word that you will find strength and direction for your life.

Regardless of whether you have been listening to the Shepherd or not, start today. His words give life. They give hope in difficult times. They give courage when you are surrounded by fearful situations. The Shepherd's voice is your anchor. Listen today.

READ PSALM 119:103–106.

THE SHEPHERD IS GIVING AN INVITATION.

Have you ever seen sheep take care of themselves? Have you seen them seek good pasture and still waters for themselves? God, Who formed us, knows how easy it is for our lives to crumble. He understands how easily we can lose direction and wander in dangerous places that subject us to relentless pressure and disappointment.

God has given us His only Son to be the Shepherd of our souls. Look at God's invitation to join His flock: "For God so loved the world, that he gave his only begotten Son, that whosoever believeth in him should not perish, but have everlasting life. For God sent not his Son into the world to condemn the world; but that the world through him might be saved" (John 3:16–17).

Do you know the Shepherd? Seek to know Him today. A life devoid of the Shepherd is a life of many struggles and endless mistakes. Only God, the Shepherd, can lead you beside quiet waters in life. Only the Shepherd can restore your soul and lead you in paths of righteousness. He never casts away those who come to Him (John 6:37). The Shepherd's arms are open to you. He is beckoning you to Himself, saying, "Come unto me, all ye that labour and are heavy laden, and I will give you rest. Take my yoke upon you, and learn of me; for I am meek and lowly in heart: and ye shall find rest unto your souls" (Matthew 11:28–29).

READ JOHN 15:5.

THE SHEPHERD IS WATCHING OVER YOU TODAY.

When God delivered His children from bondage and set them on the road to the land of promise, He did not abandon them to find their own way through the wilderness. He stood with them. Not only did He walk alongside them, but He also engulfed them with His powerful presence. "And the Lord went before them by day in a pillar of a cloud, to lead them the way; and by night in a pillar of fire, to give them light; to go by day and night: He took not away the pillar of the cloud by day, nor the pillar of fire by night, from before the people" (Exodus 13:21–22).

Life has many challenges, and in most cases, it may seem as though you are alone. Take courage; the Shepherd does not abandon His sheep on dark and treacherous paths. God will not leave you to be engulfed in the storms and flames of life. God loves you. He will stand with you. He will walk with you through those dark valleys. He will overshadow you with His presence. You will not go under. Instead, it shall be well because the Shepherd is watching over you.

Look at the Shepherd's promise to you today: "Fear not: for I have redeemed thee, I have called thee by thy name; thou art mine. When thou passest through the waters, I will be with thee; and through the rivers, they shall not overflow thee: when thou walkest through the fire, thou shalt not be burned; neither shall the flame kindle upon thee" (Isaiah 43:1–2).

The Shepherd has His eyes on you.

READ ISAIAH 49:8.

GOD IS COMMITTED TO YOUR WELFARE.

A true story is told of a forest fire that was brought under control. Firefighters walked through the devastated, black landscape to ensure that all hot spots were extinguished when one saw what looked like a large, burned-up bird. Wondering why a bird could not fly away to escape such a fire, he kicked it away. The man was astonished at the sound of chicks that scurried away seeking shelter. The firefighter was confounded to realize that a hen risked her life, endured the flames, and died to save her young ones.

God, your Shepherd, likens Himself to a mother. Like a mother, God is committed to your welfare. He oversees that you are well-fed and that your needs are sufficiently met. When a child is cradled in his mother's arms, there is no fear of anything. There is deep comfort and settled assurance that all will be well.

Find comfort in the Shepherd's words to you today: "Can a woman forget her sucking child, that she should not have compassion on the son of her womb? yea, they may forget, yet will I not forget thee. Behold, I have graven thee upon the palms of my hands; thy walls are continually before me" (Isaiah 49:15–16).

You cannot compare the Shepherd's care and protection to that of a hen. God is committed to your welfare. "When thou passest through the waters, I will be with thee; and through the rivers, they shall not overflow thee: when thou walkest through the fire, thou shalt not be burned; neither shall the flame kindle upon thee" (Isaiah 43:2).

"The Lord is my Shepherd, I shall not want" (Psalm 23:1). Stay in the loving arms of the Shepherd, and it shall be well.

READ PSALM 103:17–18.

YOUR SHEPHERD HAS SUFFICIENT GRACE TO TAKE YOU THROUGH THIS DAY.

Sheep are very delicate animals. A shepherd must carefully determine safe pasture for his sheep or else may spend most of his day rescuing and nursing them. Unlike goats and cows, which cross valleys and ascend hilly areas with ease, sheep easily stumble and get stuck in trenches. Should they fall on their backs, they remain helpless until help arrives, or else they die.

It is with such understanding that a shepherd stays vigilant and close to his sheep when the terrain is treacherous. God does the same for His children on a more intricate level. He determines the path you take and orchestrates the events of your life. He is careful with His choices, but He does not leave you at any time.

God knows what befalls you. In fact, nothing comes your way without passing through His hand. He weighs, determines, and permits only what He knows you will handle. In moments when your strength weakens and your endurance wanes, His grace prevails. When your courage diminishes and fear takes a central stage, His arms of grace hold and strengthen you. When you get overwhelmed and your spirit gets crushed within you, it is His grace that carries you.

God's grace is sufficient for your situations today. Take His Word of promise and let His grace help you. "My grace is sufficient for thee: for my strength is made perfect in weakness" (2 Corinthians 12:9).

> The Lord is my Shepherd; I shall not want . . . he leadeth me in the paths of righteousness for his name's sake. Yea, though I walk through the valley of the shadow of death, I will fear no evil: for thou art with me; thy rod and thy staff they comfort me (Psalm 23:1, 3–4).

PSALM 107:33–38.

February 5

THE SHEPHERD WILL
STRENGTHEN YOU TODAY.

God has given mothers a special place in the lives of their children. It is easy for a mother to tell when her child is distressed. As she spends time with the child, she can tell when it is time to change a diaper, play, feed, rest, give attention, or take to the doctor. The child need not tell her any of those. Because of their close interaction, the mother also knows when the child is fearful, anxious, worried, or unable to face the demands of the day. Like a good shepherd who knows when to let his sheep rest, have a drink, or graze, the mother shepherds the hearts and lives of her little ones.

What about our Chief Shepherd? Does God know us that well? Does He understand our needs, and does He meet them in a timely manner? Can we trust Him in the valleys of our lives?

God understands when you are weary and exhausted from the situations you encounter in life. In those moments, learn to sit still at the feet of the Shepherd. Allow Him to put His arms of love around you. You do not have to talk or tell Him much, for He understands. In moments when you do not know what to say, the Shepherd reads your heart and understands your intentions.

When tears roll and the anguish pains so deeply, still, He hears. Yes, tears are a language He understands. Take courage, He is with you. See His promise for you today: "For thus saith the Lord God, the Holy One of Israel; In returning and rest shall ye be saved; in quietness and in confidence shall be your strength: and ye would not" (Isaiah 30:15).

Fear not!

READ PSALM 46.

OBSERVE THE SHEPHERD TODAY.

Imagine you have been captured and taken to another country. You anticipate your release someday, even though the prospects are very low. Furthermore, you wouldn't even know how to get back home. After more than ten years of hopeful waiting, you succumb to the reality that you will be a captive for the rest of your life. You endure hard labor and the ill-treatment of your captors into your adult life.

However, your buried dream is revived when the president of your land of captivity releases all fugitives. Without warning or preparations, you are set free to return to your homeland. Since you have no means of transport, you follow a newfound leader in the group and start on a long trek back home. Your preoccupation completely shifts from the pain of the hard labor to the need for safety and sustenance.

The children of Israel faced such practical problems when Pharaoh released them from slavery. The God Who delivered His children from Egypt, the land of bondage, was not blind to what awaited His children. He led them by a pillar of cloud by day and a pillar of fire by night. His children were to watch for those pillars. Whenever the pillar of cloud lifted from above the tent, God's children knew it was time to journey forth. When the cloud stood still, they camped and waited. As long as they observed and stayed in step with Yahweh, they were safe. They were protected, and their needs were met. They enjoyed the warmth of God's presence and their hearts were at peace.

God is not blind to the dangers and difficulties on your journey. He has never been overtaken by events, and He knows what you need. Observe, see, and understand what the Lord is doing. Don't move when He is not moving. Don't act when He wants you to be still. Follow when you see Him move. Stay in step with the Shepherd today.

> I will instruct thee and teach thee in the way which thou shalt go: I will guide thee with mine eye (Psalm 32:8).

READ EXODUS 3:8–10.

February 11

THE SHEPHERD KNOWS WHAT YOU NEED AND WHAT IS IMPORTANT.

Sheep are very selective animals. Unlike pigs, goats, and even cows, which eat from a variety of choices, sheep only eat certain things. Goats can eat shrubs, briars, thistles, and other thorny vegetation without a problem. Not sheep! Many common garden plants and weeds are poisonous for sheep. Moreover, most animals can drink water that is moving and not exceptionally clean. This is not true for sheep. Their water source must be clean and still before they take a sip. A shepherd must be selective, too, in determining what to give his sheep.

A shepherd does not lead his flock to poisonous pastures. The shepherd does not offer his sheep what is harmful or dangerous. He does not withhold what is good for nourishment either.

God, your Shepherd, will not let you lack what is good and necessary for your well-being. He is your Shepherd; He will not let you be in want (Psalm 23:1). God will not give you what is poisonous or harmful either. To protect you from possible harm, there are times when God has to say no. "No" does not imply that God hates you. A "no" answer from the throne of God is true love in action. Don't insist on getting what the Shepherd does not want you to have. Remember His promise: "No good thing will he withhold from them that walk uprightly" (Psalm 84:11b).

"They shall not hunger nor thirst; neither shall the heat nor sun smite them: for he that hath mercy on them shall lead them, even by the springs of water shall he guide them. And I will make all my mountains a way, and my highways shall be exalted" (Isaiah 49:10–11).

READ ISAIAH 49:10.

THE SHEPHERD WILL WALK WITH YOU.

Shepherds are different from individuals who own horses or keep cattle on ranches. The nature of their occupation and the characteristics of the animals they keep can be seen in their character and modes of operation. Whereas cattle may not see their owner or keeper for many hours in a day and still thrive, sheep are under the constant watch and care of their shepherd. Sheep are helpless animals, and shepherds do not leave them unattended.

God is a good Shepherd. He gives His life for the sheep. He does not leave His sheep unattended. God has not left you helpless. You are not alone. Regardless of what surrounds you, you have a Helper, the Holy Spirit, Who dwells in you. God is that wonderful Shepherd Who not only walks with His children but indwells them. He understands the groans of your heart. He interprets the sighing of your heart because He resides right there.

Find help and comfort in His promise from John 14:16–18 today: "And I will pray the Father, and he shall give you another Comforter, that he may abide with you forever; Even the Spirit of truth; whom the world cannot receive, because it seeth him not, neither knoweth him: but ye know him; for he dwelleth with you, and shall be in you. I will not leave you comfortless: I will come to you."

Do not yield to fear or succumb to anxiety. God is with you. "I will never leave thee, nor forsake thee" (Hebrews 13:5). Stand still and see the salvation of God this day. Let Him hold you in His arms as you regain your confidence in His unwavering presence and help.

READ ISAIAH 46:4.

THE SHEPHERD IS LOOKING OUT FOR YOU.

Sheep are very vulnerable. Not only do they stumble easily, but they also stray from the path with similar ease. Should sheep fall on their back, they cannot get back up without support and help. It is for such reasons that a shepherd carefully searches for pasture where his sheep will not be endangered. As he leads his sheep, he cautiously looks out for cliffs, potholes, grooves, and sudden changes in terrain. He avoids paths where there is possibility of danger. He looks out for dangerous animals that can spook and hurt his flock.

God, your Shepherd, is looking out for you too. As you see Him wave and swing His staff, His aim is to protect and keep you in the way everlasting. God has your welfare at heart. You will not be surpassed. He will open the right doors for you when He determines that the time is ripe. God is protecting in ways you do not know. It is God Who has spared your life on numerous occasions that you may live and fulfill His purposes.

God will go before you. He will speak on your behalf. He will tenderize hearts and show you favor. He will give you a place. God is preparing you for the future. He sees the end from the beginning. He knows what is best for you in the days ahead. Every day is a training day in the school of God.

> The Lord is my shepherd; I shall not want. . . . Thou preparest a table before me in the presence of mine enemies: thou anointest my head with oil; my cup runneth over. Surely goodness and mercy shall follow me all the days of my life: and I will dwell in the house of the Lord forever (Psalm 23:1, 5–6).

The Shepherd is looking out for you.

READ PSALM 108:11–13.

THE SHEPHERD WANTS YOU TO HAVE THE BEST IN LIFE.

Life has glamor and a lure that tempt the heart of every Christian. Like sheep that stray from the path selected by the shepherd to pastures off to the sides, God's children are drawn away by what surrounds them. Our appetites are whet as our eyes are attracted. Sometimes, our hearts are tempted to think and believe we are missing good things within our constraints as Christians. That is not true.

God does not deny His children good things (Psalm 84:11). Contrary to popular belief, God lavishes our lives with endless treasures and looks out for us while causing boundary lines to fall for us in pleasant places (Psalm 16:5–6). To crown it all, we have a wonderful inheritance (Psalm 16:6).

The Shepherd wants you to have the best life. Your joy, comfort, and safety are a priority to the Shepherd. It is for such concerns that God gently leads His children in paths of righteousness. Your fulfillment and satisfaction in life correlate to your ability to follow the Shepherd.

God does not drive His sheep. He leads us in love, gentleness, and kindness. "He shall feed his flock like a shepherd: he shall gather the lambs with his arm, and carry them in his bosom, and shall gently lead those that are with young" (Isaiah 40:11).

When you follow Him, you are assured of having the very best life. A failure to follow the Shepherd subjects you to what is subsidiary. Look at God's testimony on behalf of those He led through the wilderness for forty long years. Stick to the Lord and your life will be guided by His Divine and powerful hand.

And I have led you forty years in the wilderness: your clothes are not waxen old upon you, and thy shoe is not waxen old upon thy foot (Deuteronomy 29:5).

READ PSALM 84.

THE SHEPHERD IS A SHELTER IN THE TIME OF STORM.

Shepherds have shelters that protect sheep from extreme temperatures. In the blazing heat, shepherds lead their sheep to large, shady trees, gullies, hedges of trees, or constructed shelters. Because sheep cannot survive well or thrive where there is a combination of extremely cold temperatures and wet and windy conditions, shepherds prepare by constructing sheds to protect their sheep. The shepherd understands his sheep. When he sees them restless, not eating well, and constantly huddling together, he steps in to meet their needs.

Our Shepherd knows and understands us better than the best shepherd out there. He prepares us for what is ahead. He knows when we need shelter. He knows when the spiritual temperatures drop very low or rise very high.

Storms of life, the cares of this world, and sin have a way of beating upon the heart of man. These things make you weary, weak, and unable to run the spiritual race with effectiveness. God, your Shepherd, is aware of that. It is for such reasons that He takes it upon Himself to restore your soul (Psalm 23:3).

Today, the Shepherd will stretch out His arm of love to you. He will soothe your sorrows. He will nurse your hurts. He will love on you. His will restore you. Enjoy God's nourishment for your heart today. Allow Him to hold you closer to Himself. Walk hand in hand with the Shepherd and let Him restore and refresh your heart. "The Lord is my Shepherd . . . He restores my soul."

"I will not leave you comfortless: I will come to you" (John 14:18).

READ PSALM 91:1–5.

YOUR SHEPHERD WILL BE FAITHFUL.

You cannot leave sheep unattended in pastures where there are predators. Sheep are defenseless animals. They lack the growling dare of other animals, and they do not have horns or teeth for defense. They depend on their master for protection. We, like sheep, are no match for the devil.

If God were to leave us alone to Satan for one day, Satan would crash and sift us like wheat. God does not leave you at the mercy of this dreadful and fierce enemy. God stands with you in battle. Satan, like Goliath the giant, likes to intimidate and prowl as he sends fear and panic. Do not fall for his dirty tricks. You are well able to mastermind his schemes and win because you have Divine help. Christ stands at the right hand of God the Father fighting for you every day. Arise and take your place in battle. Fight for the treasures with which God has entrusted you.

> But this man, because he continueth ever, hath an unchangeable priesthood. Wherefore he is able also to save them to the uttermost that come unto God by him, seeing he ever liveth to make intercession for them. For such an high priest became us, who is holy, harmless, undefiled, separate from sinners, and made higher than the heavens. (Hebrews 7:24–26)

The Shepherd will be faithful to you in battle. Christ trains us, allocates our position in battle, fights with us and for us, and prays for us. He is your Advocate. He has been faced with the temptations you are undergoing. He empathizes and steps in to strongly help you.

God knows what is ahead. Let the words of Christ to the apostle Peter encourage you to keep fighting: "And the Lord said, Simon, Simon, behold, Satan hath desired to have you, that he may sift you as wheat: But I have prayed for thee, that thy faith fail not: and when thou art converted" (Luke 22:31–32).

READ JOHN 6:60–69.

THE SHEPHERD HAS GIVEN YOU THE RIGHT ARMOR.

Sheep are vulnerable to heat and cold. God, in His great wisdom, has clothed them with enough wool to keep their body heat against blistering cold winds. This same covering is sheared when the weather is warm in order to keep them cool. God has impeccable protection for His children too.

Most enemies attack at your time of vulnerability. Robbers strike in the wee hours of the night when it is dark. They break in when you are asleep and incoherent. They may isolate and carefully entangle you in a place of little defense and where you can neither retreat nor call for help. Surprisingly, Satan uses these same tricks in order to defeat you.

What do you do when you are suspicious of an attack? You guard yourself. You safeguard your house. You secure your doors and every possible entry point. You ensure your security cameras and alarm systems are working. You may have friends, family members, and law enforcement on standby. Now, translate these preparations into spiritual preparations against Satan, who, like a robber, strikes when you least expect him. God wants you to prepare so your enemy does not find you unprepared. Look at God's admonition.

> Finally, my brethren, be strong in the Lord, and in the power of his might. Put on the whole armour of God, that ye may be able to stand against the wiles of the devil. For we wrestle not against flesh and blood, but against principalities, against powers, against the rulers of the darkness of this world, against spiritual wickedness in high places. Wherefore take unto you the whole armour of God, that ye may be able to withstand in the evil day, and having done all, to stand. (Ephesians 6:10–13)

God has provided the right armor for you to successfully fight every day. You will only stand and be safe in this battle against the devil's tricks if you put on God's armor. You need the whole armor to protect yourself fully. Use it to resist and fight back as you hold onto what the enemy is trying to steal and destroy from you.

READ 1 PETER 5:8–9.

THE SHEPHERD SAYS, "FEAR NOT."

Wolves, coyotes, foxes, bears, and wild dogs know that sheep are timid, defenseless, and fearful animals. They prey on them. They work to isolate and attack sheep. When they charge at the sheep, the fearful animals huddle together as a few flee—to the advantage of their predators.

The best way to defeat an enemy is to inflict him with fear. Fear says, "I can't. I am too small, too weak, too insignificant to make a difference." Fear is a common strategy the devil will use to make you think that God has forgotten about you. However, over 365 times, God tells us in His Word, "Fear not." He means it. He knows how easy it is for your heart to fear. Listen to Him and follow Him. "Fear thou not; for I am with thee: be not dismayed; for I am thy God: I will strengthen thee; yea, I will help thee; yea, I will uphold thee with the right hand of my righteousness" (Isaiah 41:10).

God knows what your day looks like. He knows what tomorrow holds. Remember that He sees the beginning from the end. He has already gone ahead of you. You do not need to fear. God knows what you can take. He also knows for what you are capable. It is He Who formed you and gave you your frame. He will not allow anything to come your way that you cannot handle.

Nothing will come your way that God has not allowed. For what He allows, He carefully weighs it and makes sure it is what you can handle. Take courage. You were designed with this day in mind. Walk in the strength of God and do not fear. Remember His promise: "I am with thee . . . I will help thee . . . I will uphold thee with the right hand of my righteousness."

READ ISAIAH 43:1–2.

THE SHEPHERD WILL NEVER LEAVE YOU.

A shepherd understands his role as he faces each day. He knows that he must lead his sheep to safe pasture, protect them, care for them, and look out for them. Unlike other animal keepers, a shepherd must stay close to the sheep. When they roll down gullies and valleys to freshen and cool off, he is there. While climbing hilly terrains, he looks out for them. God, our good Shepherd, does the same for His children. He does not leave His sheep alone.

Life has many rough waters. Life has many treacherous bridges to cross and dark valleys to walk. It is easy to get overwhelmed. It is easy to break under the weight of your load. However, do not lose focus of God's position in your life. He is right here with you. Find strength in His personal message to you today. "When thou passest through the waters, I will be with thee; and through the rivers, they shall not overflow thee: when thou walkest through the fire, thou shalt not be burned; neither shall the flame kindle upon thee" (Isaiah 43:2).

God will keep His promise. He will never leave you. He will walk by your side today. You will not go through this day alone at any point. As you walk through rivers of difficulty, He will be with you. The river will not overflow to drown you. He will walk with you through fires of oppression. You will come out unharmed.

"Be strong and of a good courage, fear not, nor be afraid of them: for the LORD thy God, he it is that doth go with thee; he will not fail thee, nor forsake thee" (Deuteronomy 31:6). You can count on God to walk by your side today. He is not a man who will forsake you at your greatest hour of need. Call on Him and let Him assure you of His abiding presence today. The Shepherd will not leave you.

READ DEUTERONOMY 31:8.

THE SHEPHERD IS A SHELTER AND A ROCK IN TIMES OF STORMS.

Shepherds protect their sheep from storms and hurricanes. They prepare barns and shelters in advance and move the animals from open fields to those secure locations. They feed and water the sheep in those closed areas. The sheep, too, know how to be safe. They hurdle together and remain in their circumscribed boundaries until the storm is over.

What about God's sheep? How does God deal with us when storms of life hit? God does not leave us in the open or vulnerable to the violent winds. He shelters us. He opens His arms of grace and hides us within Himself—our Rock. God gives peace in the midst of the storm.

God has the power to calm the storms that face you today. Storms of life cause turbulence and turmoil to the heart. They disrupt life in every aspect. However, look at what God desires for you amid your storms. "Let not your heart be troubled: ye believe in God, believe also in me. . . . Peace I leave with you, my peace I give unto you: not as the world giveth, give I unto you. Let not your heart be troubled, neither let it be afraid" (John 14:1, 27).

Troubled times are many. Troubled hearts even more so. God cares. God is concerned about what faces you today. He sees your troubled heart. He cares about the tears that fall deep within. He is here to stand with you and to help you today. Believe in God and count on His presence today.

God does not promise the absence of trouble, but He promises to be with you. He will not let you go through rough times alone. Hold onto His Word and walk with courage. Let Him calm your heart as He soothes you with His Word and tender love. It is He Who made the storms. He will calm the winds in your life.

READ PHILIPPIANS 4:6–7.

TRUST THE SHEPHERD.

It is not uncommon for animals to scatter, take shortcuts, and even break fences to get to their pastures. For them, all that matters at that time is the desire to satisfy their hunger. Safety is disregarded.

However, how does God deal with His children, whom He likens to sheep? God knows that we have desires, wishes, and wants. He knows what is important, what to give, what to withhold, and when to grant us our requests. He knows what is good for us and when we should have it. He also understands what can hurt us, and so He holds off some things.

The Shepherd will not take you through shortcuts. He may not allow you to break through fences to get to your desires either. Look at what He told His children thousands of years ago: "And it came to pass, when Pharaoh had let the people go, that God led them not through the way of the land of the Philistines, although that was near; for God said, Lest peradventure the people repent when they see war, and they return to Egypt: But God led the people about, through the way of the wilderness of the Red sea" (Exodus 13:17–18).

Are you walking through the wilderness? Take heart, the Shepherd may be safeguarding you from war. Does the journey seem long, torturous, and endless? Don't lose heart; God may be saving you from being maimed by your enemy. The Shepherd will not lead you to dangerous paths in life. Your safety and well-being are important to Him. Trust His leading, and you will be fine.

READ ISAIAH 40:11.

You matter to the Shepherd.

When a shepherd takes his sheep to the fields, it is not uncommon for a sheep to get lost. Sheep easily get stuck in fences, gullies, or bushes. A good shepherd inspects his flock before heading home or locking up his animals in pens for the night. When he realizes that one sheep is missing, he embarks on a journey to find it.

God our Shepherd does the same. You matter to the Shepherd. Regardless of how big a herd or a flock a shepherd may have, he does not forget one single animal. You are not just a number to God. God cares, and He knows you by name. He loves you.

The Shepherd is looking for you today. Your situations may be tough, and your heart may be tempted to think He does not care or even know about you. This is not true. God has engraved you in the palms of His hands (Isaiah 49:16). There is not a single time you are out of His Divine eye.

The troubles of this world are good at shielding our hearts from seeing and appreciating the love of our Shepherd. You are precious; you are royal. Look at how the Shepherd sees you. "But ye are a chosen generation, a royal priesthood, an holy nation, a peculiar people; that ye should shew forth the praises of him who hath called you out of darkness into his marvellous light" (1 Peter 2:9). The Shepherd knows and calls you by name each day (John 10:3).

The tough situations of life do not denote the absence of God. God is standing with you. He is holding your hand and guiding your steps. Soon, you will feel the deep warmth of His embrace. You are special to the Shepherd.

Read Matthew 11:28–29.

February 29
LEAN ON THE SHEPHERD.

In times of danger, sickness, or hunger, sheep have the shepherd as their only hope. They are dependent animals. Nevertheless, a good shepherd does not take advantage of their vulnerability to punish, discipline, or deny their needs. Instead, the characteristics of the animals propel him to prepare and perform his duties with diligence. He looks after the sick and nurses them as he feeds and protects them. The sick, weak, young, and endangered sheep stay closest to the shepherd.

God our Father is no different. He is the Good Shepherd Who lays down His life for the sheep (John 10:11). Today, the Shepherd is watching and looking out for you. He sees what surrounds you and knows the dangers in your life. He understands your weakness and weariness. He will not thrust you out of His presence into the dangers from which your heart is running.

The Shepherd will watch over you today. You can rest in His arms. He will cover you with His feathers, and He will be about your business today. God will give His angels charge to guard and guide you in all your ways.

Lean on the Shepherd today. Let your heart find peace and rest in the care of the Shepherd as you confess and depend on His Word.

> I will say of the LORD, He is my refuge and my fortress: my God; in him will I trust. Surely he shall deliver thee from the snare of the fowler, and from the noisome pestilence. He shall cover thee with his feathers, and under his wings shalt thou trust: his truth shall be thy shield and buckler. Thou shalt not be afraid for the terror by night; nor for the arrow that flieth by day; Nor for the pestilence that walketh in darkness; nor for the destruction that wasteth at noonday. (Psalm 91:2-6)

The Shepherd will rescue you. He will answer your call. He will be with you in the difficult moments of your life. He will remember you with grace and mercy. He will satisfy you and show you His salvation. Lean on the Shepherd today.

READ PSALM 121:1-8.

March

FINDING HOPE AND STRENGTH IN THE CHARACTER OF GOD

How do you deal with challenging and changing situations? Does God always stand with His children?

Your times are in God's hands. Let us find hope in His unchanging character this month.

GOD IS PRESENT DURING SEASONS OF PLENTY AND DROUGHT.

God will take care of you in moments of drought.

Droughts and hot weather pose challenges to shepherds and sheep. Sheep go through heat stress; their wool retains heat, and unless their conditions are altered, their body temperature continues to increase, and they eventually collapse and die.

A shepherd must be vigilant to look for nontraditional ways of feeding and watering the sheep. With grazing pastures dried up, he must now feed his sheep on more exotic foods like sorghum, oats, barley, or sheep nuts. The cost of maintaining sheep in such conditions is high and this can cause emotional, physical, and financial stress on the shepherd. Not only must he be extra vigilant in finding alternative ways of feeding and watering his animals, but he must monitor the sheep to ensure they are well cooled, nourished, and healthy. The shepherd is constantly present.

How does God deal with His sheep in moments of high heat and drought?

I believe God does the same for His children. In your times of drought and high heat, you have the unfailing attention of the Shepherd. Like a vessel on the wheel of a master porter, He carefully molds and works intricate designs while keeping you pliable and well cured like good clay that produces a masterpiece vessel for His use.

The Shepherd's eye is on you. Regardless of the intensity of your circumstances, the Shepherd says, "Fear not." Do not be dismayed. God will not leave you to face the fierce world with its storms alone. Instead, He will strengthen and help you with His mighty righteous right hand (see Isaiah 41:10).

He will satisfy your heart in moments of drought. The Shepherd does not take pride in malnourished sheep. God will nourish you and your little ones. God will not leave you to huff and puff like one who is destitute in a dry and scorched land. Take His promise and walk with hope and courage today:

> "And the LORD shall guide thee continually, and satisfy thy soul in drought, and make fat thy bones: and thou shalt be like a watered garden, and like a spring of water, whose waters fail not" (Isaiah 58:11).

READ 1 KINGS 17.

LISTEN TO GOD.

Sheep know and understand the voice of their shepherd. They can isolate it amid many voices. They understand and follow the cues of the shepherd too. They can tell when he wants them to lie down and rest beside quiet waters, get up, or start their journey to the grazing fields. They just follow the shepherd from one place to another. When a sheep gets hurt, it stays closer to the shepherd. This kind of communication develops over time.

God desires such a relationship with His children. To understand God, to stay and follow closely enough to know His desire and mode of operation is to be stable and secure in life.

God understands you and knows what you need at every moment and stage of life. No day goes by without His drawing your attention to Him as He works to meet your needs. He has all you need.

It is easy to miss God's voice. This often leads to frustration, distrust, and believing He does not care about us. The secret is to focus and tune in as we learn to isolate and differentiate His voice from many others.

It is easy to overlook God's voice. He may say, "Fear thou not; for I am with thee: be not dismayed; for I am thy God: I will strengthen thee; yea, I will help thee; yea, I will uphold thee with the right hand of my righteousness" (Isaiah 41:10). However, when the doctor gives his diagnosis later in the day, we may believe and act on the doctor's report with fear without remembering what God said in the morning.

God's voice is our greatest strength in life. It gives hope and courage. You can face anything however significant when you believe God's message to you each day.

Our days are filled with eventualities and God does not leave us to grope in darkness without shining His light and giving direction as needed.

"My sheep hear my voice, and I know them, and they follow me" (John 10:27).

Strive to listen to the Shepherd today.

READ PROVERBS 15:23 AND ISAIAH 30:21.

ENJOYING THE COMPANY
OF THE SHEPHERD

I have been young and now I am older, but I have never seen shepherds guarding, watching, and staying on pasturelands day after day without their sheep. When you find a shepherd all by himself in such places, he is usually on a specific mission. Conversely, it is equally rare to see sheep unattended for days in those pasturelands.

Sheep enjoy the company of their shepherd. Remember, they are dependent animals. They need a shepherd if they must thrive and stay safe. A shepherd without sheep and sheep without a shepherd are misnomers both in the literal and spiritual sense.

God delights in His children. He takes pleasure in His people (Psalm 149:4). Imagine how awful it would be for a shepherd to look forward to taking care of his sheep only for the sheep to run away from him or to walk contrary to his desires.

God enjoys the company of His children. He loves to see you walk and commune with Him.

It gives God pleasure to see your heart warmed and enchanted toward Him. Those who stay close to Him enjoy extra benefits that accompany salvation. They see His face and are strengthened in their spirits. God lightens their burdens, and they can still praise Him during tough situations (see Psalm 84).

There is no better way to go through life than to hold onto God and enjoy His company regardless of your surroundings.

God has great promises for those who enjoy His company.

> Delight thyself also in the Lord: and he shall give thee the desires of thine heart. Commit thy way unto the Lord; trust also in him; and he shall bring it to pass (Psalm 37:4–5).

READ PSALM 25:14.

TRUST THE PROTECTION OF THE SHEPHERD.

The shepherd takes it upon himself to protect his sheep. As he anticipates danger, he may lead his sheep to safety or stand against the enemy. Sheep trust their shepherd's protection. They do not hurdle together all day fearing an attack from the enemy.

God protects His children from the snares of the enemy. He does this, most of the time, by placing His holy and divine boundaries of love and protection around us. Those who identify and stay within God's secure borders are spared endless and fierce attacks of the adversary. However, to live outside God's demarcated walls of safety is to remain under the constant pursuit of this relentless enemy. God does not enjoy seeing you harassed by an enemy He has equipped you to fight and defeat. "But ye, beloved, building up yourselves on your most holy faith, praying in the Holy Ghost, Keep yourselves in the love of God, looking for the mercy of our Lord Jesus Christ unto eternal life" (Jude 20-21).

Stay within the boundaries of God's love. You will find protection and provision as you remain under the umbrella of God's love and boundaries. Outside of this are ravenous wolves seeking opportunity to hurt and drive you from God. Walk within the boundaries of God's commandments and remain secure from the luring snares of Satan. God's precepts are not burdensome. They are meant to nourish and protect and not to harm you.

God is able to keep you from falling. Christ has the power to present you faultless and undefiled before the Father. Build yourself on the most holy faith as you pray and follow God (Jude 20-24). Walking outside God's circumscribed boundary lines will leave you wounded, scarred, and unfulfilled in life. It will rob you of peace and soundness of mind. Stay within the boundaries of God's umbrella.

READ PSALM 46.

SEEK THE APPROVAL OF THE SHEPHERD.

The shepherd does not require anything out of his sheep beyond their capabilities. Sheep can neither do what a cow or a lion can. This is how our Shepherd deals with His sheep. He knows for what you are capable because He knows the weave from which you are made.

It is easy to care about how people perceive us more than what God knows and sees about us.

We enjoy great love and peace when God is pleased with our work. God is not like man who is constantly looking for something negative for which to chide you. God sees the good in you. He knows the honesty and the sincerity of your heart. Our heavenly Father not only delights in His children but blesses their efforts. There is nothing you do for Him, regardless of size or magnitude, that goes unnoticed. Look at how God deals with His servants.

> And so he that had received five talents came and brought other five talents, saying, Lord, thou deliveredst unto me five talents: behold, I have gained beside them five talents more. His lord said unto him, Well done, thou good and faithful servant: thou hast been faithful over a few things, I will make thee ruler over many things: enter thou into the joy of thy lord. (Matthew 25:20–21)

Not all comments made by people are worth trusting. You will be flattered in life. Hearts are deceitful and desperately wicked. They will say one thing and mean another.

Learn to walk and do everything as one doing it unto God. You will be frustrated when you work to win the approval and favor of man. Not many people are easy to please.

No better words can soothe your heart to restful sleep than to hear the Holy Spirit whisper, "Well done, thou good and faithful servant."

READ REVELATION 16:15.

TRUST THE WORK OF THE SHEPHERD.

One of the greatest challenges of our Christian life and walk is understanding what God is doing. Since we cannot see Him with our naked eyes, we struggle to comprehend His ways and direction. It is not unusual to wonder, "Should I move on, or should I wait?"

Does God seem slow in responding to your prayers and in fulfilling your plans and desires?

It is easy to rush, cut corners, and even skip essential steps in life to walk in stride with everyone else. However, God's plan for your life is unique. It is not like everyone else's. You must wait on God. You must be patient. Even in silence, God is still working. Can you relate to Abraham in this matter?

> And we desire that every one of you do shew the same diligence to the full assurance of hope unto the end: That ye be not slothful, but followers of them who through faith and patience inherit the promises. For when God made promise to Abraham, because he could swear by no greater, he sware by himself, Saying, Surely blessing I will bless thee, and multiplying I will multiply thee. And so, after he had patiently endured, he obtained the promise. (Hebrews 6:11–15)

Our fast-paced society works at robbing us of patience, but patience is mandatory for every Christian. There are many things that will not come your way except through the seemingly slow and painful road of patience. Like Abraham, you must patiently endure before you can obtain your promise.

Spiritual growth and spiritual fruit come through patience. Have you witnessed a tree put forth fruit in a matter of days following its planting? Just as plants are grown, cultivated, nurtured, and groomed before producing fruit, so you must exercise your heart and life in patience.

Cultivate your heart to create fertile soil for God's Word and His working in your life. Keep it tender. As He instructs and counsels, stop, listen, and follow. Before long, the fruit will show. Do not hurry what God is doing in your life. Grow in patience.

READ COLOSSIANS 3:12–13.

SEEK THE APPROVAL OF THE SHEPHERD.

We feel out of place, frustrated, and even unvalued when we do not have a clear purpose in life. Most people desire to be fruitful in addition to living a meaningful life. However, how do you face a world that is more critical than appreciative of you daily?

One secret is to seek the approval of God. We enjoy great love and peace when God is pleased with our work. God is not like man, who is constantly looking for something negative for which to chide you. God sees the good in you. He knows the honesty and the sincerity of your heart. Our heavenly father not only delights in His children but blesses their efforts. There is nothing you do for Him, regardless of size or magnitude, that goes unnoticed. Look at how God deals with His servants.

For God is not unrighteous to forget your work and labour of love, which ye have shewed toward his name, in that ye have ministered to the saints, and do minister.

Learn to walk and do everything as one doing it unto God. You will be frustrated when you work to win the approval and favor of man. Not many people are easy to please. As you walk with God it will become more important to receive His approval than that of people.

READ REVELATION 16:15.

GOD WILL NOT FAIL YOU.

It is not true that one must put God to the side in order to succeed in life. God is as interested in seeing you succeed in and fulfill His will as you are.

Our days are filled with activity. The dictates of life demand our actions and drive us in different directions. We run from morning and exhaust every ounce of energy by evening. This leaves us tired and unfulfilled. God is not blind to what faces you. He desires to help you. God wants you to walk closely with Him. Look at God's admonition today.

> What man is he that feareth the Lord? him shall he teach in the way that he shall choose. His soul shall dwell at ease; and his seed shall inherit the earth. The secret of the Lord is with them that fear him; and he will shew them his covenant. Mine eyes are ever toward the Lord; for he shall pluck my feet out of the net. (Psalm 25:12–15)

In Christ are all hidden treasures of life. It is easy to run and work so hard day and night without involving God in your endeavors. God knows what you need. He knows the best place and time to find it. Embrace God and let Him guide you. He is interested in the minute details of your life. Don't toil alone and walk away empty.

Those who fear the Lord are taught and guided of God. God's leading is precise and fruitful. It is purposeful and targeted. God entrusts His secrets to those who fear Him. No man has ever walked hand in hand with God and failed in life. *God is as interested in your success and fulfillment as you are.*

READ PSALM 86:10–11.

TRUST THE SOVEREIGN GOD.

God is sovereign. He is God. He is the high and lofty supreme One Who inhabits eternity and controls the universe by the word of His power (Hebrews 1:3). He is great and there is none like Him. Nothing occurs to God—nothing takes Him by surprise. He has power over all creation, and He takes care of every detail.

Can you trust God? Can you trust the character of God? Can you trust God when you are left to yourself amid the tough happenings of life? Is He real? Is God trustworthy?

Take time and explore God so that your heart may be anchored in Him. The world is full of turmoil, but you can trust God. "For I know that the Lord is great, and that our Lord is above all gods. Whatsoever the Lord pleased, that did he in heaven, and in earth, in the seas, and all deep places. He causeth the vapours to ascend from the ends of the earth; he maketh lightnings for the rain; he bringeth the wind out of his treasuries" (Psalm 135:5-7).

God knows what is best for you. He is not obligated to tell what He is doing. Even the hearts of kings are in His hands and He turns them wherever He wishes. God hung the earth on nothing and has held it in place by His power. He will take care of you.

READ PSALM 48:14 AND ISAIAH 57:15–16.

March 10

TRUST AND FOLLOW THE GOD OF CHANGE.

Not many people like change. Change brings uncertainty. It can take our hands off the steering wheel and expose our fears, insecurities, and inabilities while creating vulnerability. We find our bearings from mastered routines and living with familiarity.

Abraham, the great Patriarch, found himself face-to-face with the God of change in his old age. It must have been hard, for the man we now know as the father of faith. God asked Abraham to leave the land, the people, the friends, and the memories he had made and known for decades. If that wasn't a big enough challenge, God did not point to a specific place to which Abraham was to go. This is how God worded it: "Now the Lord had said unto Abram, Get thee out of thy country, and from thy kindred, and from thy father's house, unto a land that I will shew thee" (Genesis 12:1).

It will be scary when God takes you out of your familiar surroundings to the unknown. However, His intentions are good. He is not out to hurt you. You may neither know nor comprehend the next step to take, but you must remember that God Who is initiating it knows the end and He will lead you.

Change presents open doors for God's blessings. You may remain the same for years to come if God does not guide you through this open door of change. God knows what you need. He knows what is best for you. Some of His greatest blessings come through the very changes that threatened our own souls.

Little did Abraham know that through that "simple" visitation from God and the subsequent changes, he would become the father of the whole world. Out of his own barren body would proceed kings, queens, men, women, and children across the nations.

Watch out! The changes God initiates in your life may take you to places you did not dream of reaching and impact others in unfathomable ways.

"Trust in the Lord with all thine heart; and lean not unto thine own understanding. In all thy ways acknowledge him, and he shall direct thy paths" (Proverbs 3:5–6).

READ ROMANS 4:16–25.

STAND ON GOD'S SIDE.

It is not easy to talk about some things in life. However, it refreshes and anchors our hearts in God when He walks through the weird circumstances and lets you know He is watching over you.

How do you react when someone you love revolts and walks away? What do you do when the persons you help use the resultant blessings to hurt you? How about being turned in by an individual you trusted just because they are seeking a favor for themselves?

Abram found himself in such quagmire with his nephew. When disputes arose between their servants, Lot did not remember Abram's help in his life. There was no one to whisper in his ear that the whole land belonged to Abram. Maybe, there was no courageous person to remind Lot to give his uncle the first choice of where to settle. Lot chose the best of the land and departed (Genesis 13:11).

God did not leave Abram at the mercy of his little nephew. He blessed His faithful servant with much more than land and cattle (Genesis 13:14–18).

Take heart in whatever situation you face. Christ, Who sees and cares for you now, went through similar challenges. His only true friends, His disciples, turned from Him. The abundance of blessings from God in our lives drive us from Him as we seek pleasurable gratification. Judas betrayed His love for monetary gains and recognition.

Let your heart rest in the promises of God today. "For the eyes of the Lord run to and fro throughout the whole earth, to shew himself strong in the behalf of them whose heart is perfect toward him" (2 Chronicles 16:9).

God sees everything. He knows all things. You don't have to fight all battles that come your way. You cannot defend yourself against everyone. People will outsmart and outscheme you. Nonetheless, God Who is sovereign is also just. He will stand out and look out for you.

Remain true to God regardless of what people do.

READ PSALM 121.

GOD IS FULL OF IRONY.

Isaiah, the great beloved Old Testament prophet, put it in an excellent way: "For my thoughts are not your thoughts, neither are your ways my ways, saith the Lord. For as the heavens are higher than the earth, so are my ways higher than your ways, and my thoughts than your thoughts" (Isaiah 55:8–9).

When Lot parted ways with Abram, I don't think it occurred to the young man how soon he would need his uncle's help again. A coalition of kings attacked Sodom and Gomorrah, the land in which Lot settled. The Bible records that, "They took Lot, Abram's brother's son, who dwelt in Sodom, and his goods, and departed" (Genesis 14:12).

Abram did not hesitate to go for "his brother":

When Abram heard that his brother was taken captive, he armed his trained servants, born in his own house, three hundred and eighteen, and pursued them unto Dan. And he divided himself against them, he and his servants, by night, and smote them, and pursued them unto Hobah, which is on the left hand of Damascus. And he brought back all the goods, and also brought again his brother Lot, and his goods, and the women also, and the people. (Genesis 14:14–16)

The God of Abram is the one still watching out for you. The conniving, wrong intentions, schemes, and evil plots of men and women against you will not take Him by surprise.

God is the only One Who can speak to the inner fabric of your matrix. He understands the deep sighing of wonder that the heart can neither put in words nor speak about with openness.

Do not revenge or wish evil on those who despitefully use you. Give God room to avenge on your behalf. He does it better than the most skilled person you know. "O the depth of the riches both of the wisdom and knowledge of God! how unsearchable are his judgments, and his ways past finding out! For who hath known the mind of the Lord? or who hath been his counsellor?" (Romans 11:33).

READ DEUTERONOMY 32:35.

WE CAN BE HAUNTED BY WEALTH AND SUCCESS.

While fairy godmothers may not exist, it is often the case that knowing influential and important people can get you things you want. It may be alarming if we knew how many people rely on the aid of significant and influential persons for their success, positions, power, and wealth.

Abram went out with armed men from his house to rescue Lot, his nephew, who was captured by four kings. God gave Abram unsurpassed victory. He conquered their armies, retrieved Lot's family, and all they took. In addition, they plundered Sodom and Gomorrah.

On their way back home, the king of Sodom asked Abram to release the captives but keep all goods. Abram's answer was revelatory and unique, "I will not take from a thread even to a shoelatchet, and that I will not take any thing that is thine, lest thou shouldest say, I have made Abram rich" (Genesis 14:23).

Did the king of Sodom know how much God had blessed Abram? Let us think through and learn from Abram's response.

Man's help can entangle, enslave, and take away our privileges in life, leaving us prisoners for what God could have given us.

What is the source of your wealth, position, or success? Can God take credit or are you indebted to it for life?

God has good plans for you. Do not sell your soul for what God has in store for you. Look at His promise in 2 Corinthians 9:8–11: "And God is able to make all grace abound toward you; that ye, always having all sufficiency in all things, may abound to every good work: (As it is written, He hath dispersed abroad; he hath given to the poor: his righteousness remaineth for ever. Now he that ministereth seed to the sower both minister bread for your food, and multiply your seed sown, and increase the fruits of your righteousness;) being enriched in every thing to all bountifulness, which causeth through us thanksgiving to God."

READ PROVERBS 25:19 AND PSALM 147:10–11.

EXPERIENCING BREAKTHROUGHS FROM GOD.

Wonderful as money can be, it has limitations. It can buy a bed but not sleep. It can purchase clothes but not life. It will pay for great services but it will not give you peace or joy.

Abram was a wealthy man who had herds of animals, many servants, and an army for himself. However, he did not have a child. Despite God's great promises in his life, nothing could suffice the deep-seated desire for a child. Abram responded to God's promise saying, "What wilt thou give me, seeing I go childless, and the steward of my house is this Eliezer of Damascus? . . . Behold, to me thou hast given no seed: and, lo, one born in my house is mine heir" (Genesis 15:2–3).

God did not leave His beloved friend childless for life. He visited Abram in his desperate state. Look at what unfolded according to Genesis 15:4–5: "And, behold, the word of the Lord came unto him, saying, This shall not be thine heir; but he that shall come forth out of thine own bowels shall be thine heir. And he brought him forth abroad, and said, Look now toward heaven, and tell the stars, if thou be able to number them: and he said unto him, So shall thy seed be."

God cares about your deep-seated need. If He truly cares about the dead strands of hair that fall from your head, He cares more about what causes fear, anxiety, worry, and anguish.

Do not despair. God has your miracle. God is not late. Even though your situation looks humanly impossible, God has the power to move in ways you least expect. Like Abraham, believe and follow God in faith. Fear not.

READ PSALM 107:33–38.

HOLD TO THE PROMISE.

When faced with tough times, the one thing that holds and keeps you hoping and looking forward to the light of dawn is faith. However, where does such faith originate? Can we pull out faith from within and generate enough courage to navigate difficult terrains of life?

Unwavering faith has roots deeply seated in the Word of God. When God speaks to your heart, nothing will yank such promises from the heart.

Let us walk together back to the time of the resurrection for a moment.

Mary stood by the tomb of Jesus, weeping and begging to know where they had taken the Savior. The presence of angels in the tomb had no transformational effect in her situation. However, Christ's appearance changed everything. "Mary!" He called her by name and immediately, she realized she was in the presence of her Lord and Savior. Christ sent her to the disciples with a special message saying, "Go to my brethren, and say unto them, I ascend unto my Father, and your Father; and to my God, and your God" (see John 20).

Mary left that scene with courage and confidence. She could silence critics, disregard hecklers, and overlook dissuaders because of her encounter with Christ. Mary could go on to do great things for God while watchers remained mesmerized at her faith.

That is faith.

Faith, the Bible says, is the substance of things hoped for, the evidence of things not seen (Hebrews 11:1). Such faith comes by hearing from God. "So then faith cometh by hearing, and hearing by the word of God" (Romans 10:17).

When God speaks to the heart, you can arise and follow through with certainty and courage. Nothing will stand in your way to deter you from doing as God directed. However, to hold onto assumptions without hearing from God can lead to frustration, burn out and ultimate despair.

Faith is holding onto the promise just as Abram did, and it was counted to him for righteousness (Genesis 15:6).

READ HEBREWS 11.

THE LORD BROUGHT ME HERE.

God, Who is sovereign, orchestrates the events in our lives. God does not see as man sees. His ways are higher than our ways, and so are His thoughts (Isaiah 55:8–9). He sees the beginning from the end. He can therefore plan our lives with meticulous details not limited to planting us in certain places for circumscribed periods of time and meeting people for divine reasons.

When God called Abram from the land of the Chaldeans, little did Abram know what God saw as He looked at the future. Abram may have focused on his little flock and the plight of being childless. God was molding a man of faith, and a father to the nations through whom covenants of redemption could affect humankind. "And he said unto him, I am the Lord that brought thee out of Ur of the Chaldees, to give thee this land to inherit it" (Genesis 15:7).

When the children of Israel sold Joseph into slavery in Egypt, they acted in anger as they were driven by malice, hate and jealousy. I do not think it ever crossed their minds they were fulfilling God's divine purposes. Joseph who could have been overcome with grief, disbelief, and despair through numerous hardships was on the side of God. Look at what he told them.

> Now therefore be not grieved, nor angry with yourselves, that ye sold me hither: for God did send me before you to preserve life. For these two years hath the famine been in the land: and yet there are five years, in the which there shall neither be earing nor harvest. And God sent me before you to preserve you a posterity in the earth, and to save your lives by a great deliverance. (Genesis 45:5–7)

You did not plant yourself where you are today. It is God Who has placed you there for eternal and divine purposes. Find hope, strength, and courage from God to be and do what He wants. It is not time for apologies, but a time to fulfill God's purposes. God still works through awful situations to meet the needs of His people and to fulfill His eternal purposes.

READ JEREMIAH 1:5–7.

FOLLOW THROUGH WITH GOD.

It is easy to be dissuaded from your convictions, persuasions, commitments, and even covenants made with God.

God speaks in unique and definite ways to our hearts. You can tell when God cautioned you against something, stirred your heart for a cause, or even directed you to do something specific or to act on behalf of an individual.

God gives special grace, leeway, and ability to act and do as intended. That is a time to follow through with God by acting and seeking ways to fulfill those purposes. It is easy to accomplish it as you walk closely with Him, seeking His guidance and godly counsel. To look back and to toss it in the direction of those who lack a vision and devotion to God, for counsel, weakens its hold on the heart and before long, the desire to follow through with zeal also dwindles.

When God revealed to Abram that He brought him out of Ur of the Chaldees to step into His great promises and plans, Abram did not stop at that. "Whereby shall I know that I shall inherit it?" he asked (Genesis 15:8).

Abram went further to sacrifice to God and to walk closely with the author of the promise.

God uses ordinary men and women to fulfill His great purposes in life. We only read of Abram, the great father of faith, because God transformed him from a nobody to an honored man.

Follow through with God. Walk closely with Him and seek Him concerning His call on your life. What would He have you do?

"God is not a man, that he should lie; neither the son of man, that he should repent: hath he said, and shall he not do it? or hath he spoken, and shall he not make it good?" (Numbers 23:19). His work in your life is for many others whom you may or never meet. Follow through with God and lay hold of His eternal purposes.

READ JOHN 15:16.

MANY BLESSINGS GO UNKNOWN.

The heart of man deals with issues of life, most of the time, from a strange viewpoint. When someone is more powerful than you are, the human heart says, "Fight! Outsmart him, foul, trap, trick him! Undermine him, weaken, and cause him to fall out with his followers." However, God's formula says, to suppress a strong man or woman is to create opportunities for greater strength and growth. It is like pruning a fruit tree with hopes of subduing its yields. What happens to such a tree? It spreads out its branches, produces healthier limbs, and gains territory while yielding an abundance of fruit. Its roots spread farther and deeper than you expect.

God spoke prophetically to Abram concerning his offspring in Genesis 15:13, saying, "Know of a surety that thy seed shall be a stranger in a land that is not theirs, and shall serve them; and they shall afflict them four hundred years."

God, Who looks out for the poor, Who defends the fatherless, and does justice for the needy and the oppressed, did not stop at that. He told His friend, Abram, how they would triumph at the end (Genesis 15:14).

Look at what happened to this race long after Abram died: "And the Egyptians made the children of Israel to serve with rigour: And they made their lives bitter with hard bondage, in morter, and in brick, and in all manner of service in the field: all their service, wherein they made them serve, was with rigour" (Exodus 1:13–14).

God's principles stood strong for Abram's seed: "The more they afflicted them, the more they multiplied and grew. And they were grieved because of the children of Israel" (Exodus 1:12). The oppressors were left with a greater challenge of dealing with stronger men and women with perfected skills and resilience in patience, perseverance, and endurance.

God grows and matures His beloved through enormous challenges. He perfects their character and presents them to the world well equipped for greater services and purposes.

READ PSALM 115:14–15.

March 19

WE MUST NOT ACT OUT OF DESPERATION.

God's clock does not always tick at the pace we desire. What do you do when God's promise is not fulfilled within the time frames of your plans? How do you deal with life when friends and colleagues walk through open doors and prosper while yours seem closed? Think about the awkwardness of sharing in their joy while fighting tears in your heart.

The prophet Samuel, who anointed Saul to be king, gave instructions to the new king, saying, "And thou shalt go down before me to Gilgal; and, behold, I will come down unto thee, to offer burnt offerings, and to sacrifice sacrifices of peace offerings: seven days shalt thou tarry, till I come to thee, and shew thee what thou shalt do" (1 Samuel 10:8).

Saul was to go ahead of the prophet to Gilgal and wait for seven days for the man of God to show him how to sacrifice peace offerings to God—an act that would have established Saul as king in Israel.

In 1 Samuel 13:8–14, Saul went to Gilgal and waited. However, God's prophet did not show up within the agreed window of time. In that period, the Philistines assembled a large army to fight against Israel. Saul's army was terrified (1 Samuel 13:5–7). Saul panicked. He sacrificed the burnt offering and the fellowship offering, but no sooner did he finish sacrificing than Samuel appeared.

> Samuel said, What hast thou done? . . . Thou hast done foolishly: thou hast not kept the commandment of the Lord thy God, which he commanded thee: for now would the Lord have established thy kingdom upon Israel for ever. But now thy kingdom shall not continue: the Lord hath sought him a man after his own heart, and the Lord hath commanded him to be captain over his people, because thou hast not kept that which the Lord commanded thee. (vv. 11, 13–14)

God's promise to you means that God has a plan and good purposes for your life. Wait on Him. They are indicators that He is thinking about you. You are in His pipeline.

READ PSALM 27:13–14.

HELP GOD.

Our hearts rejoice and our courage rises when we understand what we are facing, or when we have control over the circumstances of our lives. We walk with a spring of confidence in our step as we take charge and dictate accordingly.

Life takes a different twist when we lose control. Reflect on how you've acted when your back was pressed against the wall.

It is in such precarious times that trusting and holding onto God's promises becomes a challenge. Your heart may scarcely remember what He said, let alone believe Him for the steadfastness of His Word and character.

Sarai, Abram's wife, found herself in such a disheartened state as she waited on God for a child. After years of holding onto God's promise without a tangible answer, Sarai stepped out with a plan to help God. Look at what she told Abram. "And Sarai said unto Abram, Behold now, the Lord hath restrained me from bearing: I pray thee, go in unto my maid; it may be that I may obtain children by her. And Abram hearkened to the voice of Sarai" (Genesis 16:2).

Sarai took Hagar, her Egyptian maid, and gave her to her husband to be his wife. Hagar conceived and gave birth to Ishmael. However, this was not the son God promised His servant Abram. Sarai's actions initiated strife, jealousy, and hatred in Abram's house. That act of helping God has subjected the world to religious wars for centuries.

Are you faced with tough circumstances today? I would like you to remember the last word God spoke to your heart regarding this situation. God's Word does not change. Do not be quick to step out and look for practical ways of dealing with it. Nothing will bring hope, restoration and healing more than God. Anchor yourself again in God's promise today.

What time I am afraid, I will trust in thee. In God I will praise his word, in God I have put my trust; I will not fear what flesh can do unto me (Psalm 56:2–3).

READ NUMBERS 23:19.

BLESSINGS MAY COME THROUGH MISFORTUNES OF LIFE.

It is hard to judge the motives and intentions of the heart. The heart can remain saddened because of truth that was twisted or because of false accusations of which you cannot exonerate yourself. Man can act on preconceived false information to pass judgments and make decisions that will affect you for many years to come. However, we can rest with this assurance that our God sees and knows everything.

When Hagar entered the servant-mistress relationship in Abram's house, I do not think she thought of falling off with Sarai as she did. It must have been a joy to serve and to live with the wealthy and well-favored couple.

After agreeing to Sarai's request to become a "wife" to Abram, Hagar conceived. A slave without personal possessions and rights soon found herself face-to-face with the inheritance that awaited her son. The unknown, low-class woman was now associated with the famous and the renown Abram. The woman who only heard of God's promises to Abram with perked ears also held an eternal promise from the very mouth of God in her heart and hand.

Wild beasts could have devoured Hagar in the wilderness, her body never to be found or anything known about the baby in her womb. Instead, the everlasting, powerful arms of the almighty God guided and watched over her in the deserted place. Today, we still read about this servant who could have remained nameless and unknown for the rest of her life.

Look at God's promise to Hagar as written in Genesis 16:10–11. Are you faced with difficult situations beyond your comprehension? Remember, not all blessings come wrapped up like gifts that cause excitement.

Look out! Today's challenges are your tomorrow's doors of blessings. Nothing is impossible with God.

READ PSALM 65:4.

DON'T FEAR THE BATTLE.

Every Christian faces fierce battles in life. Even those who are close and friends with God, like Abram, are not exempt from spiritual battles.

Not many people like war. This is no different for Christians when it comes to spiritual warfare. The most common default is to shy away or pretend that spiritual warfare does not exist. This is a trick for which Satan, your enemy, desires to see you fall. He works most in places where there is spiritual darkness or where people are oblivious to his deceitful schemes.

You do not have to fear the battle. God does not throw His children in hot battles only to leave them alone to face a fierce enemy. If your own parents would not do that, why would God dream of such a thing? God is for you. God is on your side. He is fighting for you.

> Fear not: for they that be with us are more than they that be with them. And Elisha prayed, and said, Lord, I pray thee, open his eyes, that he may see. And the Lord opened the eyes of the young man; and he saw: and, behold, the mountain was full of horses and chariots of fire round about Elisha (2 Kings 6:16–17).

It is easy to see yourself as a grasshopper whose efforts are insignificant when it comes to fighting the devil. The truth is, you can effectively engage the enemy in the battles he brings your way because you never fight alone. If God were to open your spiritual eyes, you too would realize that you are surrounded with heavenly hosts and divine power.

God fights our battles every day. None of the enemy's moves takes Him by surprise. You are God's priority, and He will not leave you to be humiliated by the enemy unless you make the choice. Stay with God. Embrace your training and witness God's presence and power as you stand your ground in battle.

READ 2 KINGS 6:1–23 AND PSALM 125:1–2.

GOD WILL KEEP HIS PROMISE TO YOU.

Life is full of different challenges. In tough times, it can be hard to pray fervently. Sometimes, all your heart may whisper repeatedly is, "God, please help me." God hears and answers those prayers. However, in those dark times, the heart looks for something tangible to hold on to until the light of dawn shines through the darkness.

It is in such moments that God's promises do what no man can do. They minister to the spirit and anchor you in trust. You remember what He told you and hold on through the dark tunnels of life. "God is not a man, that he should lie; neither the son of man, that he should repent: hath he said, and shall he not do it? or hath he spoken, and shall he not make it good?" (Numbers 23:19).

God is not a superman. He is not a legend. God is God. He is not a man who can be overtaken by the sinful, fallen nature that can cause Him to lie or forget His duties. You can trust Him to do as He has promised. You can trust His Word. It is truth by which you can order your live and be fulfilled.

"Know therefore that the Lord thy God, he is God, the faithful God, which keepeth covenant and mercy with them that love him and keep his commandments to a thousand generations" (Deuteronomy 7:9). Joshua, who succeeded Moses and led the children of Israel into the promised land, testified of it saying: "Not one thing hath failed of all the good things which the Lord your God spake concerning you" (Joshua 23:14). God will not fail you.

Do not doubt His promises just because the days are long and dark. Do not doubt His love either. He is the unchanging Rock in whom you can hide and be safe.

READ 2 CHRONICLES 6:14–15.

OUR LIVES DO NOT HAPPEN BY FATE.

God is sovereign. He is a master planner, and no one can beat Him at that.

He orchestrates events in our lives in ways that leave even the smartest people perplexed and schemers outsmarted. He can train a servant and soldier in the wilderness only to set him on the highest throne in the world. His methods are incalculable just as His ways are higher than our ways. God is at work even in the bizarre situations of your life.

Give Him time as you exercise patience, and you will behold the beauty of His doing. "And we know that all things work together for good to them that love God, to them who are the called according to his purpose" (Romans 8:28).

God averts evil and always works good out of it. If all of us were left to the fate of evil, the world would not be a place to live for a day. God cares for His children. He takes that which would have been a source of sorrow and misery and uses it to fulfill His good plans in our lives.

When Joseph walked into Egypt as a slave, little did he know the good that God would use out of the evil scheme of his brothers. Joseph could have landed in many places, but God saw to it that he was put in line to ascend to a place where his influence would save the world. Even in imprisonment, God put the right people in jail to fulfill His great purpose. God will use the same instrument intended for evil to bless you.

Life is by design. God is watching over His Word to perform and to do as He has planned for you. This may take time, but trust His wisdom. God has not left you for fate and to the scorning and laughter of your enemy. He is preparing a masterpiece for use.

READ GENESIS 50:20 AND 1 PETER 1:6–7.

FIND STRENGTH IN PRAYER.

To stand against life's challenges, a Christian must kneel in prayer. Prayer will accomplish what money and skill will not. Prayer melts hardened hearts and posts divine security against forces that can neither be overcome by tack or impeccable weapons. Prayer is an inevitable anchor for your soul. "And this is the confidence that we have in him, that, if we ask any thing according to his will, he heareth us: And if we know that he hear us, whatsoever we ask, we know that we have the petitions that we desired of him" (1 John 5:14–15).

Prayer is often God's method of choice for meeting needs in your life and in this world. God hears when we pray. He is waiting on you to pray. He can answer and respond to situations without your prayer, but many times, He waits for you to pray.

Christ prayed all night before choosing the twelve disciples (Luke 6:12–13). He got up early and prayed in a solitary place (Mark 1:35). You cannot make it without prayer. If the Son of God had to pray, how much should you and I pray?

God is waiting on you to seek Him while He can be found (Isaiah 55:6). God is waiting on you to ask (Matthew 7:7). He is counting on you to pray (1 Timothy 2:8). "Ask, and it shall be given you; seek, and ye shall find; knock, and it shall be opened unto you: For every one that asketh receiveth; and he that seeketh findeth; and to him that knocketh it shall be opened" (Matthew 7:7–8).

Prayer is a true mark of spiritual growth. This is because time spent in the presence of God yields trust and dependence on Him. Those who depend on Him pray. Those who stand pray. Those we win battles must pray.

READ EPHESIANS 6:18.

TRUST IN GOD WHILE WE WAIT.

Waiting is not easy. Imagine waiting on examination scores that will determine your acceptance to a job or school. What about waiting for results from your doctor for a condition that is keeping you sleepless in the night? Waiting is tough regardless of whether your anticipation is for something good or bad. Waiting on a flight or voyage to a dream vacation because of mechanical complications is not fun. Equally frustrating, for many, is awaiting your wedding day and saying, "I do."

Waiting can evoke ridicule and laughter. It gives food for gossip for those looking on the outside. It can make you lose friends and be held in spite and low esteem. However, how does God look at it?

When God promised in Genesis 22:17, "In blessing I will bless thee, and in multiplying I will multiply thy seed as the stars of the heaven . . . ," Abraham was faced with a situation that was humanly impossible. But because nothing is impossible with God, Sarah bore a son to Abraham in their old aged. "For when God made promise to Abraham, because he could swear by no greater, he sware by himself, Saying, Surely blessing I will bless thee, and multiplying I will multiply thee. And so, after he had patiently endured, he obtained the promise" (Hebrews 6:13–15).

God will do as He has promised. None of the good promises He has made to you will fail. God is not like a man who may promise and forget, lie about it, or even lack the ability to do it. You have no reason to fear.

Hold onto the consolation that your faith is anchored in a Savior who cannot lie. He will come through for you as promised. God's watch does not always match ours, but it is accurate and precise.

"You can be confident of this very thing, that he which hath begun a good work in you will perform it until the day of Jesus Christ" (Philippians 1:6).

READ NUMBERS 23:19.

March 27

TRUST GOD IN TOUGH TIMES.

What is your "Plan B" for today? What plans do you have in place just in case God fails to come through as He has promised? Whom do you trust most—God, your doctor, your teacher, or your friends? Most of us fear to surrender our lives and all our plans to God for fear of being stranded or being forsaken by God.

Most of us trust words of promise by men rather than the promises God made to us. God wants you to trust Him in everything. Look at His own testimony of what He will and will not do: "God is not a man, that he should lie; neither the son of man, that he should repent: hath he said, and shall he not do it? or hath he spoken, and shall he not make it good?" (Numbers 23:19).

Purpose to trust God regardless of where you find yourself today. Do not focus on the magnitude of the issues that are threatening you. God has the power to deliver and help you. He does not require the help of a human being to meet your need. He will come through for you. Find strength and hope in His promise to you, too.

> Know therefore that the Lord thy God, he is God, the faithful God, which keepeth covenant and mercy with them that love him and keep his commandments to a thousand generations (Deuteronomy 7:9).

Joshua, who stayed close to Moses and succeeded him in leading the children of Israel to the land of promise witnessed the faithfulness of God in the wilderness. He was present when God made various promises to His children, and he saw God do as He had promised.

READ 2 CHRONICLES 6:14–15.

Trust God in times of doubt and fear.

It is easy for the storms of life to cloud your view of God to the extent that you doubt His promises and the soundness of His character. It is easy to wring your hands in despair when you cannot see the end of the tunnel. It is in those dark times and when our hearts are fearful that we feel abandoned and let down by God. However, God's Word is true. His promises are sure. God has not lied to you. Look at His assurance to your heart today.

> Moreover I will endeavour that ye may be able after my decease to have these things always in remembrance. For we have not followed cunningly devised fables, when we made known unto you the power and coming of our Lord Jesus Christ, but were eyewitnesses of his majesty. (2 Peter 1:15–16)

It is easy for fear to grip us when days are cold, rainy and full of thunderous storms. On such days, we take cover as fast as our feet can carry us and remain watchful until the weather improves. The spiritual application to this is equally true. When faced with unknown and unfavorable conditions in life, it is easy to be fearful. Should those circumstances persist, our hearts can easily get desperate. It is in such times we question God's love and care. If not well anchored in Him, we seek quick and short-lived solutions fearing that He may have forgotten about us.

Take heart. Be courageous. God has not lied to you. You have not believed fairy tales either. He is trustworthy and His Word is true. You can hold to His promises in times of fear and doubt and witness His truthfulness.

God is God. He cannot lie (see Titus 1:2). Hold this truth to your heart and let it carry you in moments of doubt and fear. You have not been deceived into following Christ. Test it and be a witness who can confirm God's character and majesty. Build hope and trust in the lives of other people as they see God's faithfulness in your life.

Not only has God given us His promise, but also His oath to seal it to our hearts that He is trustworthy, and we can anchor ourselves in Him. With what are you struggling today? God has not lied to you. He will come through as He has promised. May He rise with healing in His wings for you today.

Read Hebrews 6:16–19.

THE BATTLE IS NOT YOURS.

Not many people like war or uncertainty. This is no different for Christians when it comes to spiritual warfare and daily challenges of life. No one ever feels prepared for eventualities of life. However, God does not leave us to scramble around like destitute children without hope and help.

You are more prepared than you either know or understand. God, Who sees the future, has a way of walking with us while holding our hand and training us for what is ahead.

> Fear not: for they that be with us are more than they that be with them. And Elisha prayed, and said, Lord, I pray thee, open his eyes, that he may see. And the Lord opened the eyes of the young man; and he saw: and, behold, the mountain was full of horses and chariots of fire round about Elisha. (2 Kings 6:16–17)

It is easy to see yourself as a grasshopper whose efforts are insignificant when faced with daily challenges and spiritual battles. The truth is, you can effectively engage the enemy in the battles he brings your way because you never fight alone. If God were to open your spiritual eyes, you too, would realize that you are surrounded with heavenly hosts and divine power.

God fights our battles every day. None of the enemy's moves or life's hardships take Him by surprise. You are God's priority, and He will not leave you to be humiliated by the enemy unless you make the choice. Stay with God. Embrace your training and witness God's presence and power as you stand your ground in battle. Stand still and see the salvation of God.

READ 2 KINGS 6:1–23 AND PSALM 125:1–2.

CAN YOU TRUST GOD?

Can someone trust God in a century where the tough happenings of life have left people weary, distrusting and uncertain? To echo the Word of the Savior in Luke 18:8, look at His timeless question to the disciples: "When the Son of man cometh, shall he find faith on the earth?"

Life has uncertainty. The good news is that God is never overtaken by the tough situations that face any of His children. God never leaves His children alone in those dark hours. In fact, He stands with us; He strengthens and instructs us accordingly. You, like David, can rejoice and rest in the hope of God. "I will bless the Lord, who hath given me counsel: my reins also instruct me in the night seasons. I have set the Lord always before me: because he is at my right hand, I shall not be moved. Therefore my heart is glad, and my glory rejoiceth: my flesh also shall rest in hope" (Psalm 16:7-9).

Every day is new terrain that none of us has walked before. God Who is all-knowing promises to guide us. He counsels and instructs us in the way we should go. When we take time to inquire and listen, we can walk with courage trusting His guidance.

Being guided calls for your active participation. Be keen to hear Him. Be ready to follow. Look at God's counsel for you: "I will instruct thee and teach thee in the way which thou shalt go: I will guide thee with mine eye. Be ye not as the horse, or as the mule, which have no understanding: whose mouth must be held in with bit and bridle, lest they come near unto thee" (Psalm 32:8-9).

Yes, you can trust God.

READ ISAIAH 48:17-18.

ALLOW YOURSELF TO BE MOLDED BY GOD.

God molds His children in unique ways. Each one of us is here to display God's splendor and to bring Him glory. He knows how to perfect that in His children. God uses interesting ways to get us to this point, too. Some of His methods are pleasant, while some include using the painful, harsh, or even cruel situations the enemy sent to destroy us.

You are like a bundle of treasure before God. You possess great potential in the hands of a mighty God. There is no telling what God can make of you let alone do with you as you walk and yield to Him.

God takes what looks like heartaches and misfortunes in our lives and turns them into divine purposes for the same purpose of displaying His splendor.

While we may look at the life of Joseph with wonder and amazement at the misfortunes that surrounded him, God's hand was at work. Look at the testimony of His purposes and workings on the young man's life as recorded in Psalm 81:5–6: "This he ordained in Joseph for a testimony, when he went out through the land of Egypt: where I heard a language that I understood not. I removed his shoulder from the burden: his hands were delivered from the pots."

As you pass through the great and terrible waters of life, your heart may focus on its dangers and fears, but God's eyes are fixed on the final product at His molding wheel.

As you face this day with its challenges, do not forget that God never leaves us alone to struggle in our weaknesses and troubles. Every day presents a new opportunity for us to be molded by God and to be made into something of value that is profitable to God and to the world around us. Look at God's admonition for you today.

Those who display the splendor of God are men and women with passions like yours, but they surrender and allow God to prune and shape their lives into what they could never imagine. You are God's candidate for great things. God will "remove your shoulder" from the burden at His appointed time. He will deliver you from the pots when your training and molding is over.

READ JEREMIAH 18:1–11.

April

CHRISTIAN GROWTH

What does it take for a Christian to grow spiritually? Growing is a process that takes time. It is cultivated like a garden: weeds must be pulled, plants must get nutrition and protected from disease and what can kill them.

Let us cultivate our spiritual growth this month!

GUARD YOUR HEART.

When we surrender to God and turn from our sins to walk in the newness of life that follows salvation, we soon realize that our natural flesh does not get saved. It remains a challenge amid out best efforts and genuine intentions. We also find out that God does not take away our free will to choose and to do as we wish. It can be frustrating when your spirit yearns to follow God in purity and righteousness while your heart is still enticed by lustful and worldly desires. What do you do in such cases? How do you grow despite the daily conflicts between the spirit and the flesh?

God has great answers to help us address such issues in practical ways.

> My son, attend to my words; incline thine ear unto my sayings. Let them not depart from thine eyes; keep them in the midst of thine heart. For they are life unto those that find them, and health to all their flesh. Keep thy heart with all diligence; for out of it are the issues of life. Put away from thee a froward mouth, and perverse lips put far from thee. Let thine eyes look right on, and let thine eyelids look straight before thee. Ponder the path of thy feet, and let all thy ways be established. Turn not to the right hand nor to the left: remove thy foot from evil. (Proverbs 4:20–27)

Guard your heart at all costs. Guard your desires and affections. They determine who you will be and what kind of a Christian you will be.

Guard what your eyes see. Your eyes are the gateway to the heart.

Guard your feet. Learn to tell them no. Follow God and avoid the paths of wickedness.

How is your heart?

READ COLOSSIANS 3:2.

GUARD YOUR TESTIMONY.

A good reputation and soundness of character are virtues that make significant changes in the life of an individual. Like the fruits we pick off a tree, they take time to form and mature. However, easy as it is to pluck a ripe fruit and trod into under your foot, so it is with character, our testimony, and good reputation. A testimony that was built through many years of spiritual molding and discipline can be harmed in a moment.

All God's children have one thing in common: we were once sinners walking in the filth and corruption of our flesh, but, we are washed. We are sanctified. We are justified through Christ.

> Know ye not that the unrighteous shall not inherit the kingdom of God? Be not deceived: neither fornicators, nor idolaters, nor adulterers, nor effeminate, nor abusers of themselves with mankind, Nor thieves, nor covetous, nor drunkards, nor revilers, nor extortioners, shall inherit the kingdom of God. And such were some of you: but ye are washed, but ye are sanctified, but ye are justified in the name of the Lord Jesus, and by the Spirit of our God. (1 Corinthians 6:9–11)

Christ expects us to walk after the newness of the cleansing that He did by His shed blood. God works to conform us to the image of His Son every day (Romans 8:29). Do not frustrate the grace of God and miss the incredible redemption we experience from Christ's sacrifice.

Do not return to the vomit from which you were delivered. To live a double life and secretly engage in deeds from which God saved us is to wallow in the mire of sin that not only ruins our testimony as Christians but damages the reputation of the righteous Lord Who cleansed us with His holy blood.

Call on God even in moments of temptation and you will be surprised at how present He will be in your time of weakness. Guard your testimony.

READ 2 PETER 2:20–22 AND PROVERBS 26:11.

GUARD YOUR WALK.

Most towns have dangerous alleys where people hesitate to walk when alone or when it is dark. Nonetheless, there those who opt to walk through such places despite the known dangers. Most times, they presume they will be the exceptions, and nothing will happen to them.

The Christian life has such dangerous alleys too. These are areas of known temptations in one's life. The enemy sets his traps in such places, expecting Christians to fall prey to his baits. Do not fall for the scheming of the enemy. Understand your weaknesses and stay away from dangerous spiritual alleys. Remember, you are crucified with Christ and you belong to Him. "I am crucified with Christ: nevertheless I live; yet not I, but Christ liveth in me: and the life which I now live in the flesh I live by the faith of the Son of God, who loved me, and gave himself for me" (Galatians 2:20).

Once you give your life to Christ, you no longer live to yourself. You become a bondslave to Christ. You are a slave by choice. You willingly surrender and submit not out of compulsion but out of love. A true encounter with Christ makes you a loving and liberated slave with a strong desire to follow the Master.

Our fleshly nature loves to take precedence. It easily gets puffed up and desires to walk contrary to the calling of Christ. We control it daily by:

- siding with God and saying no to our sinful fleshly desires
- keeping the body under subjection. We say no and deny it what will cause us to walk away from God (1 Corinthians 9:27)
- presenting ourselves before God as candidates of His grace and help (Romans 12:1)

READ 1 CORINTHIANS 9:25–27.

GUARD YOUR LIFE.

Most Christians desire to live a life that pleases their Master, the Lord Jesus Christ. Not every Christian succeeds in this endeavor. Like anything else in life, you do not quit after the first attempt. Those who stand strong and follow Christ diligently still face numerous spiritual struggles in their lives too. Their secret is taking one day at a time and purposing to stand as a light in a dark world while relying on God's grace and strength. God's admonition to make a difference in a dark world is their motivation. Let this be your motivation, too, as you work to guard your life.

> Ye are the salt of the earth: but if the salt have lost his savour, wherewith shall it be salted? it is thenceforth good for nothing, but to be cast out, and to be trodden under foot of men. Ye are the light of the world. A city that is set on an hill cannot be hid. Neither do men light a candle, and put it under a bushel, but on a candlestick; and it giveth light unto all that are in the house. Let your light so shine before men, that they may see your good works, and glorify your Father which is in heaven. (Matthew 5:13–16)

God in His sovereign plan has you where you are for His purpose. It is not a coincidence, luck, or even chance to be where you are today.

God understands your struggles. He also sees your effort. He knows what you can resist and guard against. Remember, it is God Who gives you the strength to say no to the enticement of the enemy.

God is counting on you to be His salt and light. Lift and exalt Him with your words and deeds. Be His hands and feet. Let His presence and impact be felt wherever He has planted you. Shine for God.

READ REVELATION 3:8.

GUARD YOUR FREEDOM.

If there is something most people enjoy in life is freedom. No one likes to be under the yoke and control of another. People flourish and step out of their comfort zones to explore new territories and come up with life-changing inventions where there is freedom to do so. Christians are no different. Imagine living under the bondage of sin and dancing to the tune of your enemy day in day out! To encounter Christ is to know freedom. "Therefore if any man be in Christ, he is a new creature: old things are passed away; behold, all things are become new" (2 Corinthians 5:17).

Christ sets us free, but our freedom has limits. There are many things you can choose to do as a child of God, but some of them are not good for you. Be wise in your choices. It is easy to develop obsessions and addictions if you do not guard your freedom. What was meant for good can turn into binding habits that will be hard to break. Look at God's admonition regarding your freedom: "All things are lawful unto me, but all things are not expedient: all things are lawful for me, but I will not be brought under the power of any" (1 Corinthians 6:12).

Yes, you may have the ability to do anything, but not everything will benefit you. Watch out for what will hurt you. Do not let your freedom be a stumbling block to God's children either. Adhere to God's guidelines below:

"But take heed lest by any means this liberty of yours become a stumbling block to them that are weak" (1 Corinthians 8:9). Do not let your choices hurt those around you just because you are free to do it.

"Wherefore, if meat make my brother to offend, I will eat no flesh while the world standeth, lest I make my brother to offend" (1 Corinthians 8:13). Restrain and even say no to yourself for the sake of those with whom God has entrusted and surrounded you.

Don't just do it because you are free to do it.

READ 1 CORINTHIANS 8:9–13.

GUARD GOD'S TEMPLE.

Wait is not a pleasant word in our fast-paced society. Why wait to bake food in an oven for hours when you can microwave it for minutes? Why dial a phone when you can make instant calls at the tapping of a button? Who wants to wait on an internet service that opens within three seconds when you can get a faster one?

This phenomenon is translated in other personal sectors of life. Why delay bodily gratification when you can indulge in pleasure and everything else at will? Despite what we are accustomed to in society, there are valuable things in life that do not come without waiting. Those who patiently wait for God to work and to display His splendor through their lives enjoy a fulfilling and fruitful life.

What does God say about gratification for our bodies? Does He have a different view from that of our "do it now" society?

> Know ye not that your bodies are the members of Christ? shall I then take the members of Christ, and make them the members of an harlot? God forbid. What? know ye not that he which is joined to an harlot is one body? for two, saith he, shall be one flesh. But he that is joined unto the Lord is one spirit. Flee fornication. Every sin that a man doeth is without the body; but he that committeth fornication sinneth against his own body. What? know ye not that your body is the temple of the Holy Ghost which is in you, which ye have of God, and ye are not your own? For ye are bought with a price: therefore glorify God in your body, and in your spirit, which are God's. (1 Corinthians 6:15–20)

Your body belongs to God. God has put His dwelling place in it. Guard and keep it clean unto God.

Sexual sins haunt and hurt deeper and longer than you may want. The devastating consequences will affect you and your family lineage for generations to come. God values you. You can wait! You can say no! Guard the temple of God.

READ ROMANS 6:12–18.

GUARD YOUR APPETITES.

A well-tested strategy for defeating an enemy is to study both his weaknesses and strengths. This is true both in the physical and spiritual aspects of our lives. Satan will use your untamed appetite to enslave and keep you miserable and defeated in life. This is because he schemes. It is not in vain that God cautions by saying, "Be sober, be vigilant; because your adversary the devil, as a roaring lion, walketh about, seeking whom he may devour" (1 Peter 5:8).

God is not oblivious to Satan's game plan. He has made provisions for us to live a victorious life as He records in Romans 6:19-20:

> I speak after the manner of men because of the infirmity of your flesh: for as ye have yielded your members servants to uncleanness and to iniquity unto iniquity; even so now yield your members servants to righteousness unto holiness. For when ye were the servants of sin, ye were free from righteousness.

God has given His children the Spirit of power, love, and of a sound mind (2 Timothy 1:7). He teaches us what to do as He gives us the will and power to do as instructed. He expects you to harness your appetites and make sound decisions in life.

"Meats are for the belly, and the belly for meats: but God shall destroy both it and them" (1 Corinthians 6:13). God has given us power to control our appetites.

"But I say unto you, That whosoever looketh on a woman to lust after her hath committed adultery with her already in his heart" (Matthew 5:28). God has given us the power and the ability to say no. Satan knows what you cannot resist. He will use it as a bait against you. Cry out to God for help!

Uncontrolled appetites will drive you to the road of sin and leave you distant from God, without whom you cannot succeed, let alone enjoy life.

READ MATTHEW 5:27–30.

GUARD YOUR PATH.

God has good plans for His children. When God brings us into this world, He does not set us out for disaster and failure. However, the paths we choose determine the course of our lives for a long time. They dictate what we become and the fulfillment we enjoy in life.

The world's philosophy says if everyone is doing it, it must be right, so let me do it. God operates on a different philosophy. Rarely do we find relying on the testimony of crowds in His earthly ministry. Regarding entry to heaven, Christ reminds us that many are called, but few are chosen. Even the chosen few are still faced with the choice of walking close to God which makes their path even narrower. He says, "Enter ye in at the strait gate: for wide is the gate, and broad is the way, that leadeth to destruction, and many there be which go in thereat: Because strait is the gate, and narrow is the way, which leadeth unto life, and few there be that find it" (Matthew 7:13–14).

You will not go through life without pressure from peers, colleagues, or even family. You do not have to go or do just because you are pressured. If it is contrary to God's Word and your conscience, do not do it. Stay away from the paths where masses walk as they degrade their bodies and yield themselves to be instruments of Satan.

Protect your feet from danger. Stick with God and be safe. What can God say about your walk today? What can He say about your choices? Will they lead you to paths of righteousness or do they lead to destruction?

READ PROVERBS 4:14, 18 AND 22:5.

GUARD YOUR EYES.

Your eyes are a quick and precise path to your heart. You can look at something and because of the powerful ability for the eyes to transport it to the heart, you may remember the image for many years to come. This means, we can control many things using our eyes. What we see affects not just the physiology of our bodies but the spiritual state of our souls.

To keep our eyes pure from the pollution of the world is to guide our hearts to have the light of God which illuminates and gives healing and joy. "The light of the body is the eye: if therefore thine eye be single, thy whole body shall be full of light. But if thine eye be evil, thy whole body shall be full of darkness. If therefore the light that is in thee be darkness, how great is that darkness!" (Matthew 6:22–23).

If you do not guard your thoughts and desires, your eyes will cause your heart to be dull and calloused. There will be spiritual darkness deep within your soul.

Make a covenant to have your eyes consecrated unto God (Job 31:1). Your eyes don't have to indulge in everything available in the world. God has given us the ability to close them, look away and even say no.

Do not let your eyes lead you from God's paths (Job 31:7). Most of what draws us away from God begins with a simple look. When the eye is left to linger, thoughts are created. Thoughts, when meditated upon, lead to actions.

Here is a practical advice to help us guard our eyes. Avoid the second look. The first look may be unexpected, unfortunate, and not deliberate. The second look is always a choice that determines your next action.

Exercise restraint today. Tell yourself, "It is enough. I will not look at what affects my heart and life in a negative manner."

Use your eyes for good today. Seek to see as God sees people and the circumstances that surround them. Let your eyes lead you to empathize with others. May what you see affect your heart in a positive way today.

READ MATTHEW 5:28–29.

GUARD YOUR FEET.

Our feet follow our eyes and heart. They only respond to the commands they receive. They can move fast, or they can be sluggish in their response. They can be excited or indifferent depending on the mission ahead. This is true in the spiritual sense too. Think about the time your heart was excited about the good news of the gospel and the divine working of God in your life. Your feet were swift to move as you told others about Christ. The same thing happens when you have exciting news to tell a friend. As your heartbeat increases, so do your steps.

Things are different when your heart is heavy, and the news is sad. Feet feel heavy, static, and somewhat unwilling to bear the weight of the message. Our spiritual feet are swift when we are excited about God and are in good communication with Him. Conversely, they become dull and heavy when our spirits are bowed down and far away from God.

So, how do you keep your feet active and ready to respond to the prompting of God? Let's look at the good answers God gives in His holy Word. "I have refrained my feet from every evil way, that I might keep thy word. I have not departed from thy judgments: for thou hast taught me" (Psalm 119:101–102).

The Christian walk is a life of restraint and refrain. You will be confronted every day with opportunities to make wise choices. Your spiritual growth will be greatly determined by what you choose to do or from what you refrain.

Think before you step out. Count the cost of your actions. "Ponder the path of thy feet, and let all thy ways be established. Turn not to the right hand nor to the left: remove thy foot from evil" (Proverbs 4:26–27).

Let your feet be swift and beautiful to carry good news of salvation and peace to heal and to refresh others (Isaiah 52:7).

Ask God to hold your feet onto His path that you may not slip (Psalm 17:5). When you hide God's law in your heart, your feet will not slide from His chosen path (Psalm 37:31).

Be firmly established in God's paths. His path yields life.

READ PROVERBS 1:15–16.

GUARD YOUR HANDS.

Many Christians want to be used by God in meaningful and tangible ways. Most of us desire to see the effectiveness of our service to God demonstrated in practical changes among the people we work with. However, why is there so much dissatisfaction in the vineyard of God? What determines the fruitfulness of our work to God? Can you work hard and still have very little for which to show? Maybe a more practical question to ask is, "Why does God seem to use some people more than others?"

God gives us a glimpse to the answers to these questions in Psalm 24:3-5. Like a parent who not only reads but understands the heart of his child, God asks and answers some interesting questions: "Who shall ascend into the hill of the LORD? or who shall stand in his holy place? He that hath clean hands, and a pure heart; who hath not lifted up his soul unto vanity, nor sworn deceitfully. He shall receive the blessing from the Lord, and righteousness from the God of his salvation."

There is no telling what God can do with a man or a woman who has covenanted to keep their hands clean before the Him. Anyone who sets himself apart for God is a spiritual time bomb in the hands of God. When you put aside dishonesty of heart to obey God, you become a candidate for His use and blessings.

Defilement is easy, but you don't have to. God, Who sees the true yearnings of your heart, will establish you and will see to it that your stand. God has so much in store for you. His admonition is strong and direct. "Come out from among them, and be ye separate, saith the Lord, and touch not the unclean thing; and I will receive you" (2 Corinthians 6:17).

Guard your hands. Keep them clean, together with a pure heart, and see what God will do with you in your lifetime.

READ 2 CORINTHIANS 6:14–18.

GUARD YOUR AFFECTIONS.

You are God's choice servant for this century. Every Christian who is washed in the precious blood of the Lord Jesus Christ is a tool for use in the Master's hands. God's vineyard is open for service to all His children. God does not hold anyone back from serving Him unless there is a good reason. Many men and women of God have been chained, disqualified from God's service, and held defeated by the enemy because they failed to guard their affections.

God, who is gracious does not cut us off from serving Him completely unless we choose to. Those who are dissatisfied with their working for God can move from dishonorable service to become vessels of honor, sanctified and ready for every good work (2 Timothy 2:20–21).

God, who does not play favorites, lays out a road map for those who will serve Him, saying, "If ye then be risen with Christ, seek those things which are above, where Christ sitteth on the right hand of God. Set your affection on things above, not on things on the earth. For ye are dead, and your life is hid with Christ in God" (Colossians 3:1–3).

Our affections play a part in how well we serve and relate to God. They can lead us to fulfillment or frustration. They cause gratification or dereliction.

> But they that will be rich fall into temptation and a snare, and into many foolish and hurtful lusts, which drown men in destruction and perdition. For the love of money is the root of all evil: which while some coveted after, they have erred from the faith, and pierced themselves through with many sorrows. (1 Timothy 6:9–10)

Our affections can either build and grow us or they hurt and deny us joy and satisfaction in life. "For all that is in the world, the lust of the flesh, and the lust of the eyes, and the pride of life, is not of the Father, but is of the world" (1 John 2:16).

God wants to trust you with true riches. Guard your affections.

READ 1 TIMOTHY 6:6–11.

April 13

GUARD YOUR CONSCIENCE.

Guard your conscience and walk in the newness of life where you are resurrected with Christ. God warns that it is possible to have a nonresponsive conscience. "Now the Spirit speaketh expressly, that in the latter times some shall depart from the faith, giving heed to seducing spirits, and doctrines of devils; Speaking lies in hypocrisy; having their conscience seared with a hot iron" (1 Timothy 4:1–2).

God has given us the inner voice that sensitively alerts us to what is right and wrong. Guard your conscience. Living in sin will desensitize your conscience. Sin hardens the heart and robs you of discernment, which accompanies a live conscience. God convicts and draws us to Himself when our walk is contrary to what He desires.

Learn to listen and obey when that warning flag appears. Proceeding to act on something despite the flaring warning sears your conscience and makes you insensitive to the future leading of the Holy Spirit.

Samson was God's man destined for great spiritual influence with a clear path set before him. He chose to walk a path that was contrary to his calling despite the counsel he received. The Bible says, "And he wist not that the Lord was departed from him" (Judges 16:20).

God is gracious to all His children. He is also a God of second chances. He does not delight in discipling His children. Most times, He warns us when we begin to follow dangerous appetites and affections. The Holy Spirit who indwells us raises red flags as He woos us back to the Father. When we recognize His voice and stop to listen and act, He restores us to Himself. However, when we deliberately press on to do what is contrary to His desire and commands despite His warning, our hearts become dull just as our conscience is seared. It becomes harder to hear and obey Him. This puts us on a dangerous path where our sin no longer bothers us. This makes us walk as powerless and ineffective servants of God.

How's your conscience? Guard it.

READ PROVERBS 29:1.

GUARD YOUR THOUGHTS.

People do not see our thoughts; however, our thoughts are judged through our actions. God reveals this for us in Genesis 6:5. The sinful actions of His people were associated with the wicked state of their minds: "And God saw that the wickedness of man was great in the earth, and that every imagination of the thoughts of his heart was only evil continually."

We live in an artificial world where many things are canned and processed. Most things appear real when they are not. Unfortunately, this phenomenon creeps into our Christian lives subtly. It is easy to put on a facade and be known for who we are not. See what God Who knows us says:

> For as he thinketh in his heart, so is he . . . (Proverbs 23:7)

> For out of the heart proceed evil thoughts, murders, adulteries, fornications, thefts, false witness, blasphemies: These are the things which defile a man: but to eat with unwashen hands defileth not a man. (Matthew 15:19–20)

Guard your thought life. Occupy your mind and thoughts with spiritual, meaningful, and positive things. Do not succumb to idleness of mind. Think on what is good, profitable, just, honest, and pure (Philippians 4:8).

Cleanse your thoughts by reading and meditating on the Word of God. Read it even in moments when you do not understand it. It will still work like water that cleans you up without even realizing it. Whatever you fill your mind with takes root and shows up eventually in your actions.

God wants you to be real.

READ PHILIPPIANS 4:8.

GUARD AGAINST PRIDE.

The proud roar like the lion in the wilderness sending its threats to those on whom they look down upon; the proud walk with deliberate strong steps trampling and belittling those they despise in their eyes . . . How does God look at pride? Who can take credit or be justified in his pride before God? The sovereign God sees our hearts for what we are. He knows and understands our thoughts right from the moment they begin to form. "For if a man think himself to be something, when he is nothing, he deceiveth himself" (Galatians 6:3).

Pride says, "Look at me! It is me, myself, and I alone; I am better than you." God deals with pride severely. He threw Satan out of heaven because of pride. He did not put Satan's position into consideration. Instead, God focused on the sin of pride.

Satan was the morning star; the anointed cherub in Ezekiel 28:14. He dwelt in God's holy presence and beheld His majesty. Cherubims covered the mercy seat in the holy of holies. This was the area filled with God's inapproachable majesty.

God has good plans for you. Do not forfeit them because of pride. Pride will deprive you of God's power, presence, and blessings.

- "Pride goeth before destruction, and an haughty spirit before a fall" (Proverbs 16:18).
- "When pride cometh, then cometh shame: but with the lowly is wisdom" (Proverbs 11:2).
- "But he giveth more grace. Wherefore he saith, God resisteth the proud, but giveth grace unto the humble" (James 4:6).

Has God blessed you with a position of honor and respect? Serve His people genuinely from your heart. Grow and build them up. Let them leave your presence strengthened and empowered for the future.

God has a very high sense of humor. He is good at making us bow before those we belittled in our hearts and minds.

READ ISAIAH 14:12–15.

GUARD YOUR WILL.

Strong-willed, stubborn, difficult to work with—where do these traits come from? How do they affect us in life?

Man is not a robot. God created us with a will. We are free to make choices. We only need to remember that our choices determine what we do and who we become. Choices have consequences, too. Guard your will and develop Godward tendencies that will lead and establish you into a reputable, God-honoring man or woman. Here are some guidelines:

Imitate John the Baptist and give God His rightful place. "He must increase, but I must decrease" (John 3:30). The urge to puff yourself up and show everyone who you are may be there, however, look at the wonderful example set for us by our Lord and Master, Jesus Christ.

Like Joshua make up your mind to follow God. "But as for me and my house, we will serve the LORD" (Joshua 24:15). A stubborn will is not always a bad thing. You can channel it into great blessings as you stand relentlessly to serve and follow God. This world will benefit from those who will stay strong in their convictions and commitments to God's service.

Have the same attitude as Christ. "Nevertheless, not my will, but thine, be done" (Luke 22:42). Remember, a servant is not greater than his master. You belong to God. Follow His leading. Your way may seem right and good, but the Master's is incomparable. Follow Him wholeheartedly. Serve His purposes.

Guard your will. You are free to choose your actions. However, remember, you do not choose the consequences. Our wills can deceive us into staying on a path that is destructive. Look at God's caution here. "Not everyone that saith unto me, Lord, Lord, shall enter into the kingdom of heaven; but he that doeth the will of my Father which is in heaven" (Matthew 7:21).

You will never go wrong succumbing to the leadership of God's mighty hand. It is the greatest liberation that will free your heart into great peace. Surrender your will to Him.

READ DEUTERONOMY 30:19–20.

GUARD YOUR WORSHIP.

God is worthy all our worship, but what exactly is worship? What kind of worship magnifies and brings glory to God? Is there such a thing as true and false worship? How does God view our worship?

True worship honors and exalts God. It does not point to the one who is worshiping. True worship fills the worshiper with awe and reverence. A heart that worships is not pompous. It does not seek to attract attention or the praise and approval of others.

True worship will draw you closer to God and make you want to live a life that is undefiled and free of sin. It is not easy to live in sin and offer true worship to God. Guard against making worship a show or a display of talent. True worship results in a changed heart.

Today, you will have many opportunities to worship and follow God. God is honored with our worship. Keep it pure and focused on Him. Enter His gates with thanksgiving and into His courts with praise (Psalm 100:4). Keep it unadulterated. Let God enjoy your praise. Remember, He inhabits the praises of His people. The only thing man can give to God is true worship. Think about it! God owns everything. He does not need anything else.

God has caution for all who will appear before Him in worship. He says,

> Keep thy foot when thou goest to the house of God, and be more ready to hear, than to give the sacrifice of fools: for they consider not that they do evil. Be not rash with thy mouth, and let not thine heart be hasty to utter anything before God: for God is in heaven, and thou upon earth: therefore let thy words be few. (Ecclesiastes 5:1–2)

God wants your heart and mind to be fully engaged in worship. He wants you to be real. Make every minute you are in His presence count. Direct all worship to Him. Avoid the desire and the temptation to draw attention to yourself.

True worship will draw you into God's presence and make you see Him for Who He is.

READ 1 SAMUEL 15:22–23.

April 18

Guard against temptation.

All God's children face temptations. Temptation is the bait which Satan uses to get to Christians. He lures in a very cunning manner as he offers what he knows will be hard to resist. Satan schemes and capitalizes on your weaknesses. Once he establishes an open door or area of weakness, he pounds his endless blows as he works to weaken and make you weary. Resist him with the Word of God. Acknowledge and speak the truth of the Word of God in response to Satan's lies.

God has a great caution regarding the working of Satan, our enemy. He says, "Be sober, be vigilant; because your adversary the devil, as a roaring lion, walketh about, seeking whom he may devour: Whom resist stedfast in the faith, knowing that the same afflictions are accomplished in your brethren that are in the world" (1 Peter 5:8–9).

God reminds us to be sober and cautious knowing that Satan literally walks by with the aim of netting you. Know your weaknesses and guard against the lusts which make you susceptible to Satan's attack. Do not give him a chance however small. He will capitalize on it.

Remember, no temptation has come to you except what God knows you can handle. God has given us the power to resist. Most Christians make the mistake of running away and hiding when temptations strike. Remember, there is no Christian who does not face temptation. It is the choice we make following the temptation that determines whether the temptation turns into sin or victory. Regardless of why and when you are tempted, God on call. He will either show you a way to get out of it or He will give you strength to stand against it.

Mastering and overcoming temptation is a clear path to spiritual growth.

Read James 1:12–15.

GUARD YOUR PURITY.

Purity is precious. Imagine being presented with drinking water contaminated with poison. Will you take it however little the poison? God enjoys dwelling in clean vessels. He delights working in and through cleaned up servants. He speaks through sanctified vessels.

> Blessed are the undefiled in the way, who walk in the law of the Lord. Blessed are they that keep his testimonies, and that seek him with the whole heart. They also do no iniquity: they walk in his ways. Thou hast commanded us to keep thy precepts diligently. O that my ways were directed to keep thy statutes! Then shall I not be ashamed, when I have respect unto all thy commandments. (Psalm 119:1–6)

It is very easy to compromise and lose your purity. All it takes is a gamble on whether you should do it or not. God is sovereign. He will not leave you to fall unless you decide to. In the day of trouble, call on Him. Look at His promise: "The eyes of the Lord are upon the righteous, and his ears are open unto their cry" (Psalm 34:15). Cry out to God for help.

There is a fight against purity in our world today. Those who keep their bodies pure and abstain from sexual defilement before and during marriage may be scorned and despised. Do not yield to such pressure. Honor God with your body. Present it as a temple and a living sacrifice to the One Who loved and saved you.

Use God's formula for guarding your purity. "Wherewithal shall a young man cleanse his way? by taking heed thereto according to thy word. . . . Thy word have I hid in mine heart, that I might not sin against thee" (Psalm 119:9, 11).

READ PSALM 119:8–17.

GUARD YOUR DESIRES.

Your desires will either lead you to or away from God. Your desires will determine what path you will walk and what you will become.

> Trust in the Lord, and do good; so shalt thou dwell in the land, and verily thou shalt be fed. Delight thyself also in the Lord: and he shall give thee the desires of thine heart. Commit thy way unto the Lord; trust also in him; and he shall bring it to pass. And he shall bring forth thy righteousness as the light, and thy judgment as the noonday. (Psalm 37:3-6)

Amnon, the son of David, lusted after his sister Tamar as recorded in 2 Samuel 13. His desire was so strong that he feigned sickness and schemed to have Tamar in his room. After committing incest, the Bible describes him saying, "Amnon hated her exceedingly; so that the hatred wherewith he hated her was greater than the love wherewith he had loved her" (v. 15).

God honors and blesses good desires. Trust in God. Commit your ways to Him. He will grant your desires in keeping with His will. God does not deny His children good things. In fact, He delights in honoring the desires of His beloved children.

God stands with His Word. Remember His promise in Galatians 6:7-8. "Be not deceived; God is not mocked: for whatsoever a man soweth, that shall he also reap. For he that soweth to his flesh shall of the flesh reap corruption; but he that soweth to the Spirit shall of the Spirit reap life everlasting."

I have seen God bless those who follow Him wholeheartedly in ways that are unconventional and not easy to fathom. God will not let you down. God honors those who honor Him. He rewards those who seek Him diligently. Remember, man looks on the outside to make his judgment. God looks on the inside. He sees and knows your desires. He will not let you down.

READ GALATIANS 6:6–8.

GUARD YOUR FRIENDSHIPS.

Do you have good friends on whom you can count? Do you have friends who can get to you at 2:00 a.m. if the need were to arise? God cares about His children. He cares that you have good friends who can stand and walk with you. The best friends ever known are honest children of God. They will remain loyal and will offer sincere advice even if it hurts.

Good friends do not just come by. You must work at it. Look at God's admonition regarding friendship in Proverbs 18:24a: "A man that hath friends must shew himself friendly." Guard your God-given friends. Cultivate godly friendships. Invest in them through prayer and quality time.

"He that walketh with wise men shall be wise: but a companion of fools shall be destroyed" (Proverbs 13:20). Take heed that you do not make friends with the world. A man's friends will reveal one's character, mind, affections, and future. Do not forget that:

- A friend of the world is the enemy of God (James 4:4). The best friend you will have is Jesus. There is nothing in the world, however valuable, that should make you forfeit your fellowship with Christ.
- Wise friends will help you to be wise (Proverbs 13:20). Good friends not only propel you to greater heights, but will help keep your feet and heart on the path of integrity, wisdom, and knowledge.
- Bad company will ruin you (1 Corinthians 15:33). No Christian is too strong to fall. An easy way to fall is to surround yourself with evil men and women. The fall will be sure.
- Real friends stick closer than a brother (Proverbs 18:24). God-given friends are more valuable than just assets in life. They spice up life and keeping you moving day after day without thinking about it.

The best way to keep and maintain your God-given friendships is to be friendly and godly.

READ PROVERBS 17:17.

GUARD YOUR MIND.

When God sanctifies us through the shed blood of Christ on the cross, He makes us spiritually minded. The Spirit of God indwells believers and quickens spiritual truths and equips us to instruct others. We also have God's Word, which reveals the mind of God to us. Yes, you have the mind of Christ!

> But the natural man receiveth not the things of the Spirit of God: for they are foolishness unto him: neither can he know them, because they are spiritually discerned. But he that is spiritual judgeth all things, yet he himself is judged of no man. For who hath known the mind of the Lord, that he may instruct him? but we have the mind of Christ. (1 Corinthians 2:14–16)

Knowing how effective believers can be with the mind of Christ; Satan targets and fights his battles in the mind. He will throw evil, false, or distorted thoughts. The mind is your spiritual battlefield. It is here you wedge war and win or succumb to the battle and surrender. The enemy understands how to plague the mind in spiritual warfare before he can wound your heart and spirit.

How then can we guard our minds and stand against the wicked schemes of our adversary? Let us look at practical approaches.

- Arrest every bad thought and counter it with the truth of God's Word.
- Do not entertain evil thoughts in your mind. If you embrace and think on them, they will become temptations. Do not be afraid to address bad thoughts audibly.
- Yielding turns temptations into sin. What began as a simple thought quickly progresses into a besetting sin if not handled right. God has given us power over our thoughts and to make them obedient and subject to God (2 Corinthians 5:3–5).

Guard your mind.

READ PSALM 119:33–34.

GUARD YOUR DOCTRINE.

There are many false prophets and teachers in the world today. The current modes of communication make it easy for such parties to propagate and spread their agenda with ease. Our microwave age that demands things to be done at supersonic speed and to walk the path of the least resistance only fuels their mission.

> But there were false prophets also among the people, even as there shall be false teachers among you, who privily shall bring in damnable heresies, even denying the Lord that bought them, and bring upon themselves swift destruction. And many shall follow their pernicious ways; by reason of whom the way of truth shall be evil spoken of. (2 Peter 2:1–2)

The devil uses false teachers to deceive the children of God. False teachers present some truth in most cases as they distort the truth of God's Word. They question what you have learned as they try to sway you to their path. They appeal to itch ears and anxious spirits which are out to only hear certain information. Such teachers and false prophets know how to excite and tell you what you want to hear. They are good at appealing to your emotions while leaving your heart hungry, dissatisfied, and looking for more.

God calls them deceivers who are cursed. They are wolves in sheep's clothing. They like to walk among God's children and pretend to be part of the flock. Remember who is behind their mission. Have nothing to do with them.

The best safeguard against such deception is to:

- Know what God's Word says. Study it! When you know what is real, it will be easy to identify counterfeits. Cross check everything you hear with the truth of God's eternal Word.
- Stay close to God. Do not run after false promises and prophesies while leaving God behind. God will satisfy your life, but false teachers and prophets will leave you empty, weak, and spiritually malnourished.

READ MATTHEW 7:15–18.

GUARD YOUR FAITH.

God has given us the most precious thing man could ever have. Salvation is precious. Our faith is precious. To belong to God is precious. The gospel is the most powerful thing ever known to transform man. Guard your faith. What an honor to belong to the family of God! There is no better place or family to belong than that of our heavenly Father.

> I thank God, whom I serve from my forefathers with pure conscience, that without ceasing I have remembrance of thee in my prayers night and day; Greatly desiring to see thee, being mindful of thy tears, that I may be filled with joy; When I call to remembrance the unfeigned faith that is in thee, which dwelt first in thy grandmother Lois, and thy mother Eunice; and I am persuaded that in thee also. (2 Timothy 1:3–5)

One way to guard your faith is live an active Christian life. To walk afar off and to straddle the fence is to be weak in your walk with God. Don't remain a nominal Christian. Be stirred for God.

The world is full of desperate people looking for what you have. Share it. God has not given you the spirit of fear; but of power, and of love, and of a sound mind (2 Timothy 1:7). Don't be ashamed of the testimony of our Lord.

Guard your faith by teaching and discipling somebody. When you know something well enough to teach others, you preserve its freshness and give it roots to spring into the next generation. Let your family and close friends benefit from your faith by sowing eternal seeds deliberately that they may come to know God, too.

READ 2 TIMOTHY 1:3–9.

GUARD AGAINST PRAYERLESSNESS.

God wants you to pray. "I will therefore that men pray everywhere, lifting up holy hands, without wrath and doubting" (1 Timothy 2:8). God acts and moves in lives and circumstances in response to the prayers of His children. He wants you to pray all the time, regardless of where you are. He is only a prayer away.

Those who become men and women of God are molded through prayer. Prayerlessness will increase worry, fear, and anxiety in your life. It will decrease faith, trust, and zeal for God. That is why we must "pray without ceasing" (1 Thessalonians 5:17).

Prayer is your spiritual oxygen without which you cannot survive. As we breathe, oxygen is dispersed to body tissues to promote cell functions which sustain body life. Prayer does the same spiritually. Without enough prayer:

- Your spiritual senses become dull.
- You increase vulnerability to Satan's deceit and attacks. This is because prayer keeps your spiritual surveillance cameras alert and working all the while.
- You lack soundness for discernment and decision-making. God gives wisdom, knowledge and understanding. Prayer is a sure way to tap these.
- You develop increased tolerance for sinful desires and habits. Prayerlessness keeps communication lines between the believer and God rusty. It dulls spiritual senses and deafens the ear to the voice of God. Sin flourishes in moments when the voice of God is silent.

It is easy to succumb to a life of prayerlessness. There are times when some quick, short prayers are good and effective. However, you cannot survive on that. You must pray. Life is fast, and unless one makes deliberate effort to pray, the prayer life withers, leaving you anxious, indecisive, and shaky.

Prayer is an anchor. There is no greater confidence than to arise from prayer with full assurance that God heard and responded in word and or deed.

Guard against prayerlessness. Pray today and continue without ceasing.

READ 1 JOHN 5:14–15 AND PSALM 55:17.

GUARD YOUR MOTIVES.

Motives are hard to discern. This is because we focus on what we see without looking intently at the reason behind what happens. What looks like an act of kindness or favor may turn out to be a selfish, self-seeking, well-calculated step when motives are revealed. It is not in vain that the Bible reminds us that the heart is deceitful and desperately wicked (Jeremiah 17:9). "All the ways of a man are clean in his own eyes; but the LORD weigheth the spirits" (Proverbs 16:2).

God, unlike man, focuses on the heart. He judges the motive before He looks at our actions. "If thou sayest, Behold, we knew it not; doth not he that pondereth the heart consider it? and he that keepeth thy soul, doth not he know it? and shall not he render to every man according to his works?" (Proverbs 24:12). A key question to ask is, "What is the motive behind my actions today?" Pursuits, policies, friendships, and actions can be deceptive when motives are hidden and not genuine. Wrong motives will make you:

- Use people
- Tramp people and disregard their feelings and hurts
- Crucify genuine love

Christ cautioned His disciples, saying, "And whosoever of you will be the chiefest, shall be servant of all" (Mark 10:44). Guard your motives as you deal with people. God Who sees the motives of our heart is always alert. God defends and fights for His children. Be kind, honest and genuine with them.

Those who honor God are honored by God. Be careful, God sets a table before His children in the presence of their enemies! He will make them sit with princes and inherit a throne of honor.

READ PSALM 55:23.

April 27

GUARD AGAINST DECEIT.

God wants to entrust you with true eternal riches. True riches are given to those who are faithful. God tests His children and sets apart the trustworthy. See what He says: "He that is faithful in that which is least is faithful also in much: and he that is unjust in the least is unjust also in much. If therefore ye have not been faithful in the unrighteous mammon, who will commit to your trust the true riches? And if ye have not been faithful in that which is another man's, who shall give you that which is your own?" (Luke 16:10–12).

When the New Testament church started, many brethren sold and shared their goods freely. Some gave money to advance the work of Christ. Ananias and Saphira sold their land too. However, they did not release all the proceeds to the work of God as purposed. Even though this was a selfless act done at will, God looked in their hearts and saw deceitfulness. God demands truthfulness from the heart. "Moreover it is required in stewards, that a man be found faithful" (1 Corinthians 4:2).

God wants every Christian to come to terms with his heart. Are you deceitful? He desires that we acknowledge who we are. Can God count us among His faithful stewards? Deceit ruins our testimonies and tarnishes the name of God. God wants us to surrender to Him. With true repentance, God will restore us. Like Jacob, He will change your name (who you really are) and give you a fresh start.

When God confronts a character trait in the life of any of His children, it is an act of love. He does not do it to embarrass and leave us desolate and humiliated but to heal and restore us to Himself. He does it to mold and prepare us for His service.

Guard against deceit today.

READ GENESIS 32.

GUARD AGAINST FRUITLESSNESS.

We have apple, pear, and peach trees in our backyard. We planted these fruit trees the same day a few years ago. Surprisingly, there is one tree that has never produced fruit despite receiving and enjoying the same conditions. We have considered cutting it down on several occasions, but we have spared it with hopes of seeing fruit someday.

How about our Christian life? Is this a true picture of spiritual unfruitfulness? How does God view fruitfulness in the lives of His children? "Herein is my Father glorified, that ye bear much fruit; so shall ye be my disciples" (John 15:8).

God has trusted every Christian with gifts, talents, work, abilities, and responsibilities for which He requires and expects fruit and faithfulness. God rewards fruitfulness. See what He told the servants from whom He was expecting fruit: "For the kingdom of heaven is as a man traveling into a far country, who called his own servants, and delivered unto them his goods. And unto one he gave five talents, to another two, and to another one; to every man according to his several ability; and straightway took his journey" (Matthew 25:14–15).

> After a long time the lord of those servants cometh, and reckoneth with them. . . . His lord said unto him, Well done, thou good and faithful servant: thou hast been faithful over a few things, I will make thee ruler over many things: enter thou into the joy of thy lord." (Matthew 25:19, 21)

A life faithfully spent listening and following God naturally produces fruit. When a child of God remains in the vine, feeds his spirit and walks with God, there is no travail in producing fruit. "But the fruit of the Spirit is love, joy, peace, longsuffering, gentleness, goodness, faith, Meekness, temperance: against such there is no law" (Galatians 5:22–23).

God wants you to be fruitful.

READ MATTHEW 25:14–29.

GUARD AGAINST SPIRITUAL MALNUTRITION.

When we feed our physical bodies a good healthy diet, we remain well nourished in order to fight off endless illnesses. However, we become anorexic when we deny ourselves essential nutrients in their rightful quantities. This can be seen clearly through an emaciated frame and resultant disorders. It stunts growth and subjects the body to undue stresses.

What about spiritual malnutrition? How can you tell when you do not feed the spiritual man? How does God evaluate our spiritual diet? "And I, brethren, could not speak unto you as unto spiritual, but as unto carnal, even as unto babes in Christ. I have fed you with milk, and not with meat: for hitherto ye were not able to bear it, neither yet now are ye able" (1 Corinthians 3:1–2).

God divides people into three major categories:

- Natural: 1 Corinthians 2:14
- Carnal: 1 Corinthians 3:1–3
- Spiritual: 1 Corinthians 15–16

The natural man is the nonbeliever who does not know God. You cannot feed him on spiritual food because he cannot appreciate it, since there is nothing to grow in him. It is like giving a tree fried chicken for dinner.

The carnal man is the Christian whose life is characterized by spiritual malnutrition. Like a baby, he must be coerced to even take milk which he needs for growth and development. He has no roots since he does not abide in Christ who nourishes and makes stable.

Hebrews 12:16 depicts Esau as a carnal man who sold his birthright for a bowl of soup. In Genesis 25:29–31, he was so hungry a birthright did not seem valuable.

Spiritual malnutrition blinds and deadens our conscience to what is important. Like Esau, we can sacrifice it for momentary fulfillment without considering its lifetime consequences. Guard against spiritual malnutrition. Seek spiritual treasures and treasure them. Feed your spirit—the inner man.

READ JOSHUA 1:8.

GUARD AGAINST GODLESSNESS.

When you compare the spiritual awakening of the eighteenth and nineteenth century, it leaves the mind wondering what is happening to the Church of Christ in this century. We live in a pleasure-filled age where sensuality is evoked and momentary thrills of the heart are pursued at all costs. Conversely, many spirits are dull, inactive, and indifferent to the things of God.

> This know also, that in the last days perilous times shall come. For men shall be lovers of their own selves, covetous, boasters, proud, blasphemers, disobedient to parents, unthankful, unholy, Without natural affection, trucebreakers, false accusers, incontinent, fierce, despisers of those that are good, Traitors, heady, highminded, lovers of pleasures more than lovers of God; Having a form of godliness, but denying the power thereof: from such turn away. (2 Timothy 3:1–5)

True to God's Word, sensuality and godlessness increase as we draw closer to the second coming of Christ. Do not let this prophecy be fulfilled in you by becoming godless every day. God loves you. Take time and think about the love He demonstrated by shedding His blood on the cross to clean you and to make you acceptable before Him. Let His love constraint and keep you within His umbrella of grace and love.

God's eyes move to and fro over the whole world to show Himself strong on behalf of those whose hearts remain steadfast toward Him. Do not miss God's blessings by being godless.

Don't miss God's blessings by being godless. Remember, a heart that is constantly seeking entertainment is a heart that is steadily drifting from God and getting calloused.

Guard against godlessness today.

READ 2 TIMOTHY 2:19.

May

GROWING IN SPIRITUAL MATURITY

Have you ever worked hard in a garden? Remember the sweating, toil, frustration, hard work, and dedication. . . . Think about the fruit of your labor as you harvested your products.

Spiritual growth takes hard work, but its fruits are compared to none in the whole world. Not even the best and most paying job offers the fulfillment that the fruit of spiritual growth will give you.

Let's tough it out this month and mature.

GROW IN FORGIVENESS.

How do you deal with life situations when people wrong you but show no remorse for their actions? How do you handle life when no one seems to care? As you may have experienced already, we live in a world of tension, resentment, and hate. As we have witnessed in this century, it is easy for even Christians to get caught up in it. However, what does God expect from His children?

The truth is, God understands the world in which we live. He knows the people who surround us and those who hurt us. Since He is sovereign and all-knowing, He even directed on how many times we must forgive. Look at this admonition: "Then came Peter to him, and said, Lord, how oft shall my brother sin against me, and I forgive him? till seven times? Jesus saith unto him, I say not unto thee, Until seven times: but, Until seventy times seven" (Matthew 18:21–22).

Those who do not know God harbor hatred and bitterness. This is not a pattern for Christians to follow. Our heavenly Father leads the way in forgiveness. Think of the numerous occasions He forgives and sets our feet on a path of hope and success.

God wants to walk, talk, and listen to you, but you must forgive. Unforgiveness is spiritual poison in the life of a Christian. It erodes trust and eats us from inside out as it spreads roots of bitterness, anger, and revenge. God has clear directions for His children on matters of forgiveness. He says, "For if ye forgive men their trespasses, your heavenly Father will also forgive you: But if ye forgive not men their trespasses, neither will your Father forgive your trespasses" (Matthew 6:14–15). This forgiveness is conditional in that God will not forgive your trespasses until you forgive others'. "Therefore if thou bring thy gift to the altar, and there rememberest that thy brother hath ought against thee; Leave there thy gift before the altar, and go thy way; first be reconciled to thy brother, and then come and offer thy gift" (Matthew 5:23–24).

Unforgiveness not only hurts our relationship with those who wrong us but also places tough communication barriers God and His children.

There is healing for your heart, but you have to receive it on God's terms. What hurts you today? God knows. Let it go, forgive, and get back into fellowship with God.

READ MATTHEW 18:23–35.

GROW IN LOVE.

The world loves, smiles, and laughs the same regardless of the geographical boundaries that separate us. This means that anyone can see love in action. True and genuine love is infectious in a positive manner. It can crack through walls of hatred to speak hope and peace to a needy heart.

Has anyone loved you at a time you felt low and discouraged? How did you feel? Love is the language that God designed to flourish among His children. He says, "A new commandment I give unto you, That ye love one another; as I have loved you, that ye also love one another. By this shall all men know that ye are my disciples, if ye have love one to another" (John 13:34–35).

God has equipped you with one of the greatest tools with which to face the unknown world—love. Love is powerful. Not many people can resist genuine love. Love disseminates feelings of sadness and hopelessness as it radiates from your heart and through your eyes and actions to bring healing and hope.

The world around stands in need of your love. God commands us to love. Let your love testify that you know Christ.

- Love is patient; it is kind. Love protects, always trusts, hopes, and perseveres.
- Love does not envy, it does not boast, neither is it proud.
- Love does not dishonor others; it is neither self-seeking, nor easily angered.
- Love doesn't keep a record of wrongs; it does not delight in evil but rejoices with the truth.

READ 1 CORINTHIANS 13:1–8.

GROW IN PATIENCE.

Does God seem slow in responding to your prayers and in fulfilling your plans and desires?

It is easy to rush, cut corners, and even skip essential steps in life in order to walk in stride with everyone else. However, God's plan for your life is unique. It is not like everyone else's. You must wait on God. You must be patient.

> And we desire that every one of you do shew the same diligence to the full assurance of hope unto the end: That ye be not slothful, but followers of them who through faith and patience inherit the promises. For when God made promise to Abraham, because he could swear by no greater, he sware by himself, Saying, Surely blessing I will bless thee, and multiplying I will multiply thee. And so, after he had patiently endured, he obtained the promise. (Hebrews 6:11–15)

Our fast-paced society works at robbing us of patience, but patience is mandatory for every Christian. There are many things that will not come your way except through the seemingly slow and painful road of patience. Like Abraham, you must patiently endure before you can obtain your promise.

Spiritual growth and spiritual fruit come through patience. Have you witnessed a tree put forth fruit in a matter of days following its planting? Just as plants are grown, cultivated, nurtured, and groomed before producing fruit, so you must exercise your heart and life in patience.

Cultivate your heart to create fertile soil for God's Word and His working in your life. Keep it tender. As He instructs and counsels, stop, listen, and follow. Before long, the fruit will show. Do not hurry what God is doing in your life. Grow in patience.

READ COLOSSIANS 3:12–13.

GROW IN MERCY.

David ascended to the throne in Israel after the death of Saul, a man who hated him with a passion. Customary in those days, kings killed family members and patriots of their predecessor to put an end to rivalry and possible coups. Despite the numerous fateful occurrences he encountered with Saul, David, the man after God's own heart, called for Mephibosheth, Saul's grandson, and showed him mercy and kindness. Mephibosheth was expecting to be killed. Instead, David set a place for him to eat with the king and to inherit great wealth.

God reminds us to be merciful because we shall receive mercy too (Matthew 5:7). Look at what else He says about growing in mercy: "Put on therefore, as the elect of God, holy and beloved, bowels of mercies, kindness, humbleness of mind, meekness, longsuffering" (Colossians 3:12).

The world is filled with those begging for mercy. Put on "bowels of mercy" and reach out to those whom God has placed on your path of life. You are God's hands and feet to them. "Withhold not good from them to whom it is due, when it is in the power of thine hand to do it. Say not unto thy neighbour, Go, and come again, and tomorrow I will give; when thou hast it by thee" (Proverbs 3:27–28).

Mercy is a virtue that is learned and cultivated. Naturally, we are mean and selfish. We wish to be first most of the time. You will not witness to those around you without mercy. Grow in mercy. Look and see with whom God is entrusting you and obey by responding as He desires. Remember, God does not treat you as your sins deserve. If it were not for His mercy, we would be consumed.

Today, you may have a reason to be angry and or to seek revenge. You have the will and power to seek justice. However, God says forgive and show mercy. Grow in mercy, cultivate it, and let it be a characteristic that defines you.

READ PSALM 18:25–28.

GROW IN KINDNESS.

Most Christians have a desire to serve God. Many want to be associated with something prominent and successful. However, not every child of God can serve in this capacity. God gifts all His children in different ways, and fills us with gifts to serve millions of His children and the people who surround us daily without making headlines or dancing in limelight.

Each one of us can excel in kindness. Not only will this make the world around us a better place, but it will minister deeply to needy hearts in ways we cannot comprehend.

When we get to heaven, I believe, we shall be surprised at how those who excelled in kindness will be rewarded. God actually gives us a glimpse of what to expect as He addresses the subject of growing in kindness in Matthew 25:37–40:

> Then shall the righteous answer him, saying, Lord, when saw we thee an hungred, and fed thee? or thirsty, and gave thee drink? When saw we thee a stranger, and took thee in? or naked, and clothed thee? Or when saw we thee sick, or in prison, and came unto thee? And the King shall answer and say unto them, Verily I say unto you, Inasmuch as ye have done it unto one of the least of these my brethren, ye have done it unto me.

Grow in kindness. Be kind and tenderhearted, seeing that Christ reckons it as service rendered to Him. There may be numerous reasons why you should be mean or even retaliate, but take a spiritual step in the right direction and chose kindness.

Be kind to God's people. "For God is not unrighteous to forget your work and labour of love, which ye have shewed toward his name, in that ye have ministered to the saints, and do minister" (Hebrews 6:10).

Watch out! God will avail opportunities for you to show kindness. Look for situations where you can sow kindness instead of hate. Choose kindness over resentment. Grow in kindness today. Cultivate it and make it a characteristic that defines you.

READ MATTHEW 25:31–46.

GROW IN MEEKNESS.

It feels good to be the best, to have an upper hand, or even the final say. It feels great to be powerful and important. However, all these feed the ego of a man and may not have eternal dividend.

God works with the meek. The works that impact us the most are not accomplished by the proud, the most notable, or even the smartest. They are done by those who are willing to lay low, to sacrifice, and to devotedly stay at it for the sake of others.

Jesus, our Lord and Savior, exemplified meekness by leaving heaven, the wonderful place that our finite minds can comprehend neither its celestial beauty or goodness, to love and live in human circumstances. God describes this in a wonderful way as recorded in Philippians 2:3-7:

> Let nothing be done through strife or vainglory; but in lowliness of mind let each esteem other better than themselves. Look not every man on his own things, but every man also on the things of others. Let this mind be in you, which was also in Christ Jesus: Who, being in the form of God, thought it not robbery to be equal with God: But made himself of no reputation, and took upon him the form of a servant, and was made in the likeness of men.

Moses, the meekest man described by God, saw himself a stammerer who could not be used to free and lead over two million people from Egypt.

To be proud and arrogant is to forfeit the working of God's might hand in our lives. To rule others with an iron hand is a sign of spiritual blindness and dullness to the richness of God's character.

Meekness is the ability to use our God-given power, position, and advantage in controlled ways as we bring glory to Him.

To what is God pointing in your life? Is pride, arrogance, power, position, or importance keeping you from being used of God? Grow in meekness.

READ PHILIPPIANS 2:1–11.

GROW IN GENTLENESS.

We live in a century and in societies that teach and emphasize looking out for ourselves. We are taught to fight and to go for it at all costs no matter what it takes. We rehearse scripts that give us an edge over others in interviews, careers, and in daily operations of life. It seems like to be gentle is to miss opportunities in life and to be mistaken for incompetence.

As a matter of fact, there are times when being rough, rude, arrogant, and unkempt in character are associated with manhood, toughness, and power that leads to respect, honor, and success.

Is there room for gentleness in our world today? What does God say about this great quality of being tender, kind and nice? "That I may make it manifest, as I ought to speak. Walk in wisdom toward them that are without, redeeming the time. Let your speech be always with grace, seasoned with salt, that ye may know how ye ought to answer every man" (Colossians 4:4-6).

God's desire is for your gentleness to be evident to all people in:

- Words: "A soft answer turneth away wrath: but grievous words stir up anger" (Proverbs 15:1).
- Deeds: "Let your moderation be known unto all men. The Lord is at hand" (Philippians 4:5).

Gentleness is nurtured while communing with God until it becomes a part of your life. It grows and matures as you chose to say yes to God and no to yourself. Self progressively dies as the inner man is renewed before God. As you obey and emulate His character, you unknowingly begin to reflect it. Other people recognize that your speech is seasoned with grace and is full of spiritual insights and soundness. Your answers are wise and full of godly counsel. Gentleness speaks for itself and you can't miss it.

It is natural to hate and to show disgust. The world if full of this. Nonetheless, to be gentle is a choice you make and purpose to cultivate until it characterizes your life. Grow in gentleness. God has many people around you who need your gentleness.

READ COLOSSIANS 3:12.

GROW IN TEMPERANCE.

Within you is great potential to do good and evil. You have power, ability, and knowledge to do as you wish. However, God calls His people to a life of self-control. Your heart must learn to say no to yourself in moments when you are tempted to do wrong. God desires to see your will controlled and your actions geared toward pleasing Him. Look at His admonition:

> And every man that striveth for the mastery is temperate in all things. Now they do it to obtain a corruptible crown; but we an incorruptible. I therefore so run, not as uncertainly; so fight I, not as one that beateth the air: But I keep under my body, and bring it into subjection: lest that by any means, when I have preached to others, I myself should be a castaway. (1 Corinthians 9:25–27)

Most dictionaries describe temperance in terms that clearly depict God's call to His children: temperance is the self-restraint, the prohibition, and abstinence for which every believer must strive and practice if he must live a life that is holy and pleasing to God. It calls for living soberly and doing everything in moderation as you analyze and make wise choices on a day-to-day basis.

God, Who understands the times in which we live, admonishes that we be temperate in all things, run the Christian race with certainty, and bring our bodies into subjection.

Be cautious and show restraint. Grow in temperance. Go against your ego, your emotions, attitudes, and even appetites and follow God's guidance today. Seek out those who have no hope or help in life. Use your muscles, power, position, provisions, and strength to be a blessing to others today.

READ TITUS 2:12.

GROW IN LONGSUFFERING.

No one likes pain. No one looks forward to troubles in this life. However, is all pain bad? Is there such a thing as good pain that grows and nurtures God's children? Are there good troubles that bring us to places of fulfillment and rest in life? Let us explore what God says. "My brethren, count it all joy when ye fall into divers temptations; Knowing this, that the trying of your faith worketh patience. But let patience have her perfect work, that ye may be perfect and entire, wanting nothing" (James 1:2–4).

God entrusts His children with certain situations that not only bring Him honor but fulfill other purposes undisclosed to us. While bragging about Job, God asked Satan, "Hast thou considered my servant Job, that there is none like him in the earth, a perfect and an upright man, one that feareth God, and escheweth evil?" (Job 1:8). Job, who was left out of this conversation, was entrusted with tragedy that deprived him of his children and possessions.

Nothing will come your way without God's approval. God does not approve what He knows you cannot handle. God's approval is a privilege, hard as it may be for us to conceive. When you pass God's tests, you shall also come out refined in other virtues, strong and resilient for Him.

With what has God entrusted you? He will not fail you.

READ 1 PETER 1:6–7.

GROW IN OBEDIENCE.

When God's eyes move to and fro over the whole world each day, does He see you as an obedient servant or as a rebel who does as you please and wish? Does God expect obedience from all or only some of His children? Exactly who should obey? Let's see true obedience from God's Word.

> Who in the days of his flesh, when he had offered up prayers and supplications with strong crying and tears unto him that was able to save him from death, and was heard in that he feared; Though he were a Son, yet learned he obedience by the things which he suffered; And being made perfect, he became the author of eternal salvation unto all them that obey him. (Hebrews 5:7–9)

You cannot be what you cannot learn, and neither can you teach what you did not learn. Learning is mandatory for you as a child of God. God will make specific opportunities available, and it is your responsibility to learn and grow in obedience. Christ, being God Himself, learned obedience from the things He suffered. He rightly has His royal position as the author of eternal salvation for all who obey.

The prophet Samuel challenged King Saul, saying, "Behold, to obey is better than sacrifice, and to hearken than the fat of rams" (1 Samuel 15:22). Saul's reply is true even today; disobedience transgresses the commandments of God.

God will speak today. Listen. Hear Him. Obey Him regardless of what He asks of you and to where He sends you.

READ 1 SAMUEL 15:20–28.

GROW IN PURITY.

We live in challenging times where the word purity does not find a place to land or settle with ease. Who can live a fresh, clean, good, and virtuous life in this century? Let us be real and ask, "Can a Christian be pure in this century?" The easiest way to answer this question is to look at God's Word: "Wherewithal shall a young man cleanse his way? by taking heed thereto according to thy word.... Thy word have I hid in mine heart, that I might not sin against thee" (Psalm 119:9, 11).

God, who is sovereign, knows when and where each one of us should live at any given point in history. He creates us with the needs of each generation in mind and lays the right matrix for us to live amid the tough challenges of each time.

Purity does not just happen. It is purposed, desired, and preserved. You will not be pure if your mind is not made up about it. If you wait for an opportunity to strike before deciding whether to remain pure or not, the chances are that you will fail.

When the young man, Daniel, was taken captive, he purposed ahead of time not to defile himself with food offered to the idols of a foreign land (Daniel 1).

Those who successfully remain pure, like Joseph, recognize that impurity is sin against God. They purpose to keep their lives free from defilement out of love, respect, and honor for God. God desires purity of:

- Heart
- Mind
- Motives
- Actions

God sees and judges your motives. Flee the lust of the flesh and the lust of the eyes. Know that our thoughts tell who we are, and actions follow our thoughts.

READ 1 CORINTHIANS 3:16–17.

GROW IN STEWARDSHIP.

We are surrounded with diverse needs on every side. God is seeking men and women whose hearts beat with love and grace to meet those needs. God seeks faithful and committed servants who will go against normal trends in life to fulfill His purposes. His eyes are looking to you today.

> And whatsoever ye do in word or deed, do all in the name of the Lord Jesus, giving thanks to God and the Father by him. . . . And whatsoever ye do, do it heartily, as to the Lord, and not unto men; Knowing that of the Lord ye shall receive the reward of the inheritance: for ye serve the Lord Christ. (Colossians 3:17, 23–24)

Spiritual growth takes place when we step out from a life of dependence on others into a life where we can serve and minister to others. Take the initiative to identify people and the things God has placed in your life that call for your service. Take responsibility and take care of them. Be dependable. It is easy to sit back and watch things happen. It is also easy to be critical when you do not share the burdens of others. Stepping into their shoes will open your eyes to prevailing needs and what it takes to have them met.

Whatever God lays on your heart to do, do it wholeheartedly as one who is doing it for God and not for man.

READ EPHESIANS 6:5–8.

GROW IN RESPONSIBILITY.

God speaks to all His children through His Word. However, it is easy to be passive and indifferent regarding the commandments of God. It is easy to assume that someone else will do as God commands while you remain on the fence. Look at God's exhortation to you today.

> I exhort therefore, that, first of all, supplications, prayers, intercessions, and giving of thanks, be made for all men; For kings, and for all that are in authority; that we may lead a quiet and peaceable life in all godliness and honesty. For this is good and acceptable in the sight of God our Saviour; Who will have all men to be saved, and to come unto the knowledge of the truth. (1 Timothy 2:1-4)

God's Word is written to you too. Do not shovel it to another as you fail to act on the demands of God. God requires you to take responsibility and do as He asks. Growing in responsibility says, "Lord, I realize You are speaking to me, and I will step out to do what You require of me whether others do it or not."

God charges you with the responsibility of praying for your leaders and your country. The peace, quietness, and godliness of this country are linked to your growing in responsibility. Don't sell out your leaders and your country out of negligence.

God wants to grow you. Most growth occurs as we step out in faith to take on the duties God assigns to us. Remember, God calls us to what He knows we can do. He formed us with precisions for different tasks. Those who take responsibility and remain faithful over little and nurtured to be faithful in greater matters.

Remind yourself of this divine revelation embedded in God's holy Word. "His lord said unto him, Well done, good and faithful servant; thou hast been faithful over a few things, I will make thee ruler over many things: enter thou into the joy of thy lord" (Matthew 25:23).

READ 2 CHRONICLES 7:14.

Grow in trust.

A character quality that can give hope in hopeless times is one of trust. Imagine holding onto someone's word with full assurance that they will be faithful to do as they promised. Unfortunately, we live in uncertainty because it is hard to trust mortal man. Even though he may have good intentions, his very nature dictates and confirms his propensity to fail.

Nonetheless, does God expect His children to be trustworthy or are they unreliable and unworthy of trust like the rest of the world?

Can God trust you? God is looking for faithful servants to trust and commission to work with Him. "Moreover thou shalt provide out of all the people able men, such as fear God, men of truth, hating covetousness; and place such over them, to be rulers of thousands, and rulers of hundreds, rulers of fifties, and rulers of tens" (Exodus 18:21).

God has notable work for all His children. God searches the heart as He examines and looks for whom to trust. He knows whom to trust with thousands, hundreds, fifties, or tens. For whatever He puts under your care, God looks for faithfulness. He wants to trust you. He reminds us in 1 Corinthians 4:2 that it is required in stewards that a man be found faithful: "Moreover it is required in stewards, that a man be found faithful."

When you are faithful in little things, God entrusts you with much more. When you are unfaithful, God finds a faithful son with whom to work and entrust your share. Testing for trust and faithfulness usually begins in very small and seemingly insignificant matters and things. God wants to trust you with His true riches. Watch out for His daily visitations and be faithful.

Read Luke 16:10–12.

GROW IN DISCIPLESHIP.

One clear way to lay a godly legacy and to influence this generation in a positive way is to invest in people. Nurture somebody. Hold someone's hand until they are stable. Instruct and mentor others into godly living. Be an example both in deed and in word. Grow faithful disciples.

"How do you this?" you may ask. Paul, a man who excelled in the practice of discipleship, has good insights from which we can learn: "Thou therefore, my son, be strong in the grace that is in Christ Jesus. And the things that thou hast heard of me among many witnesses, the same commit thou to faithful men, who shall be able to teach others also" (2 Timothy 2:1–2).

Christ came on earth with a definite mission and invested His life, time, and prayer in twelve select men. He discipled them through different circumstances and teachings within three and a half years of active ministry. Not only did Christ entrust His disciples with what He had, but He charged them with the responsibility of preserving and passing it down to other faithful people. You, like God's other children, have come to the knowledge of Christ as a result of this ministry, and God wants you to carry it forward.

Invest your life, time, and prayer in people as God leads you. Find faithful individuals who can be trusted with spiritual matters and disciple them to carry the torch to future generations. Be a leader, a mentor, and an example.

You do not have to begin big until you master your way in this area. Follow your heart as God leads and begin with those God has given you. You do not have to look very far. They are right there in your daily circles of operation. Be committed to it and see how God will grow you and the service.

READ TITUS 2:1–15.

GROW IN WISDOM.

Each generation has its share of difficulties and unique problems. You will face circumstances that demand wise actions. You will meet people with whom you must deal wisely. You cannot give what you do not have. You will not be effective in Christian ministry without wisdom. Follow the example of Christ and grow in wisdom: "And Jesus increased in wisdom and stature, and in favour with God and man" (Luke 2:52).

We live in a complex world. We live among complex people with societal norms that are ever changing. God desires for you to gain wisdom if you are to impact your society. Wisdom is knowing what to say and what to do at the right time as you judge according to the precepts of God. Wisdom honors God. It establishes the truth and guides people in the right direction.

God gives wisdom to those who desire and ask. He says, "If any of you lack wisdom, let him ask of God, that giveth to all men liberally, and upbraideth not; and it shall be given him. But let him ask in faith, nothing wavering. For he that wavereth is like a wave of the sea driven with the wind and tossed" (James 1:5–6).

- God gives wisdom to the upright in heart, to those who fear Him, who shun evil and obey His Word.
- Those who please God are blessed with wisdom.
- Ask God to give you wisdom as you weave through the situations and challenges that face you today.

Since God gives wisdom to those who ask, make it a daily endeavor to ask God for wisdom. This is because each day is not only different, but it presents us with new challenges. God created you with this century in mind. You can combat today's problems with divine help from God. Seek His wisdom. "For the LORD giveth wisdom: out of his mouth cometh knowledge and understanding" (Proverbs 2:6).

READ PROVERBS 4:7–12.

GROW IN KNOWLEDGE.

In Hosea 4:6, God laments, noting that His people perish for lack of knowledge. How is that possible? How can there be so many "smart" people in a nation and still be a significant lack of knowledge? We can draw a conclusion and say, there are many learned people in the world but not many have knowledge. According to God, knowledge does not just come by the reading of books. True knowledge is given to those who hide God's law in their hearts and live by God's commandments. It's for those who desire and look for it diligently.

God does not withhold knowledge from His people. You, too, can have knowledge with which to face the world and the tough circumstances of life. Look at God's promise:

> My son, if thou wilt receive my words, and hide my commandments with thee; So that thou incline thine ear unto wisdom, and apply thine heart to understanding; Yea, if thou criest after knowledge, and liftest up thy voice for understanding; If thou seekest her as silver, and searchest for her as for hid treasures; Then shalt thou understand the fear of the Lord, and find the knowledge of God. For the Lord giveth wisdom: out of his mouth cometh knowledge and understanding. (Proverbs 2:1–6)

Knowledge that will influence the world is found in those whose spiritual senses are sharpened by God as they consciously comprehend their responsibilities through the molding hand of God in their circumstances.

God has allowed you to live at such a time in the history of the world for a reason. You are the right person to deal with the challenges of our time. However, you cannot face such unprecedented times without knowledge from God. Do not act without knowledge today. Ask God for knowledge.

READ PROVERBS 1:7.

GROW IN DISCERNMENT.

Today, you will meet different people and you will make important decisions. Regardless of how small or big the decisions will be, your heart will rejoice when your decisions are sound and good. It is not always easy to make the right decisions. This is because, not everyone who says Lord, Lord knows God or belongs to God. Not everyone who comes or acts in the name of the Lord belongs to God.

The good news is that God does not leave His children to gamble with life and make bad decisions without stepping in to help. God gives discernment. Discernment will help you separate what's fake from what's real. Look at God's admonition.

> Beloved, believe not every spirit, but try the spirits whether they are of God: because many false prophets are gone out into the world. Hereby know ye the Spirit of God: Every spirit that confesseth that Jesus Christ is come in the flesh is of God: And every spirit that confesseth not that Jesus Christ is come in the flesh is not of God. (1 John 4:1–3)

It is easy to get deceived. You need discernment. The world around you is full of counterfeits. Discernment gives you the ability to sieve through flukes to determine what is real and right from what is fake or a masquerade. God alerts that Satan will come to you disguised as an angel of light in 2 Corinthians 11:14: "And no marvel; for Satan himself is transformed into an angel of light." False teachers and prophets like to slip in unawares. You must grow in discernment.

The Word of God will quickly and powerfully sensitize and grow you in discernment. It is powerful and sharp to expose the thoughts and the intents of the heart, to split the soul and spirit, and to bring what is hidden to light. Ask God for discernment.

READ HEBREWS 4:12.

GROW IN PRAYER.

Imagine if you got an invitation to meet and talk to the president of your nation. How would you prepare for that day? Would you be hesitant, or would you look forward to the meeting? Would you be late, or would you be a little early for the great session?

Imagine, all of God's children have divine invitations to talk with the Lord of lords and the King of kings 24/7. It is true that familiarity can breed contempt. It is easy to turn such an incredible privilege into a nominal and boring meaningless encounter. Meaningful prayer sessions that touch the heart of God are transformational and powerful.

Before you talk to people, talk to God. Before you cry out to people, cry out to God. Before you seek help from other people, seek God's help. Learn to hear from God. Learn to confide in the Lord God Almighty. Have you talked to God today? Look at God's invitation to you: "Ask, and it shall be given you; seek, and ye shall find; knock, and it shall be opened unto you: For every one that asketh receiveth; and he that seeketh findeth; and to him that knocketh it shall be opened" (Matthew 7:7–8).

Every Christian has an open invitation to ask, to seek, and to knock on God's door. God did not set a limit on how often you can talk to Him. Those who grow in prayer discover that they, too, like Elijah, although feeble and subject to human passions, can be heard of God and used to change destinies in life.

Prayer is that course you must walk if you should be bold and have power to do what God has entrusted to you. Those who become men and women of God are molded on their knees. You will not learn to stand and walk with God without learning to kneel before Him in prayer. You will learn knowledge, wisdom, understanding, and discernment as you talk with God. Grow in prayer. Commune with God today.

Do not wait for a specific time to start praying. Talk to God now and purposely set a time when you can pray and talk to Him in the coming days.

READ JEREMIAH 33:3.

GROW IN UNDERSTANDING.

The world in which we live today demands that you not only see but also understand, both with your heart and eyes. It is hard to discern or to understand the motives behind people's actions. It is easy to be deceived. You must seek and grow in understanding. Look at what a lack of understanding can do according to the following Scriptures:

> And beheld among the simple ones, I discerned among the youths, a young man void of understanding, Passing through the street near her corner; and he went the way to her house. . . . So she caught him, and kissed him. . . . With her much fair speech she caused him to yield, with the flattering of her lips she forced him. . . . He goeth after her straightway, as an ox goeth to the slaughter, or as a fool to the correction of the stocks; Till a dart strike through his liver; as a bird hasteth to the snare, and knoweth not that it is for his life. (Proverbs 7:7-8, 13, 21-23)

Mere earthly knowledge puffs men and leads to pride. God admonishes you to be full of knowledge and wisdom, which give understanding. The knowledge of God's Word leads to understanding. This understanding is the ability to have sound judgment; it's knowing what is right from wrong as you discretely establish sound precepts by which to live as a result of good discernment.

Remember, God gives wisdom. He also gives knowledge and understanding. Do not hesitate to ask God for understanding. Do not make many mistakes just because you did not ask God for understanding.

Understanding saves you from Satan's snares. To have understanding is like to have another set of eyes that help you see better, clearly and precisely. Read God's Word and pray. Let not your understanding be darkened.

READ PROVERBS 7.

GROW FROM STRENGTH TO STRENGTH.

When the spring season begins, you see a lot of new life. What looked dead because of the harsh winter springs forth into new growth. People get busy planting different things in their farms, gardens, flowerbeds and even pots. Those plants grow. They increase in size, height, structure, form and stability. Their growth is obvious. You cannot miss it.

Just as plants grow into maturity and even produce fruit and seed, God desires and expects His children to grow spiritually. God does not expect too much out of you. He just desires to see growth. Look at God's counsel that leads to spiritual growth. "Whom shall he teach knowledge? and whom shall he make to understand doctrine? them that are weaned from the milk, and drawn from the breasts. For precept must be upon precept, precept upon precept; line upon line, line upon line; here a little, and there a little" (Isaiah 28:9–10).

The Bible teaches in Isaiah 40:31 that "they that wait upon the Lord shall renew their strength; they shall mount up with wings as eagles; they shall run, and not be weary; and they shall walk, and not faint."

Spiritual growth can be likened to running long distance races. It cannot be taken like a quick sprint. It involves growing every single day. You keep adding to what you know as you practice it and acquire new knowledge to keep you strong and steady. God knows how to feed and grow you from strength to strength. Think about a little and tender newborn child who grows into a mature adult. Growth does not happen overnight. It takes daily feeds and daily tender care to grow the baby. This is how spiritual growth takes place. You consistently feed on God's Word and follow Him consistently to do as He asks and directs.

Follow God on a day-to-day basis. He will provide the right nourishment as you feed on His Word. He will lead you through choice situations to increase spiritual strength.

READ PSALM 84:4–7.

GROW IN GRACE.

Have you heard of the saying, "A surgery is major when it is done to you, regardless of how minor it may be. But it is always minor when it is done on others, regardless of how major it may be"?

God takes us through turns and twists in life for a reason. Sometimes He make us walk the tough terrains of lack, sickness, fear, pain, and anguish in order to work grace and mercy in our lives. It is by experiencing what others go through that our hearts develop genuine empathy. This is how we develop tolerance and love without sharpening our hearts and minds with criticism.

> Let no corrupt communication proceed out of your mouth, but that which is good to the use of edifying, that it may minister grace unto the hearers. And grieve not the holy Spirit of God, whereby ye are sealed unto the day of redemption. Let all bitterness, and wrath, and anger, and clamour, and evil speaking, be put away from you, with all malice: And be ye kind one to another, tenderhearted, forgiving one another, even as God for Christ's sake hath forgiven you. (Ephesians 4:29–32)

We are all recipients of God's grace. We are nothing on our own. We are forgiven, washed, and given an opportunity to walk with God as His mercies are renewed upon us today. God does not treat us as our sins deserve. We have won His unmerited favor. He wants you to practice the same.

Be merciful to others today. Put off bitterness. Control your anger and watch how you speak. Be kind. Be tenderhearted and forgive just as Christ has forgiven and given you a fresh chance today.

The day will present opportunities for you to show grace and honest love. Do not miss them. Be deliberate in your choices and actions. Allow God to use your hands, feet, mouth, and intellect to minister to others today.

READ LUKE 6:31–36.

GROW IN CHARACTER.

Character is what you are when no one is watching. Character is who God knows you to be.

God is looking for men and women of sound character with whom to work and accomplish His purposes in the world today. God desires integrity: that inner soundness of heart and spirit that fears Him and purposes to do what is right regardless of the time, the place, or who is present. God works with those who have crucified their affections and their egos and surrendered to Him in unprecedented times such as these.

God presents all His children with daily opportunities to grow in sound Christian character. This demands that we say yes to what honors Him while maintaining a firm no for what dishonors and brings shame to His name. Let us look at the words of a young man who made good use of his opportunities as we purposefully grow in ours. "There is none greater in this house than I; neither hath he kept back anything from me but thee, because thou art his wife: how then can I do this great wickedness, and sin against God?" (Genesis 39:9).

Joseph had been sold as a slave in Egypt by brothers who hated and cared little about him. He was many miles from home in a land where no one knew who he was. He could have chosen to say yes to the seductions of Potiphar's wife and kept it covered, but he didn't. Joseph saw sin as doing what was evil, wicked, and displeasing to God.

Man looks at your outward appearance, but God focuses on your heart. God wants you to honor Him in your actions and choices. He is working at building a Christlike character in you. Your godly character will be a testimony and strength for the generations to come. God molds character as you yield to Him.

READ PSALM 119:11–12.

GROW IN INTEGRITY.

What does God see when He looks in our hearts? Can He find a heart that beats with an honest desire to do right? Can He see a heart that fears sin and runs away from the slander, the malice, the deceit, the cunningness, and the conniving of the world?

Integrity is the inner beauty of having exemplary qualities held true to self in honor of God. Integrity is having a godly lifestyle, one that is without hypocrisy. Look at God's witness of integrity recorded for us to learn and follow: "But Daniel purposed in his heart that he would not defile himself with the portion of the king's meat, nor with the wine which he drank: therefore he requested of the prince of the eunuchs that he might not defile himself" (Daniel 1:8).

Daniel, a young Hebrew man who was taken captive into Babylon, did not need the coaxing of friends or colleagues to tip his scale of integrity. Deep within him was a pursuit to honor and to uphold God. He did not want to disgrace God in his choices and practices.

Sound character comes from the consistency of a personal walk with God that holds God dear to the heart. The heart gets to a point when God is the one and precious treasure it cannot do without. It leaves all else and pursues God not just as a Savior or Father but also as a dear friend.

Embrace God's deep love for you and be moved to be separated unto Him out of love, too. Remember:

- "The integrity of the upright shall guide them: but the perverseness of transgressors shall destroy them" (Proverbs 11:3).
- "He that walketh uprightly walketh surely: but he that perverteth his ways shall be known" (Proverbs 10:9).

READ 2 TIMOTHY 2:19.

GROW WITH THE MASTER.

God is always in the business of wooing His children into a closer walk and deeper relationship every day. God's ways are not our ways, and neither are His thoughts like our thoughts. Sometimes, He uses the hardships of life to draw us closer. This is contrary to what our finite human nature can understand or accept. How can a loving God use trouble to get me closer to Him, you may ask?

God never intends to hurt you when He asks you to walk with Him. It is for your good to walk close to God. Incline your heart to hear and to understand Him and He will lead you on pleasant roads to your joy and fulfillment. Let us see how He teaches such lessons to His beloved children.

> Now when he had left speaking, he said unto Simon, Launch out into the deep, and let down your nets for a draught. And Simon answering said unto him, Master, we have toiled all the night, and have taken nothing: nevertheless at thy word I will let down the net. And when they had this done, they inclosed a great multitude of fishes: and their net brake. (Luke 5:4–6)

God knows you. God knows what you need. He knows how to lead you to your needs. Walk and grow with Him. The disciples had toiled all night without catching any fish. Oh, how things changed when Christ came to the scene! From where did the fish that had been nonexistent all night come?

Stay with Christ. You never go wrong walking with the Master. Without Him you can do nothing. You will toil all day and all night and still come out empty. Your time with Him will prove to be the most treasurable, fruitful, and fulfilling. Trust His lessons and grow as He teaches you.

READ PSALM 127:1–2.

GROW THROUGH THE STORMS OF LIFE.

Life has many storms. Some storms come suddenly while others develop gradually and swell up with time. Storms create uncertainties and bring fear. They throw us off course, and some even leave us stranded.

How does God look at your storm? Do our storms of life take God by surprise? Does God have a hand in what happens to us? Let us see how God deals with storms in the lives of His beloved children:

> And straightway he constrained his disciples to get into the ship, and to go to the other side before unto Bethsaida, while he sent away the people. And when he had sent them away, he departed into a mountain to pray. And when even was come, the ship was in the midst of the sea, and he alone on the land. And he saw them toiling in rowing; for the wind was contrary unto them: and about the fourth watch of the night he cometh unto them, walking upon the sea, and would have passed by them. (Mark 6:45–48)

All of God's children go through storms. Remember, you do not go through any storm alone. It is Christ, as He did for the disciples, who maps your next destination. He knows when the winds get boisterous. He knows when you are in trouble. Remember, too, that nothing takes Him by surprise. It was Christ Jesus who sent the disciples across the sea. He knew what awaited His beloved students. Today, Christ understands what surrounds you. He also knows what is on your road of life. Just as He prayed for the disciples, He is praying for you. He will not leave you to face your storm alone. Nothing will come to you that He has not permitted.

Troubles are never meant to break and destroy you. They are specifically cultured for your path, and you were created with them in mind. God is working to grow you. You will come out stronger. You will not fail.

READ ISAIAH 43:2.

GROW THROUGH FAILURE.

Failure hurts. There is nothing more hurtful in a world that demands performance than putting your best foot forward and coming out empty. How do you proceed when you stumble day after day despite how much work or effort you put in? What do you do when you find yourself in the same spot time and time again? How do you explain to people that you are a hard worker when there is nothing in your hands to show for it?

God is not blind to the struggles and the failures that face you today. Look at His admonition:

> Not as though I had already attained, either were already perfect: but I follow after, if that I may apprehend that for which also I am apprehended of Christ Jesus. Brethren, I count not myself to have apprehended: but this one thing I do, forgetting those things which are behind, and reaching forth unto those things which are before, I press toward the mark for the prize of the high calling of God in Christ Jesus. (Philippians 3:12–14)

There is no person in the world who has never failed. Do not stop at your failure. Failure can be stepping-stones for the next great success. Failing today does not brand you a failure. Failure is God's training camp for those who will be men and women of noble service.

Do not dwell on past failures. You will miss the beauty of God today and you will be blind to tomorrow. Forget the past and look forward to what is a head as you commit everything to God and walk with Him toward your next destination. Learn from your failures and move on.

God does have to explain what He is doing and the reasons behind what you see. He is trustworthy. God is doing a new thing. Failure is not your destiny, it is a passing cloud that make room for the blessings of rain. "Remember ye not the former things, neither consider the things of old. Behold, I will do a new thing; now it shall spring forth; shall ye not know it? I will even make a way in the wilderness, and rivers in the desert" (Isaiah 43:18–19).

READ PROVERBS 24:16.

GROW THROUGH DISCIPLINE.

Discipline! Just the very mention of the word can create mixed feelings in the same heart or mind. This is because discipline is associated with pain and trouble. However, can anything good come out of discipline? Have you reaped the good fruits of disciple in life? How does God look at discipline? Contrary to what the word means, discipline is an act of God's love toward His children. Look at how God deals with His children on this matter: "As many as I love, I rebuke and chasten: be zealous therefore, and repent" (Revelation 3:19).

God disciplines His children where sin is involved. In Hebrews 12:6–11, God Word says,

> For whom the Lord loveth he chasteneth, and scourgeth every son whom he receiveth. If ye endure chastening, God dealeth with you as with sons; for what son is he whom the father chasteneth not? But if ye be without chastisement, whereof all are partakers, then are ye bastards, and not sons. Furthermore we have had fathers of our flesh which corrected us, and we gave them reverence: shall we not much rather be in subjection unto the Father of spirits, and live? For they verily for a few days chastened us after their own pleasure; but he for our profit, that we might be partakers of his holiness. Now no chastening for the present seemeth to be joyous, but grievous: nevertheless afterward it yieldeth the peaceable fruit of righteousness unto them which are exercised thereby.

God is not acting because He hates you. God disciplines His children with intentions of getting them closer to Him and farther away from the dangerous schemes of Satan. Discipline is an indication of God's protective hand of care in action.

When God disciplines you, fall back into His arms of grace in repentance. If He did not love you, He would not care to discipline you.

READ PROVERBS 3:12.

GROW INTO VESSELS OF HONOR.

When you walk through the displays of a potter's wares, your eyes may be fascinated with the art, but what is not always obvious is the thought behind the creations. What prompts a potter to make different vessels? Does he express his inner imaginations through what he makes?

You know! It is not just a potter who creates vessels for different functions and use. God, the Master Potter, likewise molds His children into vessels for His use. God decides what kind of a vessel to make, when to make it and where to best use it. This means that God can remold one vessel into a totally different vessel and use it again in whichever way He chooses. Every Christian is a good candidate in the hands of God for use.

God wants to count on you to be a vessel of honor in a century and in a society where spiritual darkness is taking the central stage. Can God find you honorable to entrust you with His spiritual torch? Can He find integrity of heart to grow you into a vessel of honor in these dark times? Look at 2 Timothy 2:20-21 to see what it will take to become God's vessel for our times.

You are designed and prepared to be a vessel of honor unto God. You have a say in the kind of vessels you become. You can be a vessel of honor or dishonor. Sin deforms and renders you good for ignoble work. Those who flee youthful lusts and follow righteousness, faith, charity, and peace with them that call on the Lord out of a pure heart purge themselves into vessels of honor. God endows them with His power and presence. He makes them honorable vessels for the times.

You were created to bring glory and honor to God. God wants to delight in you. He wants to be pleased with your service. Let Him hold your hand and lead you. Listen and do as He asks. Without even realizing, you will become a vessel of honor.

READ 2 TIMOTHY 3:16–17.

Grow in solitude.

Not many people enjoy solitude. However, God has an interesting way of growing and molding His choice servants away from the accolades of life. Daniel, a beloved servant of God, grew into a deeper relationship with God while away from home in exile. It was in Babylon that God grew the young man in wisdom and all kinds of knowledge. The divine revelations Daniel could neither comprehend nor understand while in Israel, were revealed to him in that unfamiliar environment.

Is God wooing you to spend time alone with Him? Take time to be silent today. Solitude is not a bad thing. To spend time alone in silence as your heart inclines to hear and to commune with God is an enriching encounter you should not miss. "For thus saith the Lord God, the Holy One of Israel; In returning and rest shall ye be saved; in quietness and in confidence shall be your strength: and ye would not" (Isaiah 30:15).

God shapes and grows His children in solitude. His interest is for you to walk and to grow in Him. He desires a deep relationship with you. Shake off friends and activities and be alone with God. There is time for fellowship with friends and family, but spiritual growth also demands time alone with God.

You listen and learn to hear God's voice in quiet moments. You grow in solitude. It is here that your roots deepen and get anchored in God. Most people's days are filled with action and noise. God will not howl above daily chaos to speak to you.

Retreat and listen. The truth is that you won't miss anything you leave behind to listen and to be with God. Remember, it was while alone in the desert in Midian that Moses heard God and ascertained his call. Reflect and meditate. Hear God today.

Read Mark 1:35 and Luke 5:16.

GROW IN GOD.

Life has many challenges that do not have tangible human solutions. It is easy to grow tired and faint. Difficult moments have a way of exposing the state of our hearts. They reveal from where we draw strength and our ability or inability to remain resilient in rough times.

You can have a well-anchored heart despite your surroundings. Those who stay calm amid dark and tumultuous times have the secret of placing their trust and finding stability in God. So, how do you get to such a moment of growth? Is this something that all Christians attain or is it only for a selected few?

Look at God's admonition to His disciples regarding the matter of spiritual growth:

> And he taught them many things by parables, and said unto them in his doctrine, Hearken; Behold, there went out a sower to sow: And it came to pass, as he sowed, some fell by the way side. . . . And other fell on good ground, and did yield fruit that sprang up and increased; and brought forth, some thirty, and some sixty, and some an hundred. And he said unto them, He that hath ears to hear, let him hear. (Mark 4:2–4, 8–9)

As Christ the Savior notes, growth takes place when surrounding conditions are right and favorable. This means, there are times when we may expect to see growth in vain unless we provide what is necessary.

Growing in God is not something that just happens. It is cultivated. It starts with making a move toward God as He woos your heart to Him. It also calls for purposing in your heart to hear and follow God. This is followed by the deliberate taking of steps to do as He teaches on a day-to-day basis.

Growing in God calls for cultivating your heart to form fertile soil for spiritual growth. It demands that you pull out what is ungodly. Deal with what hinders spiritual growth and keeps you from God.

READ JOHN 15:4–5.

June

CHRISTIAN RELIABILITY

Do you know Christians who are reliable? What does it take to be a reliable Christian?

Let us grow into reliable and dependable Christians this month.

STRIDE WITH PATIENCE.

Whenever I eat a juicy, tasty fruit my immediate reaction is, "I wish I can plant and have such fruits in my backyard." Little do I consider how long it may take to harvest such a fruit, let alone what it will take to get it ready and succulent. Crops do not grow in a day. Trees do not yield fruit in a matter of hours. The hardworking farmer sweats, toils and waits patiently for his crop. He must go through the emotional roller-coaster experience when drought, floods, hail, or pesticides strike. When you look at his orchard when his fruit is ready, you mind may never take you to the preceding tough months of labor and uncertainty.

It is easy to look at the coveted Bible character, Joseph, and see him lavished with all the riches and honor of Egypt and forget his long path of loneliness and disappointment along the way. It is hard to envision him, a man only second to Pharaoh, scrubbing dirty pots and mopping floors in prison. It is also easy to think that men and women who enjoy such accolades had head starts in life and their paths were full of wealthy and significant godfathers. Joseph endured many years of hard labor before getting to that position of power and influence.

What are you struggling with today? Is your path filled with uncertainty and eventualities? Have you worked hard in life, but have nothing to show for it? Are you misunderstood and faced with ridicule? Stride with patience. Joseph went through similar situations but that did not stop God from accomplishing His will and work as planned. Your current situations do not distract God from His purposes. They are part of God's package for fulfilling His plans in your life.

God will come through with His blessings as He has promised. God is not unfair. Believe His promise in Hebrews 6:10 and keep honoring Him: "For God is not unrighteous to forget your work and labour of love, which ye have shewed toward his name, in that ye have ministered to the saints, and do minister."

READ PSALM 84:11.

YOU ARE VALUABLE TO GOD.

Teenage years are vibrant and so is the young adulthood phase. Not only are we productive in this prime time but we feel valued, needed, and helpful. Our productivity and accomplishments, let alone the positive causes of our effect, give us reasons to keep moving and doing. However, this stage does not linger forever. There comes the slow phase when you can longer do as you wish. The age of the mind and body in general dictate and set your limits. As you reflect on your earlier years—the hard work, the diligence, and the lives you impacted—your spirit may sigh with mixed feelings. As you celebrate and rejoice on one hand, you may fight the sadness of feeling unproductive, less valuable, and not needed as much.

How does God look at His children in their wisdom years of life? Does He put them on the shelf only to be covered in dust?

God is very interesting. Look at what He says in Psalms 139:16: "Thine eyes did see my substance, yet being unperfect; and in thy book all my members were written, which in continuance were fashioned, when as yet there was none of them."

For every day you are alive, you are valuable and still in God's divine business. God waited until Abram was ninety years old to make a covenant that would affect all future generations. Talk about rejuvenation! God's promises to Abram were transformational: a father of many nations, abundance of blessings—wealth, riches, lands, children—circumcision, etc. (see Genesis 17).

God waited until Moses was eighty years old to lead a multitude of Israelites from Egypt to the land of promise. This same Moses was under God's surveillance, care, and protection from birth. Moses could not accomplish such a job when he was forty years of age.

As long as you are alive, you are God's jewel and vessel of honor to display His splendor and to accomplish daily purposes for Him. Age is not a factor in the vineyard of God. "And even to your old age I am he; and even to hoar hairs will I carry you: I have made, and I will bear; even I will carry, and will deliver you" (Isaiah 46:4).

God values you.

READ LUKE 12:6-7.

A CHANGE OF NAME CAN MEAN A CHANGE OF DESTINY.

Today, the King of kings may present an opportunity that will make significant changes in your life. Before the Patriarch, Abram, encountered God, he was an ordinary man living life amid idol worship in Mesopotamia—in the Persian Gulf. God said to Abram, "Neither shall thy name any more be called Abram, but thy name shall be Abraham; for a father of many nations have I made thee" (Genesis 17:5).

God transformed Jacob, Abraham's grandson, saying, "Thy name shall be called no more Jacob, but Israel: for as a prince hast thou power with God and with men, and hast prevailed" (Genesis 32:28). Jacob no longer wandered from place to place through craftiness and lying. He is the father of the twelve tribes of Israel.

God calls, cleans, and transforms ordinary people and makes them men and women of destiny. God has the power to redeem you from shame, desolation and nothingness to an honorable place. Look at His promise:

> Thou shalt also be a crown of glory in the hand of the Lord, and a royal diadem in the hand of thy God. Thou shalt no more be termed Forsaken; neither shall thy land any more be termed Desolate: but thou shalt be called Hephzibah, and thy land Beulah: for the Lord delighteth in thee, and thy land shall be married. (Isaiah 62:3–4)

You do not have to stay in your current situation forever. The many respected people you see in God's service today, have all been helped by the mighty hand of God. God will help you according to His promise in Isaiah 55:13: "Instead of the thorn shall come up the fir tree, and instead of the brier shall come up the myrtle tree: and it shall be to the Lord for a name, for an everlasting sign that shall not be cut off."

What is your name? With what is your name associated that is painful, regrettable, and undesirable? Allow God to work in your heart and do a name change. An encounter with Christ does not leave a man or woman patched up. It produces lifetime changes.

READ 2 CORINTHIANS 5:17–18.

ENCOUNTERING CHRIST CHANGES YOU.

Correction centers, laws, and discipline play crucial roles in mandating changes to people's lives. However, we also know that prisons may suppress behavior, but they do not bring lasting changes. Unless change takes place in the heart, a man will walk back into old habits and practices once the painful consequences are eliminated. So, can we expect to see true and tangible changes in a man? Is this a possibility? If yes, how does this happen? God changes men.

No man encounters Christ and remains the same. To be in the presence of God is to experience supernatural power working in every aspect of your life. God, who is light, shines in every compartment to point us to Himself and to the beauty of His glory and righteousness. The Scriptures are true in telling us, "Therefore if any man be in Christ, he is a new creature: old things are passed away; behold, all things are become new" (2 Corinthians 5:17).

Saul, a murderer, encountered Christ on the road to Damascus while on his deadly mission. There was a heart transformation. The man's zeal turned from persecuting Christians to preaching the gospel of Christ. This is the same man who wrote most of the books in the New Testament (see Acts 9).

When the Samaritan woman came face-to-face with the Savior, she saw herself for who she was. "Come, see a man, which told me all things that ever I did: is not this the Christ?" she said (John 4:29). That ended her life of adultery.

When Peter, the unlearned fisherman, met Jesus, his life was not the same again. Not only did he fish men into the kingdom of God, but he became a pillar in the establishment of the New Testament church. "And I say also unto thee, That thou art Peter, and upon this rock I will build my church; and the gates of hell shall not prevail against it" (Matthew 16:18).

Have you trusted in Jesus? With what are you struggling? Do not be afraid to seek and call on God. He will bring true change in your life.

READ JOHN 6:37.

GOD IS A GOD OF COVENANTS.

God establishes and keeps covenants with His people. God Who is faithful takes covenants seriously. Those who committedly entrust their hearts and lives to Him find Him to be a true keeper of covenants.

Many of the blessings we enjoy today as God's children can be traced to the day God made His covenant with Abram. God saw a servant and a true friend in Abram. He looked at the future in stretches of thousands of years and spoke to the faithfulness of this one man saying,

> And I will give unto thee, and to thy seed after thee, the land wherein thou art a stranger, all the land of Canaan, for an everlasting possession; and I will be their God. And God said unto Abraham, Thou shalt keep my covenant therefore, thou, and thy seed after thee in their generations. This is my covenant, which ye shall keep, between me and you and thy seed after thee; Every man child among you shall be circumcised. (Genesis 17:8–10)

As we look at Abram in retrospect, one cannot help but ask, "Has God stopped making covenants with His people? Can you make a covenant today unto God?" The answer is yes. God still makes and honors covenants with His children.

At a desperate time in Hannah's life, she cried to God and made a covenant to God saying, "If thou wilt indeed look on the affliction of thine handmaid, and remember me, and not forget thine handmaid, but wilt give unto thine handmaid a man child, then I will give him unto the LORD all the days of his life, and there shall no razor come upon his head" (1 Samuel 1:11). God heard her and gave her a son, whom she named Samuel. Samuel became a renown prophet, judge, and priest in Israel.

What about today? Does God honor covenants? God's promises are true.

As recorded in Deuteronomy 7:9, God faithfully keeps covenants with His people.

Do not be afraid to call on God and to make a commitment to Him. He is faithful. He honors and keeps covenants with those who love Him to thousands of generations.

READ ROMANS 8:31–39.

BUILD A SOUND CHRISTIAN CHARACTER.

Jacob, the patriarch, was used to a life of lying and conniving. At a young age, he followed the cunningly devised schemes of his mother and deceived his father into giving him the blessings allotted for a first born. When Esau the first born learned of the deceit, he vowed to kill Jacob, his brother (Genesis 27).

Jacob fled his home and took refuge in the home of his uncle, Laban (Genesis 31). Nonetheless, this did not solve his problem. This is because locations cannot change character. True change emanates from a heart that is transformed by God. God was gracious to Jacob. While running away from Laban after another deceitful adventure, God confronted Jacob, "What is your name?" He asked (Genesis 32:27).

It was at that time that Jacob, the deceiver, received a name change that turned his life around. "Thy name shall be called no more Jacob, but Israel: for as a prince hast thou power with God and with men, and hast prevailed" (Genesis 32:28). God responded to the honesty of Jacob.

God desires honesty from all His children. He says,

> Recompense to no man evil for evil. Provide things honest in the sight of all men. If it be possible, as much as lieth in you, live peaceably with all men. Dearly beloved, avenge not yourselves, but rather give place unto wrath: for it is written, Vengeance is mine; I will repay, saith the Lord. (Romans 12:17–19)

Develop into a reliable Christian by building a sound Christian character. It is never too early to nurture Christian virtues. Even a child is known by his doings, whether his work be pure, and whether it be right according to Proverbs 20:11. The world teaches tit for tat—get what you deserve and pay back in full. God's Word teaches the contrary. Do not repay evil for evil. Do not take the law into your own hands.

Deal honestly with all men as one who is a steward of the most High God. God fights for His children. He will fight for you. God will pay back for you in better ways than you could have imagined. Do not yield to the temptation to be cunning and deceitful.

READ ROMANS 12:17–21.

GROW IN WISDOM.

Today you will face situations that demand wisdom. Do not panic. God promises to give wisdom to those who fear and seek Him with diligence. Nonetheless, do not wait until you are confronted with tough circumstances to ask for wisdom. Take time and seek God today. Embrace Him and follow Him wholeheartedly. Let wisdom be a part of your spiritual fabric every day. Grow in wisdom.

When King Solomon ascended to the throne of Israel, he was known for his God-given wisdom. First Kings 3:16–28 records a difficult case where Solomon exemplified the worth of wisdom. Two women, who shared a house, delivered baby boys within three days. One lay on her son in the night and the boy died. She secretly exchanged her dead son for the live one, leaving her son at the breast of the other woman. In the morning, each woman claimed the living child to be their rightful son.

The matter reached the king. King Solomon opted to divide the living son into two for each mother to have half of him. The real mother pleaded with the king to give the live child to woman who had killed her son. "The fear of the Lord is the beginning of knowledge: but fools despise wisdom and instruction. My son, hear the instruction of thy father, and forsake not the law of thy mother: For they shall be an ornament of grace unto thy head, and chains about thy neck" (Proverbs 1:7–9).

God teaches us wisdom using His Word and through those He has put on our path. Wise people are few. Those who take time to follow the disciplines of attaining wisdom are few, yet the world is in great need of wise people.

The fear of the Lord is the beginning of wisdom. This fear is not an emotional threat, but reverence and honor of God. It is in holding God in high regard that His deep love compels you to love Him back and keep His commandments. Those who have true reverence for God are wise. They see and judge better as they are led of God. Their judgment is sound. They are reliable. When you grow in wisdom, you possess a treasure more precious than silver and gold.

READ PROVERBS 15:32–33.

June 8

CARE FOR THE NEEDS OF OTHERS.

Building Christian character takes time. Like anything that displays its beauty or fruits after months of hard work, Christian character follows the same principles.

Look at a practical life example when a child is born. A child starts off helpless and fully dependent on his parents. All attention is given to him; he is cuddled, carried around, fed, and made to feel special. Life is about him. If this trend continues into teenage and early adulthood years, that family will have a burden on their hands. This is because, as we grow, we decrease in our need for dependance and take on responsibilities. This is true for our spiritual growth as well. A good sign of spiritual growth is the ability to do what it takes to grow and to take responsibility over other people's growth and welfare.

This is the principle behind the parable of the talents (Matthew 25). God gives us responsibility over ones, tens, hundreds, thousands, millions, etc., according to our abilities. "Let nothing be done through strife or vainglory; but in lowliness of mind let each esteem other better than themselves. Look not every man on his own things, but every man also on the things of others" (Philippians 2:3–4).

Bear one another's burdens. Look out for the needs of others and help. Do not be overly focused on yourself until you forget those to whom you are to minister. Be driven by the love and compassion of Christ to reach out. Ask God to make it clear about whom He would like you to help, and do it heartily as one doing it to God and not unto man.

Caring for the needs of others may call for sacrifice. It may cost you time, money, prestige, or even a sneer from friends, but walk in obedience to the prompting of God and do as He says. It will be gratifying. Reaching out to the needy may be the easiest way to open a door for evangelism. It tenderizes the heart, cultivates, and makes it fertile to receive God's Word.

READ GALATIANS 6:10 AND 1 JOHN 3:17.

ACCEPT OTHERS.

After the resurrection of the Lord Jesus Christ, the early church gathered, broke bread, and fellowshiped with one another. Those who watched from outside were touched and moved with the genuine bonds of love and care.

Today, there is a deep cry in the hearts of many Christians who attend church and take part in fellowship events but still feel left out or never fully belonging. Imagine the feeling of being rejected, unaccepted, and unloved by a brother or sister in Christ!

What does God teach about such issues in His Word?

> For if there come unto your assembly a man with a gold ring, in goodly apparel, and there come in also a poor man in vile raiment; And ye have respect to him that weareth the gay clothing, and say unto him, Sit thou here in a good place; and say to the poor, Stand thou there, or sit here under my footstool: Are ye not then partial in yourselves, and are become judges of evil thoughts? (James 2:2-4)

Allow others into your circle. Do not show partiality and favoritism. Let those who desire to reach to you have access. Let them feel loved, wanted, and welcome. There are many desperate and lonely people who crave your concern. The simple gesture of welcome and love can affect them in ways you may not comprehend. Take to heart God's admonition in 1 Peter 1:22: "Seeing ye have purified your souls in obeying the truth through the Spirit unto unfeigned love of the brethren, see that ye love one another with a pure heart fervently.

Christ does not treat you as an outcast. He has shed His love abroad for you. You are special. You are loved. You belong. You are accepted in the circle of the beloved of God. Let others in as you love and serve Christ.

READ JAMES 2:1–9.

BE A HARD WORKER.

Last summer, my family had an abundance of fruits and vegetables from our backyard. The pear, apple, and peach trees were loaded with so much fruit that the branches broke at their weight. We had more corn, tomatoes, cucumbers, greens, peppers, and cilantro than we could eat. It was a delight to see counters full of fresh fruits and vegetables every day. The one thing we did not wish to remember at that time was the endless hours, days, weeks, and months of work we poured in. And yet, we could not have enjoyed the yields had we not taken time to plant and cultivate our crops.

Hard work yields good fruits (most of the time). God also rewards hard work. He notes that the farmer who works hard should be the first to eat of his crops (2 Timothy 2:6). He admonishes His children to work hard.

> For even when we were with you, this we commanded you, that if any would not work, neither should he eat. For we hear that there are some which walk among you disorderly, working not at all, but are busybodies. Now them that are such we command and exhort by our Lord Jesus Christ, that with quietness they work, and eat their own bread. (2 Thessalonians 3:10–12)

God expects His children to be diligent at their work. He does not condone laziness. God commands those who do not work when they should, and can, not to eat. Work should not be a burden but something we do in honor of God. Working is healthy. It is godly to work. It sets a good example for others and testifies well of Christ.

Idleness is not of God. God says it wastes His time (preciously given to us) and becomes an opportunity for gossiping, as it turns us into busybodies living unhealthy lifestyles. Do not depend on others if you can work. Get out and work as you honor God.

READ PROVERBS 24:33–34.

WORK TODAY AND INVEST FOR TOMORROW.

Tough times can be appreciated for the great and lasting lessons they teach us. The Great Depression, like the age of COVID-19, teaches us to stretch our cents, be good stewards of what we have, and to always have savings for a rainy day.

What do you do when troubles of life kick you out of the only job and reliable source of income? How do you face the day when you can neither afford a place to stay or decent food?

God teaches us to prepare for the future. He wants us to look at the days ahead with calmness and confidence because of the preparations we put in place. Like the woman of Proverbs 31:25, we can laugh at the days to come because of the investments, the trades, and the savings for which we have worked.

Growing up, my father drilled into us the importance of having a savings account until it became a song. "Eat 5 keep 5, eat 5 keep 5." God's Word counsels us to have savings: "Cast thy bread upon the waters: for thou shalt find it after many days. Give a portion to seven, and also to eight; for thou knowest not what evil shall be upon the earth" (Ecclesiastes 11:1–2).

Work hard today and invest for tomorrow. There is no reason why you should not make wise decisions and save part of your day's toil for the days to come. God wants you to be prepared for tomorrow. When you cast your bread upon the waters today, you will have it tomorrow. If you don't save it today, you won't have any for later either.

"The rich ruleth over the poor, and the borrower is servant to the lender," says Proverbs 22:7. You do not have to become a slave by borrowing tomorrow when you could have saved today. Like a wise man who leaves an inheritance for his children by saving and a wise woman who takes care of the affairs of her house not fearing for the days to come because she is well prepared, you, too, can prepare for the days ahead.

READ PROVERBS 13:22 AND 31:10–31.

Weigh your words.

Has anyone ever hurt you by what they said? Better still, have you ever said things you wish never left your mouth? What is the impact of words in our lives and the lives of those who listen? Words can inspire, grow, change destinies, and guide you into a bright and fruitful future.

We closed school at the end of middle school and as we waited to join high school, I had a strange visitor who presented me with an interesting gift. "I would like you to use these pens as you start a new chapter in your schooling." She said as she handed me a pack of assorted pens and squeezed me to her side. This was my primary school teacher. "I see a bright future in you," she added.

In the days that followed, I could not help but ask myself, "What did she see in me that made her say and do that?" That was not the last time I have reflected on those words.

Words can heal and words can tear and spoil that for which we have labored. God instructs us to weigh our words before we speak. God admonishes us in Proverbs 10:19–20, saying, "In the multitude of words there wanteth not sin: but he that refraineth his lips is wise. The tongue of the just is as choice silver: the heart of the wicked is little worth. The lips of the righteous feed many: but fools die for want of wisdom."

It is better to keep quiet than to speak that which hurts, tears down, or destroys. "He that hath knowledge spareth his words: and a man of understanding is of an excellent spirit. Even a fool, when he holdeth his peace, is counted wise: and he that shutteth his lips is esteemed a man of understanding" (Proverbs 17:27–28).

As you walk with God, He prepares you and fills your life with soundness of spirit so you can be a help to others. Give godly counsel. Give correct advice to those in need and help build the people of God. Weigh your words and pray for knowledge and wisdom that you may give the right and timely word.

Today you will have opportunities to sow good seeds through your words. May God help you plant eternal seeds.

Read Proverbs 25:11.

SEEK COUNSEL.

Life has many challenges through which all of us must walk. However, the journey gets bearable and weighty loads manageable when you talk and share your burdens. It is not in vain God tells us there is a friend who sticks closer than a brother (Proverbs 18:24).

This also applies to advice. You may fall into error for lack of a true friend from whom to seek counsel. Nonetheless, plans are streamlined with good advice. Our visions get clearer and our decisions more decisive when we are well advised. "Without counsel purposes are disappointed: but in the multitude of counsellors they are established. A man hath joy by the answer of his mouth: and a word spoken in due season, how good is it!" (Proverbs 15:22–23).

None of us knows what to do at all times. Seek counsel when faced with decisions and circumstances beyond your comprehension and knowledge. There is growth in seeking counsel. Do not be afraid to talk to someone.

Your plans will not go wrong when you seek the advice of honest people.

- Talk to God about your situation. God works in our hearts both to will and to do according to His good pleasure, according to Philippians 2:13. As you seek Him, He will cause your heart to incline toward the right decision. He will open your eyes to necessary details and bring the right people your way.
- Talk to godly individuals whom you respect and whose lives are a good example. God equips His children to counsel others. Those who walk with God are wise and knowledgeable. They commune with God, and you can trust their word.
- Talk to trusted experts.

READ JOSHUA 9:1–16.

DEVELOP SERVITUDE.

It feels good to be important and to be exalted above others, but that is not what life is all about. See God's formula for living in Philippians 2:4–9:

> Look not every man on his own things, but every man also on the things of others. Let this mind be in you, which was also in Christ Jesus: Who, being in the form of God, thought it not robbery to be equal with God: But made himself of no reputation, and took upon him the form of a servant, and was made in the likeness of men: And being found in fashion as a man, he humbled himself, and became obedient unto death, even the death of the cross. Wherefore God also hath highly exalted him, and given him a name which is above every name.

It is not easy to be a servant. It calls for taking the last place, if there is a place at all. It means working behind curtains without seeking acclaim. It may also mean watching people climb ladders of success while steadily stepping on your shoulders. You may do what most people hate to do! You get your feet and hands sweaty and dirty.

There is a great reward for those who will be good servants. Christ exemplified this when He washed the feet of His disciples before His crucifixion. He took the lowest possible job a man could take and washed the dust and mud of their feet. It was only a matter of time and He would seat on the highest throne both in heaven and on earth.

God gives each one of us opportunities to serve others. Purpose to serve someone today with a Christlike heart regardless of your position in life. May God smile on your service, saying, "Well done, good and faithful servant . . ." (Matthew 25:21, 23).

READ MARK 10:43–44.

GROW IN LOVE.

Love is a language that is well understood in every part of the world. Imagine how many families exist on the globe. Most of these came because of interest in another person under the big umbrella of love.

Love is powerful. It communicates affection and acceptance. It says, "You belong and I appreciate you."

It is hard to hide love. Like light, it finds ways of showing up and affecting others. You will not confuse love for hate. Regardless of age and geographical boundaries, one true mark of friendship is love.

Genuine love demands action. It is hard to love deeply while keeping hands tight to yourself. Look at what God when He loved us beyond measure! He gave His one and only Son to die and redeem us back to the Father. God desires to see genuine love from His children. "Let nothing be done through strife or vainglory; but in lowliness of mind let each esteem other better than themselves" (Philippians 2:3).

Christ taught the multitudes in Luke 6, saying, "And as ye would that men should do to you, do ye also to them likewise" (v. 31). It is easy to show love while dealing with peers and expecting something similar in return. However, God says, even the heathen can show that kind of love.

Reach out to others out of genuine love. Stoop low and hold the hand of someone lower than yourself. You will affect and influence many lives as a result of your love than with feeling high and important. In fact, your love will bring out your importance as God honors your sincere motives and actions.

- "Love your enemies, do good to them which hate you, Bless them that curse you, and pray for them which despitefully use you" (Luke 6:27–28).
- You don't have to impress anybody. Grow in love.
- Put off slander, malice, and anger. Instead, grow in love.

READ LUKE 6:26–35.

EVALUATE YOUR SALVATION.

When we travel from one place to another, we make appropriate preparations. We ensure we have all travel documents, and each is valid and up to date. We pay for the journey, pack our bags, and wait for the right time. What about heaven? How do we prepare?

Are there people who think they are headed to heaven who have neither reservations nor travel documents? I believe there are many people who have never acknowledged Christ as Lord and Savior who are on an imaginary journey to heaven.

In Matthew 7:21–23, God makes an astounding revelation that makes us know there will be surprises in heaven. He says, "Many will say to me in that day, Lord, Lord, have we not prophesied in thy name? and in thy name have cast out devils? and in thy name done many wonderful works? And then will I profess unto them, I never knew you: depart from me, ye that work iniquity."

God does not want anyone to assume they are going to heaven without checking themselves out to be sure. "Wherefore, my beloved, as ye have always obeyed, not as in my presence only, but now much more in my absence, work out your own salvation with fear and trembling" (Philippians 2:12).

Work out your own salvation with fear and trembling. Let your salvation be real, producing the evidence of fruit, as you obey God and walk in deep reverence. Walk the talk. Let your lifestyle testify that you know Christ.

Do not frustrate the grace of God. Don't use God's grace as a license to sin. You have been forgiven and washed. Live as a child of the light. Sin crucifies the Savior again and subjects the gospel to scorn and ridicule.

When you live in sin, enjoy sin, and the sin does not bother you, you may need to evaluate your salvation. That may be evidence that you never had salvation in the first place. Those who are born again have a desire to please their Savior. They may fall in sin but as they grow in grace and knowledge of God they sin less.

READ 2 TIMOTHY 2:19.

SEEK GOD'S APPROVAL.

How do you measure the worth of what you do every day? Do you get a daily evaluation? If yes, who does it and what does it say? There are millions of people who quit their jobs on a daily basis because they are frustrated. Some leave because they feel unappreciated, while others never go back because of poor compensations and bad working environments, among other reasons.

Since we are hired by human bosses and we have human emotions, you can expect this trend to stay the same. The one thing that can change this is to seek approval from God. God guides us toward this principle in Colossians 3:23–24, saying, "And whatsoever ye do, do it heartily, as to the Lord, and not unto men; Knowing that of the Lord ye shall receive the reward of the inheritance: for ye serve the Lord Christ."

God knows how hard it is to please mortal man. It is no wonder He says, "Study to shew thyself approved unto God, a workman that needeth not to be ashamed, rightly dividing the word of truth" (2 Timothy 2:15).

Make it your life's pursuit to seek the approval of God rather than the approval of men. It will liberate you from the bondage of man and set you free to enjoy your walk with God. You will never measure up to the standards of many people. People are their own yard sticks, and they will move the bar every time you get closer.

When your quest is to show yourself a servant who is approved by God, you will not want to be measured by other people's yard sticks. You will surpass them by far. Like Enoch in Hebrews 11:5, enter God's Hall of fame for His servants with this description: "He had this testimony, that he pleased God."

To seek the approval of men and women in this world is to live a frustrated life. God appreciates your love and work for Him. He encourages those who work for Him. He is tender and loving and does not deal with us like a shrewd master who is not easy to please. Remember, you are a coworker with Christ in the vineyard of God. He deals with you with love and respect.

READ 1 THESSALONIANS 2:4–8.

SHOW EVIDENCE OF GROWTH.

It is easy to tell the difference between something that is growing and something that is stunted. We can tell when our children are growing by their changes in height and weight. We can tell when they no longer fit in their clothes or shoes. I have been in homes where children's growth was monitored by making check lines on walls.

How about our Christian life? What determines spiritual growth? Can we draw lines to evidence our growth from one year to another? How does God measure spiritual growth?

In 1 Corinthians 3:1–3, God refers to different things that denote spiritual immaturity. Among them are envy, strife, and divisions. He likens them to a baby who is dependent on milk for growth.

Our lives do not show spiritual growth until we begin to live what we teach and desire to see in others. It is easy to operate on the principle, "Do as I say," but that is not God's method for His children. Evidence of growth will show as we practice what we hear or teach.

> Thou therefore which teachest another, teachest thou not thyself? Thou that preachest a man should not steal, dost thou steal? Thou that sayest a man should not commit adultery, dost thou commit adultery? thou that abhorrest idols, dost thou commit sacrilege? Thou that makest thy boast of the law, through breaking the law dishonourest thou God? (Romans 2:21–23)

Evaluate your life to see if you are where you were last year at such a time spiritually. A good way to do it is to see if you are still struggling with the same issues with which you struggled last year, or if you have you made spiritual strides.

What is the evidence of spiritual growth in your life? Take spiritual steps. Select areas that require growth and work on them diligently. The evidence of spiritual growth reflects a godly heart full of desire to follow and please God. It is a sign of walking toward maturity. It leads to reliability.

READ JAMES 1:22–25.

WATCH YOUR CHOICES.

We evaluate the maturity of our children by the choices they make. The choice of a car for a twenty-year-old will be different from that of a thirty- or forty-year-old married man or woman. The same goes for clothes, house, and even work. This is because we learn from the poor choices we make as we grow.

God opens our eyes to the importance of choices in Genesis 13:10–11:

> And Lot lifted up his eyes, and beheld all the plain of Jordan, that it was well watered everywhere, before the LORD destroyed Sodom and Gomorrah, even as the garden of the LORD, like the land of Egypt, as thou comest unto Zoar. Then Lot chose him all the plain of Jordan; and Lot journeyed east: and they separated themselves the one from the other.

Lot was given a chance to choose a place where he would settle with his family. His choice proved very costly down the road as he pitched his tent toward Sodom, which was later destroyed. The Bible does not reveal a time when Lot took time to inquire of God or to seek counsel regarding where to settle.

God made man will a free will to make choices. Free though it is, God expects us to honor Him with our choices. Choices which honor God prove to be the best and most fruitful in life. The choices you make today will influence your decisions, your lifestyle, and the quality of life you will live in future. Involve God in your choices. Seek His counsel. Honor Him and He will in turn honor you.

Look at His open invitation for help as recorded in Psalm 32:8–9: "I will instruct thee and teach thee in the way which thou shalt go: I will guide thee with mine eye. Be ye not as the horse, or as the mule, which have no understanding: whose mouth must be held in with bit and bridle, lest they come near unto thee."

Remember, choices have consequences. We can make choices, but we cannot choose the consequences.

READ 1 KINGS 18:21 AND ISAIAH 30:21.

RESIST TEMPTATION.

Every Christian faces temptation. As matter of fact, Christ faced temptation too. Satan is careful when and how to tempt. He makes the most of every opportunity and schemes in clever but cunning ways. For example, when Christ was hungry after forty days of prayer and fasting in the wilderness, Satan knew that Jesus—who was fully man—was weak, hungry, and lonely. Look at the prime choice of his temptations in Matthew 4:1–10:

> If thou be the Son of God, command that these stones be made bread. . . . If thou be the Son of God, cast thyself down: for it is written, He shall give his angels charge concerning thee: and in their hands they shall bear thee up, lest at any time thou dash thy foot against a stone. . . . All these things will I give thee, if thou wilt fall down and worship me." (vv. 3, 6, 9)

Christ showed us His power over temptation as He unfolded its mystery to Peter:

> And the Lord said, Simon, Simon, behold, Satan hath desired to have you, that he may sift you as wheat: But I have prayed for thee, that thy faith fail not: and when thou art converted, strengthen thy brethren (Luke 22:31–32).

Satan frequently uses the same pattern he used on Eve in the garden of Eve when tempting us today. He begins by throwing an evil thought in our minds—this is his greatest battlefield. This is the first step toward either falling or resisting the temptation. The battle can end right there by resisting and counteracting the thought with the truth of God's Word.

When we entertain the evil thought, it leads into desire. This is when lusts develop and with time you begin to crave what is sinful. When desire is ripe, it leads to a dangerous road when the right opportunity unfolds.

You will be faced with diverse temptations regardless of how spiritual you may be. Resist temptation. Resist thoughts that are evil. Remember, Christ is praying for you. He desires to see you stand.

READ 1 CORINTHIANS 10:13.

FEED THE INNER MAN.

When a child does not eat good nutritive foods in their rightful amounts, we see him lose weight and remain mere skin and bones. We call this malnutrition. Such a child is weak and unable to fight off most common ailments, including common colds.

Likewise, spiritual malnutrition takes place when we do not feed our spirits adequately on foods that anchor the heart firmly in God. Like a malnourished child, we cannot weather the storms that life throws at us without crumbling and hurting badly from their weight.

Spiritual malnutrition is a cause of spiritual defeat, apathy, and fruitlessness. A well-fed inner man is a strong, valiant, courageous, and decisive, who can walk with God to witness many victories in his life.

God cautions us to walk close to Him, saying,

> This I say then, Walk in the Spirit, and ye shall not fulfil the lust of the flesh. For the flesh lusteth against the Spirit, and the Spirit against the flesh: and these are contrary the one to the other: so that ye cannot do the things that ye would. But if ye be led of the Spirit, ye are not under the law. Now the works of the flesh are manifest, which are these; Adultery, fornication, uncleanness, lasciviousness, Idolatry, witchcraft, hatred, variance, emulations, wrath, strife, seditions, heresies, Envyings, murders, drunkenness, revellings, and such like: of the which I tell you before, as I have also told you in time past, that they which do such things shall not inherit the kingdom of God. (Galatians 5:16–21)

The flesh is always at war with your spirit. When you feed your heart with solid spiritual food, the flesh is weakened and your spirit wins as you thrive in your spiritual walk. If you starve your spirit, you suffer spiritual weakness and increase this war.

Feed the inner man.

READ ROMANS 7:21–25.

HAVE A TEACHABLE SPIRIT.

Spiritual growth is embedded in the seedbeds of our ability to learn. As a common joke goes, all we know we learned from someone, read from someone, or heard from someone. It is hard to grow when you cannot learn. It is not easy to learn when you cannot listen to the teacher either.

God cautions us in Psalms 32:9 not to be like a horse or a mule, which have no understanding. Their mouths must be controlled with a bit and bridle before they can obey and follow their master.

Such control can leave those animals with busted and bleeding mouths that hinder the enjoyment of daily meals and activities. Since we are not controlled with such instruments, God cautions us not to be wise in our own eyes but to listen and follow at will. "Be not wise in thine own eyes: fear the Lord, and depart from evil. It shall be health to thy navel, and marrow to thy bones" (Proverbs 3:7–8).

You will never be too old to learn. Make every day a learning day. Do not be wise in your own eyes; it cultivates a haughty spirit devoid of learning. Learn from the Lord. Depart from evil as you follow God's teaching and see it bring health, nourishment, and fulfillment in your life.

You learn from those with whom you associate whether you know it or not. "He that walketh with wise men shall be wise: but a companion of fools shall be destroyed. Evil pursueth sinners: but to the righteous good shall be repayed" (Proverbs 13:20–21).

God is your Shepherd. He will lead you beside quiet waters as He instructs and teaches you in the way you should go. He knows what you need at this point in your life. He knows whom to use to teach you. Humble yourself before God and be taught of Him.

READ 1 PETER 5:5.

June 23

GROW THROUGH REBUKE.

Rebukes are hard and painful to take. Matthew 16:22–23 records a funny incidence where the apostle Peter pulled Christ, the Savior, to the side and began to rebuke Him. Christ did not wait to see the end of all that! He turned and rebuked Peter, instead saying, "Get thee behind me, Satan: thou art an offence unto me: for thou savourest not the things that be of God, but those that be of men." I have always wondered how the apostle Peter reacted at that time.

The Bible has a lot to say about rebukes. Knowing how hard rebukes can be, God cautions us to be careful about who and how we rebuke. Proverbs 9:7–9 says, "He that reproveth a scorner getteth to himself shame: and he that rebuketh a wicked man getteth himself a blot. Reprove not a scorner, lest he hate thee: rebuke a wise man, and he will love thee. Give instruction to a wise man, and he will be yet wiser: teach a just man, and he will increase in learning."

Rebukes yield different results depending on how they were done and received. Spiritual growth takes place through learning from our rebukes.

You are never too spiritual to receive a rebuke. If Christ could admonish and rebuke the disciples through whom the gospel was given and spread in the world, we should not expect to be exceptions.

Rebukes and corrections are part of growing in our spiritual journey. One key mark of spiritual maturity is the ability to take rebukes graciously and act on them accordingly.

Step back and evaluate your rebukes. Were they honest and genuine? Is there need for rebuke in your life? Is God pointing to what can be self-destructive in your life? Grow through your rebukes.

READ PROVERBS 29:1.

RESPECT AUTHORITY.

The mention of the word respect in our modern-day society carries with it different associated meanings and reactions. It is not uncommon to hear statements like, "Respect! Why should I respect them when they do not have my best interests at heart? Who said I have to respect them? I will only respect those who respect me! Sorry, they do not deserve my respect."

How does God look at this term? What is His stand on respect? Does He have any commands for His children on respect?

God asks us to respect authority. He says, "Let every soul be subject unto the higher powers. For there is no power but of God: the powers that be are ordained of God" (Romans 13:1).

It is God Who sets up governments. Your vote is important, but the final answer comes from God. God's ways are higher than our ways, just as His thoughts are higher than our thoughts. He knows whom to put in power. Respect those in authority.

> Whosoever therefore resisteth the power, resisteth the ordinance of God: and they that resist shall receive to themselves damnation. For rulers are not a terror to good works, but to the evil. Wilt thou then not be afraid of the power? do that which is good, and thou shalt have praise of the same: For he is the minister of God to thee for good. But if thou do that which is evil, be afraid; for he beareth not the sword in vain: for he is the minister of God, a revenger to execute wrath upon him that doeth evil. (Romans 13:2–4)

It takes a humble spirit to respect the people God has placed in leadership and to honor and pray for them as He commands. It honors God to honor and respect authority. Remember, it is God Who sets and establishes leadership.

READ DANIEL 2:21.

TELL THE TRUTH.

Have you ever told a lie because you were afraid to tell the truth? Imagine what happens when the truth comes out anyway, because eventually it does. You feel embarrassed and wish you had braced up and told the truth.

As Christ proclaimed the gospel of the kingdom of God to the Jews, He told them, "If ye continue in my word, then are ye my disciples indeed; And ye shall know the truth, and the truth shall make you free" (John 8:31–32). The gospel, which is true, frees man from the inner chains of sin. He notes that truth sets us free. In fact, God notes that truthfulness leads to spiritual growth:

> That we henceforth be no more children, tossed to and fro, and carried about with every wind of doctrine, by the sleight of men, and cunning craftiness, whereby they lie in wait to deceive; But speaking the truth in love, may grow up into him in all things, which is the head, even Christ. (Ephesians 4:14–15)

Two lies do not make up for the truth. Tell the truth. Be honest in the sight of God even when you have made a mistake. Repent of your shortcoming and ask God to help your face or tell the truth. There is no need to be cunning. God Who sees the heart can take wheels off your chariot and cause the truth to come out. When you honor Him He promises to be merciful and to honor you in turn.

It is better to be poor and honest than to have riches and be dishonest. A righteous and good man is known by his truthfulness. The truth will set you free (John 8:32). It will leave you with a clean conscience and peace at night.

Today, you may be confronted with situations that demand truth. Purpose to tell the truth and set your heart free to grow and thrive with God. God will honor you as you choose His way of truth and honesty.

READ ZECHARIAH 8:16.

CONTROL YOUR TONGUE.

A quick and easy way to know a person is to listen to him. The tongue has a way of articulating feelings, emotions, and desires. This is revealed through the choice of our words, the intonation and volume of our voices. The words that roll off our tongues give insight to our character too.

A man who has control of his tongue is wise. The tongue is a little world of iniquity. It is boastful unless brought under subjection. It defiles the whole body and can cause great destruction in your life and that of others. It is not easy to retrieve that which has left your mouth. Controlling the tongue is not easy. It is something on which we must work every day.

The Bible correctly notes that "The heart is deceitful above all things, and desperately wicked: who can know it? I the Lord search the heart, I try the reins, even to give every man according to his ways, and according to the fruit of his doings" (Jeremiah 17:9–10).

Our tongues have power. The words we speak leave lasting impacts on those who hear them. A child who hears hurtful and demeaning words be it from parents or peers ponders on their truth especially when faced with tough situations in life. They may easily succumb to failure and defeat unlike one who hears encouraging words that stir action and courage.

The tongue is controlled by the heart. "A good man out of the good treasure of his heart bringeth forth that which is good; and an evil man out of the evil treasure of his heart bringeth forth that which is evil: for of the abundance of the heart his mouth speaketh" (Luke 6:45). Control your tongue by filling your heart with godly treasure.

READ JAMES 3:3–12.

June 27

DIE TO SELF.

David, a young boy, killed the giant Goliath at a time in the history of Israel when God's people faced scorn and defeat. Israel was weary from endless wars with the Philistines. King Saul promised to reward anyone who would take away the contempt from the land. David did it but that did not go well with the king.

After a historic slaughter of the Philistines that day, the women went out to meet the men with dance and song, saying, "Saul hath slain his thousands, and David his ten thousands" (1 Samuel 18:7). The Bible notes that Saul was very angry at the refrain in the song. He said, "They have ascribed unto David ten thousands, and to me they have ascribed but thousands: and what can he have more but the kingdom? And Saul eyed David from that day and forward" (v. 8).

What should have been a joyful celebration and acknowledgment of true heroism turned into a lifelong battle between Saul and David.

We crave popularity at some point in life. We desire to be highly esteemed and set in a bracket of our own. John the Baptist had the noble job of being the forerunner of Christ, but he did not struggle with gaining popularity over Christ. John the Baptist understood what it means to give people opportunities as you retreat from the spotlight.

He said, "He must increase, but I must decrease. He that cometh from above is above all: he that is of the earth is earthly, and speaketh of the earth: he that cometh from heaven is above all" (John 3:30–31).

Be careful. Craving popularity will desensitize your heart to the needs of your spirit. If you continue feeding it, your flesh will have an edge over your spirit and before long, you will be following Christ from a far off. You will succumb to temptation easily. In fact, popularity must die before you can follow and do God's will. Christ will not fight for preeminence in your life. You must surrender at your own will. Learn to die to self and let Christ be Lord. He must increase, but you must decrease.

READ GALATIANS 2:20.

BELIEVE GOD AND GROW.

Lazarus, the friend of Jesus, died and was buried four days. Martha and Mary wept bitterly at the death of their only brother. This was a difficult time as they could not understand why Christ did not go to see and heal Lazarus when they called for Him. When the Savior finally appeared, their faith was low and their grief immense. Little did they know, it was an exercise to increase their faith and grow their trust in the Savior.

Christ challenged Martha, saying, "Said I not unto thee, that, if thou wouldest believe, thou shouldest see the glory of God?" (John 11:40). This is a good matrix for our faith. To believe God is to grow. Faith in God deepens our roots of dependance and cause us to trust more. Those who believe God, despite their age see the power of God and witness spiritual growth in their lives.

You are special before God. You are here for God's special purpose. God uses people like you to do His work. God has equipped you with what you need to serve Him. Let no man despise you. Believe God and grow to be an example to other believers in word, in conversation, in love, in faith, and in clean thoughts.

This will be attained as you give attention to reading, practicing, and teaching God's Word. Continue in sound doctrine and stir up the gifts of God in you. No one will despise your age as you get hold of God and pursue righteousness out of a sincere heart. Believe God and grow.

Regardless of your age and status, you too can follow God wholeheartedly as you learn from Paul's advice to Timothy:

> Let no man despise thy youth; but be thou an example of the believers, in word, in conversation, in charity, in spirit, in faith, in purity. Till I come, give attendance to reading, to exhortation, to doctrine. Neglect not the gift that is in thee, which was given thee by prophecy, with the laying on of the hands of the presbytery. (1 Timothy 4:12–14)

READ HEBREWS 6:1.

PRACTICE SELF-CONTROL.

Solomon is the wisest king who has ever lived on earth (1 Kings 3:12). God chose and equipped him to lead Israel. However, the man who wrote and taught the proverbs of wisdom to an entire land walked away from God because of a lack of self-control.

First Kings 11:1–9 records that Solomon had seven hundred wives and three hundred concubines. In his old age, those wives turned his heart from God to worship idols. Solomon fell to the very things from which God warned him to stay away.

Life calls for self-control. This is the power to say no to yourself even when you can do or get it. It is strength under control.

All of us are subjected to similar experiences most of our lives. Those who succeed and proceed to be fruitful in their Christian lives practice self-control. We are confronted with the same temptations day in and day out. Those who practice self-control win more than they lose.

Practice what you have learned from God and work on your self-control. Self-control says, "I can do as I please, but I choose to do what God says. I am in a position to get it or do it, but I will listen to God."

Self-control is not easy, but it is not impossible. God Who asks it of His children helps us in our moments of need and temptations. He even gives us a good formula to help us stand strong in this fight. Think on things that are honest, just, pure, lovely, true, good, and right. Bring God praise as you practice what you have learned and received. Practice self-control.

> Finally, brethren, whatsoever things are true, whatsoever things are honest, whatsoever things are just, whatsoever things are pure, whatsoever things are lovely, whatsoever things are of good report; if there be any virtue, and if there be any praise, think on these things. Those things, which ye have both learned, and received, and heard, and seen in me, do: and the God of peace shall be with you. (Philippians 4:8–9)

READ 1 CORINTHIANS 9:24–27.

PUT OFF STUBBORNNESS AND REBELLION.

The prophet Samuel anointed Saul to be king over Israel. God had good intentions for the king and His people, Israel. When Saul prepared for his battle with Amalekites, God gave him clear instructions to utterly destroy everything in the land without sparing any man, woman, child, ox, sheep, camels, and donkeys (1 Samuel 15:3).

Saul did not execute the orders. He spared the king of the Amalekites, and spared the best of the sheep, cattle, fat calves and lambs (1 Samuel 15:9). God was displeased. He reminded the new king that to obey was better than sacrifice, and to hearken than the fat of rams. For rebellion is as the sin of witchcraft, and stubbornness is as iniquity and idolatry (vv. 22–23). Saul's stubbornness and rebellion cost him the kingdom. God rejected him.

A stubborn spirit defies everything and says, "I will do as I please. Who are you to tell me what to do? Why should I listen to you? Who are you and what have got to do with you?"

God warns that "whosoever shall exalt himself shall be abased; and he that shall humble himself shall be exalted" (Matthew 23:12).

God is not willing that any of His children miss the path designed for them. He is ready to instruct and guide as He walks with you. Listen and live. Humble yourself under His mighty hand and He will lift you up in due season. Look at His promise: "I will instruct thee and teach thee in the way which thou shalt go: I will guide thee with mine eye. Be ye not as the horse, or as the mule, which have no understanding: whose mouth must be held in with bit and bridle, lest they come near unto thee" (Psalm 32:8–9).

God is more interested in your listening and obeying than anything else you may be compelled to offer. To obey is better than sacrifice, and to listen than the fat of rams. God sees rebellion like the sin of witchcraft, and arrogance as wickedness and idolatry. Put off stubbornness and rebellion. It is time to grow.

READ JAMES 4:6.

July

FINDING SPIRITUAL STRENGTH IN THE PROMISES OF GOD

God has many promises to help you go through life each day. Find strength this month as you embrace what God has for you in His Word.

"Fear not."

The best way to defeat an enemy is to inflict him with fear. Fear says, "I can't. I am too small, too weak, too insignificant to make a difference." Fear is a common strategy the devil will use to make you think that God has forgotten about you. However, over 365 times, God tells us in His Word, "Fear not." He means it. He knows how easy it is for your heart to fear.

Listen to Him and follow Him: "Fear thou not; for I am with thee: be not dismayed; for I am thy God: I will strengthen thee; yea, I will help thee; yea, I will uphold thee with the right hand of my righteousness" (Isaiah 41:10).

God knows what your day looks like. He knows what tomorrow holds. Remember, He sees the beginning from the end. He has already gone ahead of you. You do not need to fear. God knows what you can take. He also knows for what you are capable. It is He who formed you and gave you your frame. He will not allow anything to come your way that you cannot handle.

Nothing will come your way that God has not allowed. For what He allows, He carefully weighs it and makes sure it is what you can handle. Take courage. You were designed with this day in mind. Walk in the strength of God and do not fear. Remember His promise: "I am with thee . . . I will help thee . . . I will uphold thee with my right hand."

Read Isaiah 43:1–2.

July 2

"I WILL NEVER LEAVE YOU."

Life has many rough waters. Life has many treacherous bridges to cross and dark valleys in which you must walk. It is easy to get overwhelmed. It is easy to break at the weight of your load. However, do not lose focus of God's position in your life. He is right here with you.

Find strength in His personal message to you today: "When thou passest through the waters, I will be with thee; and through the rivers, they shall not overflow thee: when thou walkest through the fire, thou shalt not be burned; neither shall the flame kindle upon thee" (Isaiah 43:2).

God will keep His promise. He will never leave nor forsake you. He will walk by you today. You will not go through this day alone at any point. As you walk through rivers of difficulty, He will be with you. The river will not overflow to drown you. He will walk with you through fires of oppression. You will come out unharmed.

"Be strong and of a good courage, fear not, nor be afraid of them: for the LORD thy God, he it is that doth go with thee; he will not fail thee, nor forsake thee" (Deuteronomy 31:6). You can count on God to walk by your side today. He is not a man who will forsake you at your greatest hour of need. Call on Him and let Him assure you of His abiding presence today.

READ DEUTERONOMY 31:8.

"ASK AND IT SHALL BE GIVEN."

Imagine the honor of presenting a deep, pressing need to someone who can help you. What would you do if the president invited you to his house and gave you a chance to make one request! For what would you ask? Wonderful as that may be, you have a greater and better opportunity.

Today you have a great personal invitation from the King of kings. He is not kidding with you. He is real. He means it. Take Him at His Word and respond to Him.

> Or what man is there of you, whom if his son ask bread, will he give him a stone? Or if he ask a fish, will he give him a serpent? If ye then, being evil, know how to give good gifts unto your children, how much more shall your Father which is in heaven give good things to them that ask him? (Matthew 7:9–11)

One of the greatest privileges you have as a child of God is the access to God through prayer. Many people would love to be in the presence of important and influential people, but you have an open invitation to the King of kings. Let your request be made known to God. Ask and it shall be given.

God delights in your talking with Him. He has good things for you. If your parent cannot give you a stone when you ask for bread how much more can you expect from God? "Hitherto have ye asked nothing in my name: ask, and ye shall receive, that your joy may be full" (John 16:24).

READ 1 JOHN 5:14–15.

"Seek and you will find."

Is there a deep hunger within your soul you do understand? Is your heart searching and looking for something of meaning to satisfy your spirit? Does your heart long to hear from God? Are you desirous of answers to the paradoxes surrounding you today?

God is ready for you. God is waiting for you to incline your whole heart in honest search and call on His name. "Then shall ye call upon me, and ye shall go and pray unto me, and I will hearken unto you. And ye shall seek me, and find me, when ye shall search for me with all your heart. And I will be found of you, saith the Lord: and I will turn away your captivity" (Jeremiah 29:12–14).

Seek the Lord while He may be found. Call upon Him while He is near. Seek God while He woos your heart and extends His scepter of grace and love. It means He is eagerly waiting for you. Walk through this open door and find peace and rest for your soul.

God expects His children to seek Him. He unfolds Himself to those who seek Him. He reveals His secrets those who diligently seek Him. "The Lord is good unto them that wait for him, to the soul that seeketh him. It is good that a man should both hope and quietly wait for the salvation of the Lord" (Lamentations 3:25–26).

Seek and you will find.

Read Isaiah 55:6–7.

"KNOCK AND THE DOOR SHALL BE OPENED."

Have you knocked on some doors with hopes of finding help only for them to close before your eyes? Have you looked to a friend with hopes of finding help only for your heart to be crushed? God is not so. He is who He says He is, and He does as He promises. Try Him today. "Ask, and it shall be given you; seek, and ye shall find; knock, and it shall be opened unto you: For every one that asketh receiveth; and he that seeketh findeth; and to him that knocketh it shall be opened" (Matthew 7:7–8).

You have an open invitation to knock on God's door today. He is waiting for you. Knock and the door will be opened unto you. You need God. You need His help. He knows it and that is why He is waiting on you.

Knocking takes an act of the will. You must purpose to go and knock as you ponder what exactly you will say when the door is opened. It is a privilege to be invited. It is an opportunity to get into God's arms of grace and love. Knock and enter His favor. He has abundant knowledge, wisdom, and understanding awaiting you. It is only sin that will separate you from God. Sin causes God to hide His face and not hear when you knock. Knock!

READ PSALM 66:18.

"Ye have not because ye ask not."

It is easy to look at some people and believe they have more access to God than you do. It is also easy to believe that God hears certain individuals more than you. Not only do such notions lead to frustration, but they also breed a discontented spirit that easily departs from God. They can lead to envy, covetousness, anger, and bitterness. Interestingly, God reminds us that many bad things can result from our inability and our unwillingness to ask Him for our needs.

> From whence come wars and fightings among you? come they not hence, even of your lusts that war in your members? Ye lust, and have not: ye kill, and desire to have, and cannot obtain: ye fight and war, yet ye have not, because ye ask not. Ye ask, and receive not, because ye ask amiss, that ye may consume it upon your lusts. (James 4:1–3)

God expects His children to ask for what they need. It is true He already knows your needs, but it is also true that He can grant those needs without your asking, and many times He does. However, asking is part of His divine plan for you.

God waits to for you to ask before He will meet some of your needs. Can you imagine, God looking at you and telling you, "You do not have this because you did not ask me for it"? You have not because you ask not.

There are some wars and turmoil in your life that have resulted from your unmet needs. You have committed some sins that could have been avoided simply by asking God to meet your needs. God has what you are looking for. Ask. Don't miss God's open invitation today.

Read John 16:24.

God gives wisdom.

Do you know what tomorrow holds for you? Can you predict how this day will end? How will you navigate through the challenges of each day this week? You know, God does not want you to struggle through life alone. God wants to show you what to do, when to do it and how you should proceed each day of your life. Look at what God has for you:

> If any of you lack wisdom, let him ask of God, that giveth to all men liberally, and upbraideth not; and it shall be given him. But let him ask in faith, nothing wavering. For he that wavereth is like a wave of the sea driven with the wind and tossed. For let not that man think that he shall receive any thing of the Lord. A double minded man is unstable in all his ways. (James 1:5–8)

Life is complicated and full of mystery and ups and downs. You cannot make it without wisdom. God gives wisdom. From His mouth comes knowledge and understanding. God does not want you to go through life like one groping in darkness. Ask Him for wisdom.

God is interested in the decisions you make and the actions you take. He wants you to do it right. Develop a close relationship with Him as you seek and depend on His help. He gives wisdom not just to those who lack but to those who ask. Ask.

Read Proverbs 2:6–7.

"My peace I give unto you."

God has the power to calm the storms that face you today. Storms of life cause turbulence and turmoil to the heart. They disrupt life in every respect. However, look at what God desires for you amid your storm: "Let not your heart be troubled: ye believe in God, believe also in me. . . . Peace I leave with you, my peace I give unto you: not as the world giveth, give I unto you. Let not your heart be troubled, neither let it be afraid" (John 14:1, 27).

Troubled times are many. Troubled hearts even more so. God cares. God cares about what faces you today. He sees your troubled heart. He cares about the tears that fall deep within. He is here to stand with you and to help you today. Let not your heart be troubled. Believe in God and count on His presence today.

God does not promise the absence of trouble, but He promises to be with you. He will never leave nor forsake you. He will not let you go through rough times alone. Hold onto His Word and walk with courage. Let Him calm your heart as He soothes you with His Word and tender love. It is He who made the storms. He will calm the winds in your life.

Read Philippians 4:6–7.

GOD WILL MEET YOUR NEEDS.

All creation waits and looks to God for the supply of every need. God cares that your needs are met. If God were to close His loving and mighty hand of supply, the entire world would come crumbling down in unbelievable ways. God meets needs in a timely manner. Look at His promise: "These wait all upon thee; that thou mayest give them their meat in due season. That thou givest them they gather: thou openest thine hand, they are filled with good" (Psalm 104:27–28).

God will meet your needs. God has never been negligent. You can trust His promise from Luke 12:27–31:

> Consider the lilies how they grow: they toil not, they spin not; and yet I say unto you, that Solomon in all his glory was not arrayed like one of these. If then God so clothe the grass, which is today in the field, and tomorrow is cast into the oven; how much more will he clothe you, O ye of little faith? And seek not ye what ye shall eat, or what ye shall drink, neither be ye of doubtful mind. For all these things do the nations of the world seek after: and your Father knoweth that ye have need of these things. But rather seek ye the kingdom of God; and all these things shall be added unto you.

READ PHILIPPIANS 4:19.

GOD WILL GUIDE YOU.

Life has uncertainty. The good news is that God is never overtaken by the tough situations that face any of His children. God never leaves His children alone in those dark hours. In fact, He stands with us; He strengthens and instructs us accordingly. You, like David, can rejoice and rest in the hope of God. "I will bless the Lord, who hath given me counsel: my reins also instruct me in the night seasons. I have set the Lord always before me: because he is at my right hand, I shall not be moved. Therefore my heart is glad, and my glory rejoiceth: my flesh also shall rest in hope" (Psalm 16:7–9).

Every day is new terrain that none of us have walked before. God, who is all-knowing, promises to guide us. He counsels and instructs us in the way we should go. When we take time to inquire and listen, we can walk with courage trusting His guidance.

Being guided calls for your active participation. Be keen to hear Him. Be ready to follow. Look at God's counsel for you: "I will instruct thee and teach thee in the way which thou shalt go: I will guide thee with mine eye. Be ye not as the horse, or as the mule, which have no understanding: whose mouth must be held in with bit and bridle, lest they come near unto thee" (Psalm 32:8–9).

READ ISAIAH 48:17–18.

GOD GIVES ETERNAL LIFE.

Heaven is real. It is true there is eternal life for all who know and follow God. It is true that there is eternal rest from turmoil, sorry, pain, and sin. You, too, can have eternal life just as God has promised in His Word. See it for yourself:

> And as Moses lifted up the serpent in the wilderness, even so must the Son of man be lifted up: That whosoever believeth in him should not perish, but have eternal life. For God so loved the world, that he gave his only begotten Son, that whosoever believeth in him should not perish, but have everlasting life. (John 3:14–16)

God gives eternal life to all who believe on the Lord Jesus Christ, who repent of their sins to be cleansed by His shed blood on the cross. God does not cast those who come to Him away.

God watches over His children and preserves them until they inherit heaven as promised. God does not lose any who are His, those who are called by His name. Those who are truly born again of the Spirit of God cannot lose salvation. Those who are born again will never perish. They have "eternal life, which God, that cannot lie, promised before the world began" (Titus 1:2). You are secure in God. Walk in His ways and trust Him.

READ JOHN 10:27–29.

Nothing will separate you from God.

You are secure in Christ. Nothing can separate you from God. When you surrender to God, your life is hid in Christ. Christ who covers you is in the Father. Not even the devil will molest you unless they go through the Son and get permission from the Father. "Who shall separate us from the love of Christ? shall tribulation, or distress, or persecution, or famine, or nakedness, or peril, or sword?" (Romans 8:35).

God does not leave you to do the best you can as you walk to heaven. He has adequate provisions for your journey and He will take care of all that comes your way. Embrace His promise: "For I am persuaded, that neither death, nor life, nor angels, nor principalities, nor powers, nor things present, nor things to come, Nor height, nor depth, nor any other creature, shall be able to separate us from the love of God, which is in Christ Jesus our Lord" (Romans 8:38–39).

You are more than a conqueror through Christ who has loved and redeemed you.

READ PSALM 139:1–3.

GOD IS YOUR REFUGE.

Are you faced with troubles and turmoil today? Are you afraid? Is your future uncertain? You have One Who cares. He is your refuge. He will help you today. Look at His faithful promise to you: "The Lord is my rock, and my fortress, and my deliverer; my God, my strength, in whom I will trust; my buckler, and the horn of my salvation, and my high tower" (Psalm 18:2).

God is your refuge. He is your high and mighty tower, your rock, a sure fortress in whom to hide. He is your sure help in times of trouble. This is part of His goodness which He has laid up for them that fear Him. He hides His children in His pavilion and saves them from the pride and strife of men's tongues. This is God's kindness to you.

There may be cause for you to fear today, but there is a reason for you to face this day and the days to come with courage. Draw strength and courage from God's promise. He is your refuge and strength, a very present help in times of trouble. Fear not even when the waters seem to rage high. God is in your midst, and He will help you right on time.

READ PSALM 46:1–5.

GOD DOES NOT FORGET THE NEEDY.

Have you prayed but it looks like God has remained silent? Have you waited on God until you feel like He has forgotten about you? Are you desperate to hear from the God of heaven? Do you feel overwhelmed with your needs?

God is not silent. God is not deaf. He has not trodden over your prayers and moved on to more important business. You are His business. Look at His promise to you today: "The wicked shall be turned into hell, and all the nations that forget God. For the needy shall not always be forgotten: the expectation of the poor shall not perish forever" (Psalm 9:17–18).

You are God's responsibility. Do your part and trust God to be faithful to you. God has your best interests at heart. He is not blind to your needs, neither will He turn a deaf ear to your plea.

This is God's Word to you today: "Are not five sparrows sold for two farthings, and not one of them is forgotten before God? But even the very hairs of your head are all numbered. Fear not therefore: ye are of more value than many sparrows" (Luke 12:6–7).

God has not forgotten about you. Stand still and see the salvation of God. He is faithful. He will come through for you in ways you least expect. Remember, God is able to do exceedingly abundantly above all we can ask or think according to His power that works in us (Ephesians 3:20).

READ ISAIAH 41:13.

GOD WILL PRESERVE YOU.

Are you perplexed with the occurrences you see in the world? Do you wonder what tomorrow holds and what to expect from the future? God is not wringing His hands over your life. Nothing occurs to God. Nothing takes Him by surprise. He has never been caught off guard. God is watching over you. Find strength and hope in His promise for you today:

> For the oppression of the poor, for the sighing of the needy, now will I arise, saith the Lord; I will set him in safety from him that puffeth at him. The words of the Lord are pure words: as silver tried in a furnace of earth, purified seven times. Thou shalt keep them, O Lord, thou shalt preserve them from this generation forever. (Psalm 12:5–7)

God will preserve you in this generation. You are not alone. Despite the oppression and difficulty that may prevail, God will not be overtaken with evil. God will come to your rescue. He will not allow anything to come your way that is too hard to handle. He will preserve and protect you through every trial and bring you out just as He has planned.

You are well equipped for today. You are the right person living in the right place and at the right time in the right generation just as it was planned by God. Take courage. God is with you. He is watching over His Word to perform it. God will preserve you.

READ PSALM 71:3.

GOD FAVORS YOU.

When God delivered the children of Israel from their land of bondage, He led those millions of people with His outstretched hand and by the power of His might. He defeated their enemies and led them safely to the Promised Land. God gave them lands, cities, houses, grooves and many other things for which they did not labor. He was their portion in life. God's favor on His children did not stop with that generation.

Today, God treats you will favor. Look at where you are today because of the favor of God: "The Lord is the portion of mine inheritance and of my cup: thou maintainest my lot. The lines are fallen unto me in pleasant places; yea, I have a goodly heritage" (Psalm 16:5–6).

You are favored by God. God is sovereign and has the power to do whatever He desires for you. He can see to it that you have the best brooks and lands. He has power to give you the best position. No one can stand in His way. He can outsmart the best schemes in the world and make His way stand for you. He makes the boundary lines to fall in pleasant places for His children.

So, what is the secret of gaining God's favor? "By mercy and truth iniquity is purged: and by the fear of the Lord men depart from evil. When a man's ways please the Lord, he maketh even his enemies to be at peace with him" (Proverbs 16:6–7). Make God your portion. God is dependable. Love Him and walk tall as He showers you with His blessings and favor.

READ PSALM 37:1–4.

GOD HAS FULLNESS OF JOY AND PLEASURES.

Christians are the most blessed people on earth. Sin, and only sin, hinders God's children from experiencing the fullness of joy in God and enjoying life in abundance. God's design and pleasure are for you to be the most contented person on earth. "Thou wilt shew me the path of life: in thy presence is fulness of joy; at thy right hand there are pleasures for evermore" (Psalm 16:11).

You have access to the God Who made the earth and holds all its treasures in His hands. "The Lord God is a sun and shield: the Lord will give grace and glory: no good thing will he withhold from them that walk uprightly" (Psalm 84:11).

God gives joy. He gives peace that surpasses all human understanding. He calms our storms and walks with us through the fires of life. He hides us in the cleft of the Rock—Himself—and ensures our stability and safety. God cares for His beloved children.

The world does not give joy. It robs you of God's treasure of the fullness of joy. The world does not give pleasure. The pleasures of sin are momentary; they deny you true pleasure, fulfillment, and the enjoyment found in Jesus Christ. God does not deny you anything good.

In His presence is fullness of joy. Much more awaits us in heaven.

READ PSALM 84:10–11.

GOD HEALS.

Are you sick today? Have you talked to your heavenly Father about your illness? Have you sought His face and asked for His touch? God wants you to involve Him in everything that goes on in your life, including sickness. His desire is for you to talk to Him first before you consult and seek the help of doctors. Do not underestimate what He will do for you! "And Asa in the thirty and ninth year of his reign was diseased in his feet, until his disease was exceeding great: yet in his disease he sought not to the Lord, but to the physicians. And Asa slept with his fathers, and died in the one and fortieth year of his reign" (2 Chronicles 16:12–13).

God heals. Christ healed many sick people as He walked in this world in His earthly ministry. "The woman who had a blood issue for twelve years said within herself, If I may but touch his garment, I shall be whole. . . . Jesus turned . . . and said, Daughter, be of good comfort; thy faith hath made thee whole. And the woman was made whole from that hour" (Matthew 9:20–22).

Christ is our great physician; the healing balm. There is healing in His Word. "Is any sick among you? let him call for the elders of the church; and let them pray over him, anointing him with oil in the name of the Lord: And the prayer of faith shall save the sick" (James 5:14–15).

READ MARK 6:53–56.

GOD HEALS NATIONS.

Do you like what surrounds you? Do you desire to live in a peaceful and prosperous country? Does your heart long for a time when you can go out and come back without fear? God's will is for you to live in a peaceful environment. However, you have a role to play in determining the kind of environment you will enjoy. Look at God's formula:

> If my people, which are called by my name, shall humble themselves, and pray, and seek my face, and turn from their wicked ways; then will I hear from heaven, and will forgive their sin, and will heal their land. Now mine eyes shall be open, and mine ears attent unto the prayer that is made in this place. (2 Chronicles 7:14–15)

God heals and restores nations. Every Christian has a part to play in the healing of the nation. The outline is laid out: humble yourself, pray and seek God's face, and turn from wicked ways. God never meant for nations to walk estranged from Him. It is God Who prospers and preserves nations with His grace and mercy.

Do your part and foster the healing of your nation. A God-favored nation is the right place for God's children to live and prosper. Look at God's call today: "Seek the peace of the city whither I have caused you to be carried away captives, and pray unto the Lord for it: for in the peace thereof shall ye have peace" (Jeremiah 29:7).

READ DEUTERONOMY 28:1.

Christ is a Rock to the Overwhelmed.

Are the winds of life blowing and beating vehemently on your boat? Is there no rest for your soul? Are your dreams deem and your hopes shuttered? Is your heart overwhelmed with seemingly no place to anchor and find rest? God has not left you to face the angry waves of life alone. God is near. God's ear is attentive to your call.

He understands what is facing you today and He is here to stand with you. Find rest in His promise today: "Hear my cry, O God; attend unto my prayer. From the end of the earth will I cry unto thee, when my heart is overwhelmed: lead me to the rock that is higher than I. For thou hast been a shelter for me, and a strong tower from the enemy" (Psalm 61:1–3).

God hears the cry of His children. His ear is attentive to their prayer. When your heart is overwhelmed, He is right there. Don't be afraid. Fall into His arms. He is your Rock. He will remain a shelter and a strong tower to shield you from the enemies and angry waves rocking your boat. They will not get to you.

God will lift you out of your pit of despair. He will not leave you in the mire. He will put a new song in your mouth. He will establish your going again and set your feet upon His perfect path. Wait patiently, He will not let you down, He is a Rock to those who are overwhelmed (see Psalm 40).

Read Psalm 31:1–3.

GOD IS TRUSTWORTHY.

Is your heart troubled? Are the situations of life causing fear and anxiety? Are you wondering whether to hold on and to wait on God or to move on to "Plan B"? Do not despair. God is trustworthy. Wait. Hold onto God. Look at His promise today; you can trust God: "What time I am afraid, I will trust in thee" (Psalm 56:3).

God is trustworthy. You don't have to be afraid of man. No man will come to you unless God permits Him. Neither will any situation come your way that He cannot see you through. In moments when you cannot see Him, trust Him. God laughs at the plans of the wicked (Psalms 2:4; 59:8). He knows them too well and can foil them anytime.

God sees the tossing that goes on in the night. He knows how your thoughts are troubled. He will not put you to shame. He will not let your enemies to triumph over you. God Who has delivered your soul from eternal death out of His deep love will preserve your life and keep you from falling. You, too, will rejoice and say: "I sought the Lord, and he heard me, and delivered me from all my fears. They looked unto him, and were lightened: and their faces were not ashamed" (Psalm 34:4). Taste and see that the Lord is good. God is trustworthy!

READ PSALM 34:4–9.

"ALL THINGS WORK TOGETHER FOR GOOD."

God has no intentions of hurting you. What He allows to come to you, He will turn for your good. God does all things well. He knows your frame. He knows how to prune and mold you into His desired vessel. He knows how much pressure you can take and for how long. "And we know that all things work together for good to them that love God, to them who are the called according to his purpose" (Romans 8:28).

It does not matter the intention with which people deal with you. God can make those situations work for your good. Joseph was sold into Egypt by malicious brothers who hated and envied him. Grim though his circumstances were, Joseph was able to face many years later, saying: "But as for you, ye thought evil against me; but God meant it unto good, to bring to pass, as it is this day, to save much people alive" (Genesis 50:20).

Face today with courage. Approach the circumstances of your life with the realization that God is aware of them. Commit your fear and anxiety to God knowing that He understands what surrounds you. Regardless of what you are going through, remember, God is not out to hurt you. Instead, God will stand with His promise to work it all out for your good.

READ 1 CORINTHIANS 10:13.

GOD SATISFIES.

No one will satisfy your life like God. No one will give you joy, fulfillment, and contentment like the Lord. Try Him. Put Him to the test and see. Follow Him wholeheartedly and see that none of His good and great promises for your life will fall to the ground (see Joshua 21:45).

God satisfies. "Oh that men would praise the Lord for his goodness, and for his wonderful works to the children of men! For he satisfieth the longing soul, and filleth the hungry soul with goodness" (Psalm 107:8–9). There is no excuse for you to loiter in Satan's camp looking for satisfaction. The most fulfilled and satisfied people on earth today are Christians who are walking in obedience to God's Word. In the presence of God there is fullness of joy and at His right hand are pleasures for evermore (Psalm 16:11). God satisfies the longing heart. He fills the hungry soul with goodness. He lavishes His children with His goodness.

God pours contempt upon princes, and causes them to wander in the wilderness, where there is no way. Yet He sets the poor on high from affliction, and makes him families like a flock. God makes our borders peaceful. He satisfies with abundance.

You have not followed cunningly devised fables by coming to Christ. Christ is real. He will meet your physical, emotional, and spiritual needs. God satisfies.

READ PSALM 107:9.

GOD TRAINS YOU.

Can you remember the meals you ate this past month on a daily basis? I highly doubt that we would be able to remember half of the meals we ate. Nevertheless, every bite you took was used to nourish your body. Your body shows detailed evidence of what you ate. Body functions were sustained, processes were renewed, and there was new growth.

This phenomenon works the same when it comes to spiritual growth. Feeding your spirit on a daily basis nourishes your life, strengthens you, and equips you for spiritual battles. Without even realizing it, you will stand amid great battles.

> It is God that girdeth me with strength, and maketh my way perfect. He maketh my feet like hinds' feet, and setteth me upon my high places. He teacheth my hands to war, so that a bow of steel is broken by mine arms. Thou hast also given me the shield of thy salvation: and thy right hand hath holden me up, and thy gentleness hath made me great. Thou hast enlarged my steps under me, that my feet did not slip. (Psalm 18:32–36)

The Christian journey is a spiritual battle. We are faced with an enemy who is cunning and well disguised. Satan targets you every day. God does not leave His children at Satan's mercy. He teaches and trains us for this battle. He points us to His formidable armory and shows us how to use weapons of spiritual warfare (Ephesians 6:10–18).

Every teaching God gives you is meant to train and prepare you to face the enemy with strength and confidence. When you listen and obey, you will pursue the enemy and overtake him. Embrace your training.

READ PSALM 18:32–50.

GOD GIVES JOY.

Let the joy of the Lord carry you through the circumstances of your life today. Life may be tough. The turns in your life may be uncertain and even painful. However, lean on God and allow the Holy Spirit to radiate His divine light into your soul and give you joy and hope. Do not inhibit the song God puts in your heart. Take it! Sing it! "Then he said unto them, Go your way, eat the fat, and drink the sweet, and send portions unto them for whom nothing is prepared: for this day is holy unto our Lord: neither be ye sorry; for the joy of the Lord is your strength" (Nehemiah 8:10).

The joy of the Lord is strength to God's children. Joy comes from the deep settled confidence and assurance resulting from the unchanging character of God, who can be trusted. The circumstances should not dictate your joy. Instead, let the joy of the Lord carry you through the circumstances.

Today, you can agree with the prophet Habakkuk and say:

Although the fig tree shall not blossom, neither shall fruit be in the vines; the labour of the olive shall fail, and the fields shall yield no meat; the flock shall be cut off from the fold, and there shall be no herd in the stalls: Yet I will rejoice in the Lord, I will joy in the God of my salvation. The Lord God is my strength. (Habakkuk 3:17–19)

READ PSALM 28:7–8.

TO THE MERCIFUL, GOD IS MERCIFUL.

To whom can you extend God's mercy today? Are there people looking and desiring your mercy and help? It is because of the Lord's mercy that we can stand and be a people of honor today. Do the same to somebody today. Look at how God will respond to your act of mercy.

> Therefore hath the Lord recompensed me according to my righteousness, according to the cleanness of my hands in his eyesight. With the merciful thou wilt shew thyself merciful; with an upright man thou wilt shew thyself upright; With the pure thou wilt shew thyself pure; and with the froward thou wilt shew thyself froward. (Psalm 18:24–26)

God is merciful. When you choose to follow His precepts, you can be sure that He will show Himself faithful. He shows His mercy to the merciful, just as He shows Himself upright to the upright. God's ways are perfect. They have been tried and found true. He honors those who honor Him.

Whatever you do to the least of God's children, God takes note and counts it toward Himself. When you give a glass of water to His servants, it is counted as a glass given to the Lord and it is worth a prophet's reward. Be careful therefore how you treat those who will pass your way today. Remember, some have entertained angels without knowing (Hebrews 13:2).

READ MATTHEW 25:43–45.

GOD DOES NOT FORSAKE US.

God stands with His children. God does not leave you to grope alone in darkness when your life is tossed by storms. God does not remain distant in your moments of need or despair. God takes full responsibility for you. He stands with you. He feeds, encourages, and strengthens your heart every day. Look at His promise for you today: "For the Lord will not forsake his people for his great name›s sake: because it hath pleased the Lord to make you his people" (1 Samuel 12:22).

God does not forsake His children. You can serve the Lord with joy and confidence knowing that He is trustworthy. God has been put to the test for centuries but has never been found guilty of failing anyone. King David testified to the world in Psalm 37:22–26, saying:

> The steps of a good man are ordered by the Lord: and he delighteth in his way. Though he fall, he shall not be utterly cast down: for theLord upholdeth him with his hand. I have been young, and now am old; yet have I not seen the righteous forsaken, nor his seed begging bread. He is ever merciful, and lendeth; and his seed is blessed.

You are not a burden to God. As a matter of fact, you did not choose God. God Who chose you will meet your needs. He will never leave you desolate. God will not forsake you.

READ HEBREWS 13:5.

July 28

GOD WILL NOT WITHHOLD GOOD.

Many people hold the false notion that God does not lavish His children with good things. I have met brethren who believe that God sustains His children with the bare necessities of life. To some extent, they consider this as a mark of true spirituality. This is far from scriptural truth. God desires to see you fulfilled and satisfied in life.

He is not a tyrant who cannot give you anything good. Look at His written Word today and judge for yourself: "For the Lord God is a sun and shield: the Lord will give grace and glory: no good thing will he withhold from them that walk uprightly. O Lord of hosts, blessed is the man that trusteth in thee" (Psalm 84:11–12).

God delights in His children. His children give Him pleasure. It is for this very reason they were created, and He rejoices in that. He cannot withhold good from those who give Him satisfaction. Get close to God, love Him; follow Him and hold Him in high esteem and see for yourself that He does not withhold anything good from those whose walk is upright. "O taste and see that the Lord is good: blessed is the man that trusteth in him. O fear the Lord, ye his saints: for there is no want to them that fear him. The young lions do lack, and suffer hunger: but they that seek the Lord shall not want any good thing" (Psalm 34:8–10).

Those who look to Him are radiant; their faces are not covered with shame. God will not withhold good things from you.

READ PSALM 36:7–9.

YOU ARE IN GOD'S HANDS.

Many people in the world are known by a number. You are identified in most places using a social security number, an identification number, a driving license number, or even a tally number to determine when you can be served. That is not how God deals with you. You are not just a number before God. He knows you by name. You are His, and He deals with you as if you were His only child. You never have to wait in line. You never have to feel overshadowed or like a second-class individual.

Look at His promise to you today: "Can a woman forget her sucking child, that she should not have compassion on the son of her womb? yea, they may forget, yet will I not forget thee. Behold, I have graven thee upon the palms of my hands; thy walls are continually before me" (Isaiah 49:15–16).

God has engraved you in the palms of His hands. Engraving symbolizes the permanency of your position, just as you have entered a covenant relationship of Father and son. In the same way, God does not disown you. He cannot forget about you. You have been engraved as God's signet ring, signifying one who is greatly loved by Him.

As you embrace God's commandments, He in turn engraves you in the palms of His hands so that your needs and interests are ever before Him (Isaiah 49:16). You are in God's hands. Impossible as it may seem that a woman can forget the child who is sucking on her breast, it is more impossible for God to forget you. Your times are in His hand and so is everything about you (Psalm 31:15).

READ ISAIAH 43:1–3.

GOD GIVES REST.

Are you faced with difficult situations that have endured for a very long time? Is your heart weary? Is your strength dwindling? Does it seem like you are hanging on for one last time?

Your situation will not last forever. God will give you rest. God knows how long the night season has been in your life. God understands the toiling and how tired you feel. God is not blind to your plight, and neither is He deaf to the honest cries of your heart. Allow His Word to soothe your heart today: "Let not your heart be troubled: ye believe in God, believe also in me" (John 14:1).

Your Christian walk with the Lord can be likened to walking on earth. There are times when your walk is along a flat surface. Other times you have to climb hills and into deep valleys. No one terrain remains forever. God knows when you need to go through mountains and valleys, but He also gives you rest. He will make you to lie down in green pastures. He will restore your soul (Psalm 23).

God invites you to Himself in moments when you are weary: "Come unto me, all ye that labor and are heavy laden, and I will give you rest" (Matthew 11:28). Wait on the Lord and be of good courage (Psalm 27:14).

Rest is on the way. God gives power and strength to the weary. Yes, they that "wait upon the Lord shall renew their strength; they shall mount up with wings as eagles; they shall run, and not be weary; and they shall walk, and not faint" (Isaiah 40:31). God will not make you stay in your situation longer than He desires. The God Who loves you is looking out for you today. God will give you rest.

READ ISAIAH 40:28–31.

July 31

THE LORD IS GOOD.

God has called you to a life of joy, fulfillment, and contentment. You can taste the goodness of God regardless of what surrounds you today. God is in charge of all things. He lightens your burdens, gives you direction, soothes your sorrow, and comforts and carries you in times of great difficulty. He calms the raging storms and fills your heart with peace. He fills you with abundant blessings and keeps you safe in His arms. "O taste and see that the Lord is good: blessed is the man that trusteth in him. O fear the Lord, ye his saints: for there is no want to them that fear him. The young lions do lack, and suffer hunger: but they that seek the Lord shall not want any good thing" (Psalm 34:8–10).

Taste for yourself and see that the Lord is good. You cannot enjoy swimming when you stay in the shallow waters. It works the same way with your Christian life. Those who live lukewarm and shallow lives barely get to know their Savior. A deep relationship with God is an adventure that will leave you satisfied and fulfilled. The more you know Him the more you will love and Him and discover the hidden treasure that is found by few who dare to go for it.

Seek the Lord and you shall not want for anything good. "The angel of the Lord encampeth round about them that fear him, and delivereth them" (Psalm 34:7). God is good, taste it for yourself!

READ PSALM 100.

August

TRUSTING THE CHARACTER OF GOD

Who is God? Whom have you believed and what is His character like? Can a Christian trust the character of God? Is the God of Abraham and Isaac still trustworthy in such times?

GOD IS SOVEREIGN.

Can you trust God? Can you trust the character of God? Can you trust God when you are left to yourself amid the tough happenings of life? Is He real? Is God trustworthy? Take time and explore God so that your heart may be anchored in Him. The world is full of turmoil, but you can trust God.

> For I know that the Lord is great, and that our Lord is above all gods. Whatsoever the Lord pleased, that did he in heaven, and in earth, in the seas, and all deep places. He causeth the vapours to ascend from the ends of the earth; he maketh lightnings for the rain; he bringeth the wind out of his treasuries. (Psalm 135:5-7)

God is sovereign. He is the high and lofty supreme One Who inhabits eternity and controls the universe by the word of His power (Hebrews 1:3). He is great and there is none like Him. Nothing occurs to God. Nothing takes Him by surprise. He has power over all He has created and takes care of every detail.

God knows what is best for you. He is not obligated to tell what He is doing. Even the hearts of kings are in His hands and He turns them wherever He wishes. God hung the earth on nothing and has held it in place by His power. He will take care of you.

READ PSALM 48:14 AND ISAIAH 57:15–16.

GOD KEEPS HIS PROMISES.

What is your "Plan B" for today? What plans do you have in place just in case God fails to come through as He has promised? Whom do you trust most; God, your doctor, your teacher or your friends?

Most of us fear to surrender our lives and all our plans to God for fear of being stranded and or being forsaken by God. Most of us trust words of promise by men than the promises of God made to us. God wants you to trust Him in everything. Look at His own testimony of what He will and will not do: "God is not a man, that he should lie; neither the son of man, that he should repent: hath he said, and shall he not do it? or hath he spoken, and shall he not make it good?" (Numbers 23:19).

God is not a superman. He is not a legend. God is God. He is not a man who can be overtaken by the sinful fallen nature that can cause Him to lie or forget His duties. You can trust Him to do as He has promised. You can trust His Word. It is truth by which you can order your live and be fulfilled. "Know therefore that the Lord thy God, he is God, the faithful God, which keepeth covenant and mercy with them that love him and keep his commandments to a thousand generations" (Deuteronomy 7:9).

Joshua, who succeeded Moses and led the children of Israel into the promised land, testified of it saying: "Not one thing hath failed of all the good things which the Lord your God spake concerning you" (Joshua 23:14).

God will not fail you.

READ 2 CHRONICLES 6:14–15.

GOD IS TRUSTWORTHY.

Men and women of integrity are few in our modern-day world. It is disheartening when institutions and those you would have expected to uphold the law and live truthfully fall way below your lines of trust. But how does God measure up to all these?

When all fails, when those you trusted fail you and your heart is frustrated, you can have a strong and secure anchor in the character of God. God is trustworthy. You can take Him at His Word and you will not be disappointed. "God is faithful, by whom ye were called unto the fellowship of his Son Jesus Christ our Lord" (1 Corinthians 1:9).

You have believed on One Who is a solid rock in whom there is no offense. God is trustworthy. His Words are true. That is His character and He cannot deny it. David testified of God saying, "I have been young, and now am old; yet have I not seen the righteous forsaken, nor his seed begging bread" (Psalm 37:25).

This is the same David whom God lifted from a shepherd boy to kingship; a royalty and splendor that has left an unmatched legacy to this day.

You can trust God to be whom He has said He will be to you. He will do as He has promised. You can be "confident of this very thing, that he which hath begun a good work in you will perform it until the day of Jesus Christ" (Philippians 1:6).

You have been called into fellowship with a trustworthy God. God is reliable. He is dependable. He is truthful. Trust Him.

READ PSALM 22:4–5.

GOD CANNOT LIE.

It is easy for the storms of life to cloud your view of God to the extent that you doubt His promises and the soundness of His character. It is easy to wring your hands in despair when you cannot see the end of the tunnel. It is in those dark times and when our hearts are fearful that we feel abandoned and let down by God. However, God's Word is true. His promises are sure. God has not lied to you. Look at His assurance to your heart today:

> Moreover I will endeavour that ye may be able after my decease to have these things always in remembrance. For we have not followed cunningly devised fables, when we made known unto you the power and coming of our Lord Jesus Christ, but were eyewitnesses of his majesty. (2 Peter 1:15–16)

God is God. He cannot lie (Titus 1:2). Hold this truth to your heart and let it carry you in moments of doubt and fear. You have not been deceived into following Christ. Test it and be a witness who can confirm God's character and majesty. Build hope and trust in the lives of other people as they see God's faithfulness in your life.

Not only has God given us His promise but His oath also to seal it to our hearts that He is trustworthy, and we can anchor ourselves in Him. With what are you struggling today? God has not lied to you. He will come through as He has promised. May He rise with healing in His wings for you today.

READ HEBREWS 6:16–19.

August 5

GOD TAKES CARE OF HIS CHILDREN.

God has promised to take care of you even in old age. He is not planning on abandoning you in your adult life. He will take care of you until He receives you up in glory.

We face every day with some plans in place. We plan what to do, where to go, what to buy, what to eat, and even what to wear. We do the same for our children and those in our families. We plan for their upkeep, their schooling, and their future. However, we forget that God, our Father, does the same for His beloved children. Have you seen a mother give birth and thrust her babies out of the house to fend for themselves in their helpless state? Unfortunately, this is how our fallen minds envision God in moments of difficulty. We look at Him like one who abandons and leaves you to struggle all alone in life.

Just like you plan and take care of your children, so does God plan and take care of you. Look at God's promise to take care of you even when you are old and frail: "And even to your old age I am he; and even to hoar hairs will I carry you: I have made, and I will bear; even I will carry, and will deliver you. To whom will ye liken me, and make me equal, and compare me, that we may be like?" (Isaiah 46:4–5).

No one takes care of his children like God. "The young lions do lack, and suffer hunger: but they that seek the Lord shall not want any good thing" (Psalm 34:10). Yes, God will take care of you even in old age. He will not abandon you when you are weak and old. He will take care of you until you die.

There is not a moment when God wrings His hand in confusion as He wonders how to take care of you. God has made good plans for you. Everything is secure. Give your burdens to the Lord and let Him take charge. Trust Him for who He is and what He has said.

READ PHILIPPIANS 4:19.

GOD KNOWS WHAT IS BEST.

God's training and evaluation are unlike what you have had in your life. Teachers present relevant content to you and evaluate you to see how much you learned. Most tests and examinations are predictable and expected. God on other hand is good at testing when you least expect it. Most times you never know when you are under His examination.

Look at how He did it to His beloved children as they journeyed through the wilderness: "And thou shalt remember all the way which the Lord thy God led thee these forty years in the wilderness, to humble thee, and to prove thee, to know what was in thine heart, whether thou wouldest keep his commandments, or no" (Deuteronomy 8:2).

God sees the beginning from the end. He knows you. He knows what is best for you. He plans your life and carefully chooses what to bring before you at appropriate times. The children of Israel wandered in the wilderness for forty long years without many knowing that God was humbling and testing their hearts.

Do not waste the circumstances of your life. God will use them, too, to see what is in your heart and whether you can keep His commandments or not. Sometimes, God chooses to take us through moments of lack as He teaches us to depend on Him. He uses different situations to draw our attention back to Him and to keep a clear focus on what is important and eternal.

Trust His choices for you. Follow Him wholeheartedly and you will be ready for His examination at any time.

READ DEUTERONOMY 8:1–6.

GOD IS FAITHFUL.

God is faithful; you can take Him at His Word. The hardships of life have a clouding effect on our view of God, and the disappointments we face with people also have their share in affecting our trust in God. We equate God to mortal man to some extent, and fear that He may not come through for us. It is easy to despair and lose sight of God when your back is pressed to the wall. It is easy to suppress His voice as you seek what looks like solutions to carry you through those difficult moments.

Quiet your spirit today and allow God's Word to impact your heart. Reflect on what He has said and trust Him for every word: "God is faithful, by whom ye were called unto the fellowship of his Son Jesus Christ our Lord" (1 Corinthians 1:9).

We can affirm Paul's words in Romans 3:4 and say: only God is true, and every man is a liar. God is faithful. He has never lost any of His children, and you can trust that He will carry you to the end. "Know therefore that the Lord thy God, he is God, the faithful God, which keepeth covenant and mercy with them that love him and keep his commandments to a thousand generations; And repayeth them that hate him to their face, to destroy them: he will not be slack to him that hateth him, he will repay him to his face" (Deuteronomy 7:9–10).

God promises to love you, bless you, and multiply you. He has also promised to bless the fruit of your womb and the fruit of your land (see Deuteronomy 7:13). God is your Rock; His work is perfect. All his ways are judgment. He is a God of truth. There is no iniquity in Him. God is just and right (Deuteronomy 32:4).

God is faithful. You can trust Him with all your tough situations today.

READ DEUTERONOMY 7:6–12.

GOD IS LOVE.

When man sins against God, his first reaction is to run away. Like Adam and Eve, he looks for an excuse with hopes of winning the heart of God again. While estranged and far away from God, he bruises his heart with many sorrows. This is not God's desire for your life. He knew you would sin before you did it. There is a better solution to sin's solution according to God's holy Word. It is called repentance.

> Beloved, let us love one another: for love is of God; and every one that loveth is born of God, and knoweth God. He that loveth not knoweth not God; for God is love. In this was manifested the love of God toward us, because that God sent his only begotten Son into the world, that we might live through him. Herein is love, not that we loved God, but that he loved us, and sent his Son to be the propitiation for our sins. (1 John 4: 7–10)

God has intense and unfathomed affection for His people. His love is unconditional. Love is part of His divine nature. That is why He loved us while we were still sinners by sending Christ to die for us. We couldn't merit God's love. Our human nature can't earn enough to win His love. Even at our very best, our righteousness is like filthy rugs before a holy God (Isaiah 64:6).

It is true! God loves you! He loves you when you are good and even when you have blown it. Stay under His umbrella.

READ JOHN 3:16–18.

GOD IS HOLY.

It is not easy for the heart of man to fathom the holiness of God. God is so holy that you cannot be in His true presence and remain on your feet gazing at Him. If He wouldn't welcome us into His presence because of the covering of the blood of Christ with which we are adorned, His holiness would instantly slay us. God is so pure and holy that He shines like the sun in its most brilliance. It is no wonder heaven is preoccupied with the holiness of God. "And one cried unto another, and said, Holy, holy, holy, is the Lord of hosts: the whole earth is full of his glory" (Revelation 4:3).

God is sinless. He is perfect without any spot or wrinkle of wrongdoing in His nature. On the other hand, man is born a sinner (Romans 3:23). God uses the human analogy of light and darkness to help us understand. Man is like total darkness while God is total light. The two cannot dwell together. It is for this reason that Christ had to reconcile man to God through His shed blood to banish darkness and cause us to live as children of light. God is light and in Him there is no darkness at all (1 John 1:5).

You have been cleansed and reconciled to God. You can fellowship with God. Just as there's no fellowship between light and darkness, God cannot fellowship with you if you continue living in sin. His holy nature banishes and punishes sin. He does not need to contemplate it; it is a natural spiritual phenomenon. Think about it. When you jump up you land right back on the ground. You do not fly. This is because the law of gravity is in operation. God's spiritual laws work the same.

READ 2 CORINTHIANS 6:14–18.

August 10

GOD IS KIND.

Man is quick to write you off and tear you down for the slightest mistake you make. Man is easy to criticize, to mock, and to discipline you whenever you mess up. God is not so. God is kind. He looks at you with compassion. God knows how frail you are and how easy it is for you to mess up and even fall. He deals with your graciously. In fact, He knows how stubborn your heart is, too, yet that does not stop His kindness toward you. Even with all you harbor in your heart, He still shows His love and kindness to you daily. God treats us better than we deserve. See this for yourself:

> But they and our fathers dealt proudly, and hardened their necks, and hearkened not to thy commandments, And refused to obey, neither were mindful of thy wonders that thou didst among them; but hardened their necks, and in their rebellion appointed a captain to return to their bondage: but thou art a God ready to pardon, gracious and merciful, slow to anger, and of great kindness, and forsookest them not. (Nehemiah 9:16–17)

We are a living testimony of God's kindness. The prophet Nehemiah, who had gone to rebuild the wall of Jerusalem after they had been burnt down as God's people were taken into captivity, knew how proud Israel was. God did not deal with them after their rebellion. He was merciful, slow to anger, and great in kindness. He did not forsake them.

God has not dwelt with you as your sins deserve. He has been kind and longsuffering. He stands with outstretched arms as He beckons you into His love. Let His love melt your heart into His arms of grace.

READ TITUS 3:4–6.

GOD IS ETERNAL.

We live in an ever changing world. People change. Things change. Policies change, and so do governments. Celebrities come and go and so go great shows and operations. Inventions change and so do the minds of men and women. However, amid all these changes, there is one reliable and unchanging God. You can trust Him when your world is tossed up and down. You can lean on Him when all else has given way.

Find strength in the immutability of God today. "Lord, thou hast been our dwelling place in all generations. Before the mountains were brought forth, or ever thou hadst formed the earth and the world, even from everlasting to everlasting, thou art God" (Psalm 90:1–2).

God was here long before the earth was formed. Moses was very reluctant to take his God-given role to lead Israel out of Egypt. As he argued against going back to Egypt from where he had fled, "Moses said unto God, Behold, when I come unto the children of Israel, and shall say unto them, The God of your fathers hath sent me unto you; and they shall say to me, What is his name? what shall I say unto them? And God said unto Moses, I Am That I Am: and he said, Thus shalt thou say unto the children of Israel, I Am hath sent me unto you" (Exodus 3:13–14).

In essence, God was telling Moses, "I am God. I have always been. I have neither beginning nor end." You belong to an eternal God. Love Him. He will not change.

READ ISAIAH 57:15.

GOD IS A JEALOUS GOD.

God demands single-minded worship from those who have willingly entered His covenant relationship through the atoning blood of His Son. God does not condone spiritual adultery. Not only has God saved you from the filth of sin, but He has showed you His goodness and greatness. All His children enjoy His love and faithfulness. Do not cross boundaries by departing from God to do what is dishonoring and displeasing to Him. He will not hold you guiltless. Some sins have lasting consequences from which you cannot escape. They will affect your family and the generations to come.

> Take heed to thyself, lest thou make a covenant with the inhabitants of the land whither thou goest, lest it be for a snare in the midst of thee: But ye shall destroy their altars, break their images, and cut down their groves: For thou shalt worship no other god: for the Lord, whose name is Jealous, is a jealous God. (Exodus 34:12–14)

God is love, but He is also a jealous God. He is a consuming fire (Deuteronomy 4:24; Hebrews 12:29). God is pure, and His nature cannot tolerate sin. He is like the sun in its most brilliance. Darkness cannot stay in His presence. It flees.

Sin provokes jealousy in God. In Exodus 20:5, God warned against idol worship as He gave the Ten Commandments: "For I the Lord thy God am a jealous God, visiting the iniquity of the fathers upon the children unto the third and fourth generation of them that hate me" (Deuteronomy 5:9).

As the apostle Peter cautions, depart from sin and live a life that is pleasing to God if you have truly tasted and seen that God is good (1 Peter 2:3). Take heed to the words of Joshua to God's children in Joshua 24:15: "And if it seem evil unto you to serve the Lord, choose you this day whom ye will serve; whether the gods which your fathers served that were on the other side of the flood, or the gods of the Amorites, in whose land ye dwell: but as for me and my house, we will serve the Lord."

READ DEUTERONOMY 6:12–17.

GOD IS JUST.

When you look at yourself in comparison to other people, it is easy to think that God is unfair. Some people think and reason better. There are those who have more success than others. Some are better at teaching, leading, planning, and implementing plans. Some are better looking. The truth is that God does not deal with anybody unfairly.

God knows you better than you know yourself. He knows what you can and what you cannot do. He knows what to entrust to you and what to give to someone else. He knows where you will serve Him best and where you cannot thrive. God knows your capabilities. He formed you. He knows what treasures are in your deposit.

> But the Lord shall endure for ever: he hath prepared his throne for judgment. And he shall judge the world in righteousness, he shall minister judgment to the people in uprightness. The Lord also will be a refuge for the oppressed, a refuge in times of trouble. And they that know thy name will put their trust in thee: for thou, Lord, hast not forsaken them that seek thee. (Psalm 9:7–10)

God has always been and will continue to be fair. He is God and knows what to do, and when and how to do it. He is always right and fair. God rules over the affairs of men justly. "Good and upright is the Lord: therefore will he teach sinners in the way. The meek will he guide in judgment: and the meek will he teach his way. All the paths of the Lord are mercy and truth unto such as keep his covenant and his testimonies" (Psalm 25:8–10).

God knows whom to lift or whom to bring low. He knows whom to punish and whom to bless. You can trust Him to be just. Regardless of how far gone things may seem to be in your life, you can depend on God to be just.

READ 2 THESSALONIANS 1:6–10.

GOD IS OMNIPRESENT.

God is everywhere. His eyes are in every place. He sees everything that happens every moment. He sees what takes place in every nation, every community, every home, and in every individual's life at the same time. This is good news; however, it is also scary. He knows everything. God is near. All you need is to call on Him. Reach out and let Him hold your hand. He wants to guide you. He sees the path of life as it stretches before you. Let Him walk with you.

> Whither shall I go from thy spirit? or whither shall I flee from thy presence? If I ascend up into heaven, thou art there: if I make my bed in hell, behold, thou art there. If I take the wings of the morning, and dwell in the uttermost parts of the sea; Even there shall thy hand lead me, and thy right hand shall hold me. If I say, Surely the darkness shall cover me; even the night shall be light about me. Yea, the darkness hideth not from thee; but the night shineth as the day: the darkness and the light are both alike to thee. (Psalm 139:7–12)

God is present everywhere at all times. He fills up the entire universe. The devil can only be at one place at a time. That is why he uses demons to fulfill his missions.

You are always in the presence of God. God is literally everywhere you go. He witnesses all that goes on in the world, whether done in secret or on the roof tops. No wonder He is just!

READ JEREMIAH 23:23–24.

GOD IS OMNISCIENT.

Who can understand God? Who can tell His workings? When He chooses to do His work in the world, He does it in ways that man cannot fathom. When He chooses a vessel to do His work, He surprises people with His pick and leaves them marveling. When He chooses to work in a community, He uses the most uncertain and unconventional means. He works in ways that no man expected. God is all-knowing. God knows the hearts of His people.

> O the depth of the riches both of the wisdom and knowledge of God! how unsearchable are his judgments, and his ways past finding out! For who hath known the mind of the Lord? or who hath been his counsellor? Or who hath first given to him, and it shall be recompensed unto him again? For of him, and through him, and to him, are all things: to whom be glory for ever. Amen. (Romans 11:33–36)

God knows everything. He is full of knowledge, wisdom, understanding, revelation, and discernment. When He looks at the world and all the inhabitants, He knows all about their past, their present, and even what is yet to take place. Paul put it right. The depth of His wisdom, knowledge, and judgment is so immense that it is impossible for us to understand it. That is why He is God. You can neither understand nor explain Him.

God knows us well. He knows the thoughts and intents of our hearts (see Hebrews 4:12). He weighs the motives behind our actions. He knows who loves Him.

READ 2 TIMOTHY 2:19.

GOD IS OMNIPOTENT.

It feels wonderful to be associated with someone important and very powerful. You feel protected and covered. You are assured of your voice being heard. You anticipate good treatment and favors. Imagine if you had personal connections with the most powerful men and women of the world. However, for the child of God, you are better placed than knowing such personalities. You belong to God—the Almighty—to whom no man can compare. He is more powerful than all the powerful people who ever lived put together. He is the only trustworthy person you will ever meet. He is your God.

> Ah Lord God! behold, thou hast made the heaven and the earth by thy great power and stretched out arm, and there is nothing too hard for thee. . . . Great in counsel, and mighty in work: for thine eyes are open upon all the ways of the sons of men: to give everyone according to his ways, and according to the fruit of his doings. (Jeremiah 32:17, 19)

God is all-powerful. There is nothing impossible with God. He made the heavens and the earth by the power of His might. The design and operation of His creation are impeccable. When God moves on the scenes of human impossibility, there's no doubt that the work was done by God. He is just thus cannot do what is evil.

God has power to do as He has promised. There is nothing that will take Him by surprise. Nothing is too hard for God. He asks the same question He had for Sarah when He announced that she would bear Abraham a son in old age: "Is anything too hard for the Lord?" (Genesis 18:14).

READ EPHESIANS 3:20.

GOD USES EVIL FOR YOUR GOOD.

God will use what is intended for evil to bless you. God has the power to use an evil path, a wicked scheme, manipulation, a hateful act, a denied opportunity, frustration, and even a closed door to do you good. God works in mysterious ways. Who can understand His doings? His doors of blessings are not obvious to the human eye. Sometimes, He presents His greatest opportunities, to us, disguised as big challenges. "And we know that all things work together for good to them that love God, to them who are the called according to his purpose" (Romans 8:28).

God averts evil and works good out of it most of the time. If all of us were left to the fate of evil, the world would not be a place to live for a day. God cares for His children. He takes that which would have been a source of sorrow and misery and uses it to fulfill His good plans in our lives.

When Joseph walked into Egypt as a slave, little did he know the good path onto which God would use the evil scheme of his brothers. Joseph could have landed in many places, but God saw to it that he was put in line to ascend to a place where his influence would save the world. Even in imprisonment, God put the right people in jail to fulfill His great purpose.

God will use the same instruments intended for evil to bless you. Watch out for God's working in your life? His ways are past finding out!

READ GENESIS 50:20 AND 1 PETER 1:6–7.

GOD PROTECTS HIS CHILDREN.

God will not leave you to fate. He will not leave you under the terror of your enemies either. God will protect you. You are the apple of God's eye. His presence shall overshadow you. His mighty hand shall fight for you. He does not need to let you know He is near. Trust His presence and promise. God stands with His children. Look at His promise today:

> He that dwelleth in the secret place of the most High shall abide under the shadow of the Almighty. I will say of the Lord, He is my refuge and my fortress: my God; in him will I trust. Surely he shall deliver thee from the snare of the fowler, and from the noisome pestilence. He shall cover thee with his feathers, and under his wings shalt thou trust: his truth shall be thy shield and buckler. (Psalm 91:1–4)

No one can protect like God. God protects His children from plague, traps of Satan, and the evil intentions of men. His methods are hard to comprehend. When He wanted to protect Moses from Pharaoh's decree that all male children should be drowned in the Nile River, it was the same Nile He used to save the child. Moses was protected and raised in Pharaoh's house at the wicked ruler's expense (see Exodus 1–2).

It is hard to trust when your guts are trembling, and your heart is fearful. Trust God's promise and rest in Him: Remember, He does not lie. He is right there with you. "There shall no evil befall thee, neither shall any plague come nigh thy dwelling" (Psalm 91:10).

READ PSALM 91.

August 19

GOD WILL WATCH OVER YOU.

Have you walked through dangerous territories at dangerous times when you had to look over your shoulder from time to time? Have you faced terrifying situations that left your heart trembling? Are you afraid to pass through certain places because of the cold shivering memories they hold? Are you fearful and anxious about tomorrow?

Life is full of uncertainties. However, God knows every terrain that stretches before you. God understands your fears and that is why He has a special promise for you today. God will not leave you to walk the dreadful valleys of life alone.

> The Lord is thy keeper: the Lord is thy shade upon thy right hand. The sun shall not smite thee by day, nor the moon by night. The Lord shall preserve thee from all evil: he shall preserve thy soul. The Lord shall preserve thy going out and thy coming in from this time forth, and even for evermore. (Psalm 121: 5–8)

Stop and comprehend this truth: God, the great Jehovah Himself, is watching over you. He is the one defending and protecting you. He watches over you as you come and go out every day. He is diligent to keep you from evil and to preserve your life.

God will not let you slip or fall. He will not sleep about His duties and let evil befall you. You can comfortably say that He is your help. "He shall give his angels charge over thee, to keep thee in all thy ways. They shall bear thee up in their hands, lest thou dash thy foot against a stone" (Psalm 91:11–12). God will watch over you.

READ PSALM 121.

GOD IS TRUE.

Has God ever lied to you? Has God given you His Word but failed to come through as He promised? Has God failed you in any way? It is hard to find truthful men and women. It is even harder to find men and women of integrity. It is hard to trust when you cannot hold what is spoken to be true. In a world where truth is relative, can you trust God? Can you take God at His Word? What is the testimony of those who have walked with God? Did they find Him true as He says?

> For when God made promise to Abraham, because he could swear by no greater, he sware by himself, Saying, Surely blessing I will bless thee, and multiplying I will multiply thee. And so, after he had patiently endured, he obtained the promise. For men verily swear by the greater: and an oath for confirmation is to them an end of all strife. Wherein God, willing more abundantly to shew unto the heirs of promise the immutability of his counsel, confirmed it by an oath. (Hebrews 6:13–17)

Lying is a sinful human attribute which is foreign to God. God cannot lie (Titus 1:2; Hebrews 6:18). God's Word is spoken to many people who do not stop to understand and act on it because their lack of understanding of God.

God is true and He will make everything come to pass as promised. He promised heaven to all who believe on Him. Heaven is real, and we can anticipate His second coming when we shall go to be with Him forever. You can take God's promises to the bank as you discard unbelief. What has He spoken to your heart? Don't act in unbelief. He is true.

READ NUMBERS 23:19.

GOD IS INVISIBLE.

The presence and the workings of the invisible God are witnessed and enjoyed every day by everybody. Who can run away to avoid the presence of God? When you ascend to the hills and to the mountains, you will find Him there. When you go down to the beach and in the ocean, you will find Him even in the deep waters. When you hide from the light of day to dwell in darkness, even there, His presence shines through. Your mouth may deny Him, but your heart cannot. The evidence of His presence is everywhere. Let your heart see and understand the invisible God today.

> For the wrath of God is revealed from heaven against all ungodliness and unrighteousness of men, who hold the truth in unrighteousness; Because that which may be known of God is manifest in them; for God hath shewed it unto them. For the invisible things of him from the creation of the world are clearly seen, being understood by the things that are made, even his eternal power and Godhead; so that they are without excuse. (Romans 1:18–20)

We cannot see God with our human eyes, but He makes Himself so well-known that it is hard to refute His existence. The invisible things about Him right from creation are clearly seen and understood that it makes it hard for any skeptic to have a reason for unbelief.

Invisible though God is, He puts His knowledge in the heart of man so distinctly that those who adamantly push Him aside still have His witness against their actions. Every person is created with the awareness of God. God breathed in you His breathe before you became a living soul.

READ 1 JOHN 4:12.

GOD IS SPIRIT.

He can be any place at any time. He can be everywhere, in the capacity He desires, at the same time. This means you have access to Him wherever you are and whenever you want. You, too, can have Him all the time. You do not have to wait in line. However, He is holy. God is so holy that sin cannot dwell in His presence. His holiness is so pure that sinful man cannot approach Him and remain alive without the atoning blood of God's precious Son, Jesus Christ. Look at the description of God in the following Scripture:

> That thou keep this commandment without spot, unrebukable, until the appearing of our Lord Jesus Christ: Which in his times he shall shew, who is the blessed and only Potentate, the King of kings, and Lord of lords; Who only hath immortality, dwelling in the light which no man can approach unto; whom no man hath seen, nor can see: to whom be honour and power everlasting. Amen. (1 Timothy 6:14–16)

God is not made of flesh and blood like us. Christ only took on the form of man for the time He came on earth to reconcile us to God by paying the death penalty on the cross as the perfect sacrifice. Otherwise, God does not possess matter that requires space. This is how Christ could appear to His disciples behind closed doors after His resurrection.

Spirit though He is, God reveals Himself so carefully and intricately that He develops an intimate relationship with His children. He makes Himself so real that His eternal presence is true, comforting, and very reassuring.

READ JOHN 4:24.

GOD IS IMMUTABLE.

God does not change. You can count on Him to be there and to do as He has promised.

People change but God remains the same. Governments change, but God is the same steady Rock in whom you can hide. Seasons change, but God is the same trustworthy, reliable, and unchanging hope for His children.

> I said, O my God, take me not away in the midst of my days: thy years are throughout all generations. Of old hast thou laid the foundation of the earth: and the heavens are the work of thy hands. They shall perish, but thou shalt endure: yea, all of them shall wax old like a garment; as a vesture shalt thou change them, and they shall be changed: But thou art the same, and thy years shall have no end. (Psalm 102:24–27)

God does not change. He is the same yesterday, today, and shall remain forever (see Hebrew 13:8). God is perfect. He has no need for change. Only the imperfect require change. God does not grow older or wiser. He does not change His mind or gamble with right and wrong choices. He knows everything, He is all-powerful, and sees everything.

It is because of God's immutability that we are not consumed. You can trust God's inability to change. He will there tomorrow just as He was today to keep watch and meet your needs.

READ HEBREWS 6:17–18.

GOD IS LIGHT.

There is something about light that brings hope and courage to the heart of every man. Have you been sick in the deep and dark hours of the night when the outside was pitch dark? Those are the moments you long for light. Light dispels gloom. Light suppresses evil. Light erects boundaries for things that like darkness. Light vanishes fear. Now take a moment and think about it—the God Who gives light is light Himself. How does this relate to His children according to His holy Word?

> This then is the message which we have heard of him, and declare unto you, that God is light, and in him is no darkness at all. If we say that we have fellowship with him, and walk in darkness, we lie, and do not the truth: But if we walk in the light, as he is in the light, we have fellowship one with another, and the blood of Jesus Christ his Son cleanseth us from all sin. If we say that we have no sin, we deceive ourselves, and the truth is not in us. (1 John 1:5–8)

Light denotes God's character. God is clean, pure, and untouched with evil. He signifies His presence with light. The burning bush that was not consumed caught Moses's attention (Exodus 3:1–12). The pillar of fire led the children of Israel in the wilderness (Exodus 13:21, 22; Numbers 14:14). Saul was struck by God's presence in the form of light from heaven before his conversion (Acts 9:3–4).

Light also denotes God's relationship with His children in the Christian walk. The closer you get to Him, the more you desire to depart from sin and its darkness.

Walk like one who has been drawn from darkness into His glorious light.

READ PSALM 119:105, 130.

GOD IS IMMORTAL.

The world is desperate for hope. People are weary of cunningly devised lies that fill most arenas with personal propaganda and self-driven agendas. Where can man anchor his soul? Where does the heart of man turn when everything is illusional and hopeless? The God Who created this world knew you would be faced with unprecedented times. That is why He is immortal. He is not like vain men and women in whom you cannot put your trust.

God is the same yesterday, today, and forevermore. You can trust Him. See God for who He is today: "Who only hath immortality, dwelling in the light which no man can approach unto; whom no man hath seen, nor can see: to whom be honour and power everlasting. Amen" (1 Timothy 6:16).

God is eternal. God is everlasting and He endures forever. He will never die or cease to be. He is immortal. It is only God—Yahweh—who possesses this attribute. There have been many self-proclaimed gods in the world. They all die and move out of the scene, leaving followers deceived and jaded. God lives in His glorious light forever, clothed in power and majesty. He is divine. His followers join Him in His heavenly dwelling and continue to live forever.

The immortal God gives eternal life to all who come to Him. Those who do not know Him suffer condemnation because, despite the intense revelation which leaves all men without excuse, they fail to believe on the only true God. Every created thing will pass away, but God Who is eternal will endure forever. You can put your trust in Him.

READ 1 TIMOTHY 1:7.

GOD IS LIFE.

When man is desperate, he searches for hope in places and in things that may surprise you. Desperation will drive you to seek help from idols, charms, creeds, spirits, the dead, and harmful individuals. When a man's life is hanging in the balance, it is not unusual to see panic, fear, and anxiety reaching out for anchoring limbs on which to hold. None of these things give hope.

This is not so for those whose hearts are anchored in God. In desperate moments of life, they grasp firmly to the Solid Rock—Jesus Christ. They stick closer to God and fix their eyes on Him for mercy, grace, strength, and help.

> But our God is in the heavens: he hath done whatsoever he hath pleased. Their idols are silver and gold, the work of men's hands. They have mouths, but they speak not: eyes have they, but they see not: They have ears, but they hear not: noses have they, but they smell not: They have hands, but they handle not: feet have they, but they walk not: neither speak they through their throat. They that make them are like unto them; so is every one that trusteth in them. O Israel, trust thou in the Lord: he is their help and their shield. (Psalm 115:3–9)

Life starts with God and can only be found in Him. In Genesis 2:7, "The Lord God formed man of the dust of the ground, and breathed into his nostrils the breath of life; and man became a living soul."

Idols, carved images, charms, and fortune secrets are all powerless and deceptive. They do not give life. You are alive today because you still have the breath of God within you.

READ PSALM 84:2.

GOD IS INFINITE.

God is limitless. He is immeasurable. He is boundless and omnipresent. God has neither beginning nor end. He is infinite—that is why He tells us He is the Alpha and Omega, the beginning and the end. You cannot determine where He begins or ends.

God's character is infinite. He can never be less of who and what He is. You cannot exhaust His knowledge, wisdom, love, mercy, or patience. You cannot empty Him. He remains the same yesterday, today, and forevermore.

> Behold, he cometh with clouds; and every eye shall see him, and they also which pierced him: and all kindreds of the earth shall wail because of him. Even so, Amen. I am Alpha and Omega, the beginning and the ending, saith the Lord, which is, and which was, and which is to come, the Almighty. (Revelation 1:7–8)

You cannot exhaust God. Man runs out of patience and expresses frustration and lack of restraint of character. Finances run out and you must work and wait until they are replenished. Man, who is mortal, has a beginning and an end. His flesh wastes away and his spirit returns to God, His Maker.

The great infinite God seeks a personal relationship with you. Imagine the comfort and strength, the joy and hope, the guidance and teaching He has for all who will dare to know Him intimately.

READ PSALM 147:5.

GOD IS SOVEREIGN.

God, who has called and redeemed you, is supreme. He is sovereign over all the earth. He created all things by the power of His might. He knows everything. All things hold together in Him. He is all-powerful, all-knowing, and the self-existing One Who inhabits eternity. He is mighty and powerful. He cannot be overcome by evil. Nothing occurs to Him. Nothing catches Him by surprise. Your situations and the circumstances of your life are before Him. He knows everything about you.

> Circumcise therefore the foreskin of your heart, and be no more stiffnecked. For the Lord your God is God of gods, and Lord of lords, a great God, a mighty, and a terrible, which regardeth not persons, nor taketh reward: He doth execute the judgment of the fatherless and widow, and loveth the stranger, in giving him food and raiment. (Deuteronomy 10:16–18)

God is who is says He is. He is great and lifted high above everyone and everything. God does not need anyone's help. He can defend Himself. He has proved to be the Rock of offense to those who don't believe.

We can join the David in Psalm 95:3–6 in saying, "For the Lord is a great God, and a great King above all gods. In his hand are the deep places of the earth: the strength of the hills is his also. The sea is his, and he made it: and his hands formed the dry land. O come, let us worship and bow down: let us kneel before the Lord our maker."

READ DANIEL 4:35 AND JOB 9:12.

August 29

GOD IS YOUR FATHER.

When you choose to repent and turn from sin to follow Christ, believing in your heart that He shed His blood on the cross, died, and was raised again to ransom you, you enter a new father-son relationship with God.

Just as earthly children have special rights and privileges, you, too, become a member of the royal family of God. You have unlimited access to God, and you become a coheir with His only begotten Son—Jesus Christ. As a son, God desires a close walk with you. Look at God's witness according to His holy Word.

> For as many as are led by the Spirit of God, they are the sons of God. For ye have not received the spirit of bondage again to fear; but ye have received the Spirit of adoption, whereby we cry, Abba, Father. The Spirit itself beareth witness with our spirit, that we are the children of God: And if children, then heirs; heirs of God, and joint-heirs with Christ; if so be that we suffer with him, that we may be also glorified together. (Romans 8:14–17)

Do not live like a destitute child who is without a father. God is your Father. You are loved. You belong to Him. He takes full responsibility for you. You are His son. Develop a strong relationship with Him and enjoy the privileges of your heavenly citizenship. Ask and allow Him to fill you with His wisdom and knowledge that you may know how to live in this world. Learn to hear His voice that He may guide you every day. Enjoy His presence that turns fear into hope and courage. Let Him hold your hand and lead you through the bends of life with divine assurance of His power, might, and His presence.

READ COLOSSIANS 2:6–13.

GOD DELIGHTS IN HIS CHILDREN.

Do not allow the world to dictate how you relate to God. The world—those who do not know God and who have never encountered Him at a personal level—would love to hear you make apologies for loving and following God. They think it is naive and cowardly to love and follow God. The world desires to make you look miserable, unfashionable, uncultured, and even foolish for associating yourself with God. The truth is that the world desires what God has so lavishly given you. Eternal life, love, peace, hope, protection, faith, knowledge, wisdom, understanding, discernment, and numerous blessings are things that the heart of man covets. He strives and works hard for them his entire lifetime.

God takes pleasure and delights in His children. God enjoys fellowship with His chosen people. God wants you to enjoy your Christian walk with Him. He wants you to rest in His love. He wants you to know that you are special to Him. His desire is to deliver you from the sorrow and oppression of the enemy so you can serve Him with joy and gladness. "The Lord thy God in the midst of thee is mighty; he will save, he will rejoice over thee with joy; he will rest in his love, he will joy over thee with singing. I will gather them that are sorrowful for the solemn assembly, who are of thee, to whom the reproach of it was a burden" (Zephaniah 3:17).

You see, when a man's ways please the Lord, he makes even his enemies to be at peace with him (Proverbs 16:7). "The Lord taketh pleasure in them that fear him, in those that hope in his mercy" (Psalm 147:11). God delights in your relationship with Him.

READ PSALM 18:16–21.

GOD CHOSE YOU.

Growing up, we played all kinds of games. Usually, two leaders had to select members for their teams. They took turns to call out the names of those they wanted on their teams. The leaders scrambled for the best team players. However, imagine what it would be like not to be selected on any team. Imagine how crushing that would be to a young heart and mind to know they were neither wanted nor valued—they were not chosen.

Imagine God, the mighty King of all the earth, wanted you and chose you for Himself. Even before you were born, He desired you. He made you and called to Himself by His own holy name. You belong to God.

> Blessed be the God and Father of our Lord Jesus Christ, who hath blessed us with all spiritual blessings in heavenly places in Christ: According as he hath chosen us in him before the foundation of the world, that we should be holy and without blame before him in love: Having predestinated us unto the adoption of children by Jesus Christ to himself, according to the good pleasure of his will, To the praise of the glory of his grace, wherein he hath made us accepted in the beloved. (Ephesians 1:3–6)

You did not choose God, instead God chose you before the foundation of the world out of love to walk with Him in holiness. God did not choose you because you were better than others, but because He loved you. He chose you out of His good pleasure. "Ye are a chosen generation, a royal priesthood, an holy nation, a peculiar people; that ye should shew forth the praises of him who hath called you out of darkness into his marvellous light" (1 Peter 2:9).

READ JOHN 15:16.

GROWING IN SPIRITUAL WARFARE

Do you know you are fighting in the Lord's army? What are your weapons for this war and whom are you fighting? How do you train for battle? Do you know you are guaranteed to win?

Train for battle this month! Do not remain behind. Commit to train faithfully for the next thirty days. Practice what you learn and grow as a good soldier of God.

YOU ARE IN A WAR. WHAT IS SPIRITUAL WARFARE?

Every Christian is engaged in spiritual warfare every day. You are fighting an enemy who is cunning and wise. Satan knows how to disguise himself in order to get to you. He is good at fooling God's children and keeping them preoccupied with nonessential matters as he draws their attention away from his attacks.

So who exactly is Satan and what is his warfare like? Look at how God's refers to this enemy: "And the great dragon was cast out, that old serpent, called the Devil, and Satan, which deceiveth the whole world: he was cast out into the earth, and his angels were cast out with him" (Revelation 12:9).

Satan was once a cherub—a highly positioned angel—who ministered before God in the holy of holies. He revolted against God as he got puffed up with pride. See what God said of Him:

> For thou hast said in thine heart, I will ascend into heaven, I will exalt my throne above the stars of God: I will sit also upon the mount of the congregation, in the sides of the north: I will ascend above the heights of the clouds; I will be like the most High. Yet thou shalt be brought down to hell, to the sides of the pit. (Isaiah 14:13–15)

Satan was cast on earth, and he has waged war against God, His work, and His followers ever since. This puts you in opposition to Satan as God's child.

Satan targets Christians who are walking far away from God. Christians who are carnal, who indulge in sin, and who do not enjoy a close walk and communion with God are easy prey for Satan. You must guard your spiritual walk if you will prevail in this warfare.

READ ISAIAH 14:11–16.

HOW DOES SPIRITUAL
WARFARE APPLY TO YOU?

Your fight is against an enemy whom you cannot see with your physical eyes but whose effects are visible and well manifested to be understood. Satan, together with his angels, do not have physical bodies, but they are the evil and hostile powerful spiritual beings who rule and govern over this world. Satan is called the prince of the power of the air, the god of this world, and the prince of this world (Ephesians 2:2; 2 Corinthians 4:4; and John 14:30, respectively).

You fight against the wicked schemes of Satan every day. You fight against spiritual wickedness aimed at thwarting God's work, the spread of the gospel, and your living a victorious Christian life. "For we wrestle not against flesh and blood, but against principalities, against powers, against the rulers of the darkness of this world, against spiritual wickedness in high places" (Ephesians 6:12).

Satan works to get you on his side and to propagate his agenda without even realizing it. Instead of sowing love, and reaching people with the gospel of Christ, he will get you into a corner where the most natural thing for you to do is hate, fight, and talk ill of your brothers and sisters.

Stand your ground as a true follower of Christ and shine your light in the dark world to expose and dispel the forces of evil.

READ EPHESIANS 2:1–9.

THE TRUTH ABOUT SPIRITUAL WARFARE . . .

Once you surrender to follow Christ, you automatically enlist in the army of God. You become an enemy of Satan. Satan seeks opportunities to ferociously destroy as he tears you apart. Satan makes time to scheme and walk around as he looks for ways and reasons to attack you. He seeks to quench your fervor for God, plant doubt in your mind, stunt your spiritual growth, and take control of your life.

How do you stop him? What does the Bible say? How does God equip you for this? Look at God's clear answer! "Be sober, be vigilant; because your adversary the devil, as a roaring lion, walketh about, seeking whom he may devour: Whom resist stedfast in the faith, knowing that the same afflictions are accomplished in your brethren that are in the world" (1 Peter 5:8–9).

We fight back by resisting steadfastly in the faith. Resisting means you are countering what Satan is doing. It means you are stopping him from hanging around you and from taking the good with which God has blessed you. You resist by closing the doors through which Satan attacks you.

Resisting means you are not listening to Satan's suggestions that are contrary to God's Word and instructions. Resisting means you stand for your family and safeguard it from worldliness. You depart from secret sins and follow God out of a pure and sincere heart. Resisting also means you stand firm, take God at His Word, and live by it.

A Christian who is washed by the blood of the Lord Jesus Christ, filled with His Spirit, and living by the precepts of God is a great threat to the devil.

Stay spiritually alert, be vigilant and watch out for attacks.

READ ROMANS 13:12–14.

SATAN'S GREATEST STRATEGY IS DECEPTION.

Satan's greatest strategy in spiritual warfare is deception. He disguises himself and works in situations making them to appear real while he launches his wicked attacks. His packages and deals are attractive, appealing, and enticing.

> For such are false apostles, deceitful workers, transforming themselves into the apostles of Christ. And no marvel; for Satan himself is transformed into an angel of light. Therefore it is no great thing if his ministers also be transformed as the ministers of righteousness; whose end shall be according to their works. (2 Corinthians 11:13–15)

Satan knows that you will identify him for who he is, so he masquerades and twists the truth as he makes you gamble with the truth of God's Word. He has used this war strategy from the garden of Eden—when he confronted Eve and challenged what God had said—throughout history, to this day.

Stay with the truth of God's Word. Watch out for those who give partial truths and guard your conscience from Satan's attack. Don't gamble with God's Word. Whatever God says is settled as truth.

READ GENESIS 3:1–7.

Your mind is a battlefield.

How does Satan fight? Exactly where does he stage his war?

The devil's greatest and favorite battlefield is your mind. Christ, knowing the bad thought being contemplated, challenged the Pharisees in Matthew 9:4 saying, "Wherefore think ye evil in your hearts?" Most battles begin with entertaining the wrong thoughts in our minds. Satan throws evil thoughts to Christians and challenges what God has outlined in His law. But look at God's promise for you today: "Thou wilt keep him in perfect peace, whose mind is stayed on thee: because he trusteth in thee. Trust ye in the Lord for ever: for in the Lord Jehovah is everlasting strength" (Isaiah 26:3–4).

You can win your battles at this grass root level by identifying the thought as being evil and casting it out and refusing to entertain and nurse it in your mind. God has equipped us to identify, cast out evil imaginations, and cause our thoughts to be obedient to Christ, according to 2 Corinthians 10:3–5:

> For though we walk in the flesh, we do not war after the flesh: (For the weapons of our warfare are not carnal, but mighty through God to the pulling down of strong holds;) Casting down imaginations, and every high thing that exalteth itself against the knowledge of God, and bringing into captivity every thought to the obedience of Christ.

Failure to combat evil thoughts will lead you to the next stage, where they turn into temptations.

Let your mind stay on Christ and enjoy His peace as you trust in Him.

Read Ephesians 6:10–17.

WE MUST DEAL WITH TEMPTATION.

Every child of God is subjected to the schemes of the enemy. We are bombarded with appearances of evil every day. God wants us to have victory. He does not want you to give in to temptation. Satan entices us through what we see. When he throws his wicked thoughts, avoid the second look and encounter. The first look or encounter may be unavoidable, but the second is a choice we make that can open the floodgates of trouble. "Blessed is the man that endureth temptation: for when he is tried, he shall receive the crown of life, which the Lord hath promised to them that love him" (James 1:12).

Be wise, Satan throws his baits one at a time at intervals well disguised to conceal his presence and working. Heed God's caution: "Let no man say when he is tempted, I am tempted of God: for God cannot be tempted with evil, neither tempteth he any man: But every man is tempted, when he is drawn away of his own lust, and enticed" (James 1:13–14).

There is a reward for resisting and standing against temptation. God has a crown of life for you. He knows what faces you each day. Remember, He will not allow you to be tempted above what you can stand or bear. God stands with you during every temptation. Call on Him. God desires to see you master and overcome the temptations that come your way every day. Look back at what you are battling one year from today and bear a good testimony that God helped you overcome that temptation.

READ JAMES 1:12–16.

BEWARE AND GUARD YOUR WEAPONS.

You cannot effectively fight any battle without weapons. This is true for both physical and spiritual warfare. The Bible gives us an interesting narration of how God's children found themselves in a situation where they were faced with a fierce enemy yet without weapons. The Philistines, gathering to fight Israel, had defeated God's children before and taken control of their ability to make weapons of war.

There was not a man found in Israel who could make weapons, as all of them together with their booths had been taken captive. Look at a brief section of this narrative: "So it came to pass in the day of battle, that there was neither sword nor spear found in the hand of any of the people that were with Saul and Jonathan: but with Saul and with Jonathan his son was there found" (1 Samuel 13:22).

On the day of battle, Israel was faced with an army of thirty thousand chariots, and six thousand horsemen, and people as sand on the seashore in multitude, yet only Saul and his son had swords. You can read how God used Saul's son to gain victory over the enemy in 1 Samuel 13.

You cannot win spiritual warfare without spiritual weapons. You cannot wing this war and survive. There are many casualties among Christians because the enemy knows us. He knows when we do not have enough weapons with which to fight him. Satan knows when your heart and hands are empty, void of spiritual ammunition. That is when he strikes.

God's Word is your most powerful weapon. Acquire and store it. Guard it. Live by it. Take God at His Word and follow Him wholeheartedly. Depart from sin. This is what dulls your spiritual senses and denies you weapons with which to fight. Feast on God's Word and store ammunition for spiritual warfare.

READ 1 SAMUEL 1:5–22.

September 8

SPIRITUAL WARS ARE REAL.

Imagine receiving a call informing you that a wild bear identified at the entrance of your home was in a ferocious attack mode. Your three children who had gone jogging are on their way home. What will you do? Will you sit still and pray for God to provide a detour, or will you do something? I presume you will take the deadliest weapon you can find and head for the entrance for the sake of your children. Now imagine, God likens our adversary, the devil, to this bear. The fierce and untamed enemy gives no warning as to when he will attack.

God reminds us of this truth, saying, "The thief cometh not, but for to steal, and to kill, and to destroy: I am come that they might have life, and that they might have it more abundantly" (John 10:10).

How do you face such an enemy? Will you sit down and surrender in defeat, or will you try to pray him away? Let us face practical facts about this warfare.

Spiritual wars are as real as physical wars. You have casualties with visible evidence of wounding and maiming. The devil does not play fair. He comes with a clear motive and intention of stealing, killing, and destroying. God warns that Satan walks around as a roaring lion seeking whom to devour. To devour is defined by most dictionaries as to eat up hungrily, to engulf, eat wantonly, and destroy recklessly or voraciously. That defines the enemy who looks for you every day.

You must be spiritually alert. Walk circumspectly as wise men, and not as fools (Ephesians 5:15). It is sin that exposes us the most to the attacks of the enemy. Act thoughtfully as you endeavor to do what God has laid down in His law and save yourself untold turmoil and wounding from your adversary. Don't be a willful spiritual casualty. Guard your walk. Arm yourself with spiritual ammunition from God's Word every day.

READ 1 PETER 5:8–9.

GOD TRAINS HIS CHILDREN FOR BATTLE.

God trains us for spiritual battles in different ways. Sometimes He uses the tough situations He allows to come our way to train us in patience, temperance, focus, and dependence on Him. Sometimes, He allows conflicts in our lives in order to train us in resilience, integrity, honor, truthfulness, and faithfulness. Many times, He trains us using His Word, which is given by divine inspiration. As we read and embrace His Word, to live by it, He trains us in His doctrine. He uses His Word to reproof, to correct, and to train us in all righteousness (2 Timothy 3:16–17).

God's Word is our manual of instruction and training for spiritual wars. His way is simple, clear, and very effective. God admonishes us to be strong in Him. To learn of Him and teach what we have learned to faithful Christians as we endure hardships as good soldiers without entangling ourselves in things which give Satan grounds to attack us. God stresses the need and importance of following Him for those who will fight to win spiritual battles (2 Timothy 2:3).

God does not want you to be ignorant of the devil's devices (2 Corinthians 2:11). He does not want you to be unprepared for spiritual battles either. God gives us strength and equips us with sufficient skills for this battle as He towers over us as a mighty fortress in whom we hide as we fight. Here is your witness that God trains us for battle: "Blessed be the Lord my strength which teacheth my hands to war, and my fingers to fight: My goodness, and my fortress; my high tower, and my deliverer; my shield, and he in whom I trust; who subdueth my people under me" (Psalm 144:1–2).

READ PSALM 18:32–35.

WATCH AND PRAY.

Prayer is God's divine deadly ammunition for believers against Satan. Many spiritual battles are won on your knees as you tarry with God in prayer. The weakest Christian is a great spiritual soldier to reckon with when actively engaged in prayer. Prayer forms a hedge of protection and erects walls that stand strong against our enemy. Prayer places strong boulders in weak areas that serve as entry points for the invasion of the enemy.

What is God's evaluation of your prayer life? Can God charge you with neglect when it comes to the protection of your family through prayer? Can God hold you responsible for the turmoil in your home because you have left things to chance instead of praying earnestly? "Pray without ceasing. In everything give thanks: for this is the will of God in Christ Jesus concerning you. Quench not the Spirit" (1 Thessalonians 5:17–19).

Christ set the example of prayer for us to follow while here on earth. He tarried all night in prayer before choosing His disciples in Luke 6:12–13. In Matthew 14:23, He awoke while still dark to be alone in prayer. After a hard day's work, Christ retreated to pray in Mark 6:46. Sometimes, prayer took the place of His meals. He challenged His disciples, saying, "What, could ye not watch with me one hour? Watch and pray, that ye enter not into temptation . . . " (Matthew 26:40–41).

Every Christian can pray and safeguard against certain spiritual attacks. God asks you to pray without ceasing. He wants you to pray and maintain the vigilant attitude and thought of prayer that keeps you alert and in constant communion with Him. Have your set time for prayer but breathe endless, sincere, and honest heartfelt prayers throughout the day as you go about your business and witness situations for which to pray.

READ MARK 14:37–38.

September 11

PRAYER IS EFFECTIVE.

You are not too weak to pray. God has given you a treasure with which to work wonders and propagate His kingdom while holding the forces of evil at bay. This great treasure, which is also a weapon, is prayer. Every Christian has equal access to the power of God through prayer. There is so much that can change in your life, home, and society if you understand the mighty force behind this weapon. A great percentage of our daily troubles and struggles stem from prayerlessness. God wants you to be a man or woman of prayer. If your heart is pure before God, your prayers will remain deadly. Look at God's admonition to you today regarding prayer:

> Confess your faults one to another, and pray one for another, that ye may be healed. The effectual fervent prayer of a righteous man availeth much. Elias was a man subject to like passions as we are, and he prayed earnestly that it might not rain: and it rained not on the earth by the space of three years and six months. (James 5:16–17; see also 1 Kings 17)

Prayer is that effective, deadly spiritual ammunition that knows no bounds. It is precise and gets to the enemy however disguised and transcends geographical boundaries. The effectual earnest prayers of those who keep themselves from the entanglement of sin possess great power and accomplish wonders.

Your prayers will rout the enemy and send him fleeing. That is why Satan works hard to keep you from praying. Wishy washy prayers are ineffective. Satan likes the lukewarm, dull-minded, and bored Christians whose prayers are nothing short of a joke and an abomination before a holy God.

Prayer that fights the enemy must be definite, purposeful, fervent and heartfelt. You must pray fervently and protect yourself and your family.

READ LUKE 22:31.

OUR WEAPONS ARE MIGHTY.

You are not too weak to engage in spiritual warfare. This is a lie the enemy propagates and uses to keep you subdued and defeated. This is how he enslaves and keeps us helpless. God cannot thrust you into a fierce battle for which He does not provide impeccable artillery and protection. God has given us weapons that subdue vile men at their own will. God's weapons break the well-known, sought-after wicked men and women and cause them to surrender. God has given us His Word by which to live and wage spiritual warfare. How are you using your spiritual weapons? Look at the power of the weapons with which God has equipped you.

> For though we walk in the flesh, we do not war after the flesh: (For the weapons of our warfare are not carnal, but mighty through God to the pulling down of strong holds;) Casting down imaginations, and every high thing that exalteth itself against the knowledge of God, and bringing into captivity every thought to the obedience of Christ; and having in a readiness to revenge all disobedience, when your obedience is fulfilled. (2 Corinthians 10:3–6)

Throughout the years, men and women have tried to set aside God's weapons of choice to tackle life's problem their own way and failed terribly. Spiritual wars are won using spiritual weapons as you follow God's formula. Trust them.

God has given you power. Take charge of your thoughts. Cast down and resist evil thoughts. Resist the evil plans and schemes formulated by Satan against you, those with whom you live, and your surroundings. Resist what is evil and work to let your desires and thoughts be obedient to Christ. It will call for saying no to self many times and yes to God. Stand up and fight for what matters in your life. Use your spiritual weapons today.

READ MATTHEW 18:18–19.

September 13

GOD HAS PROVIDED THE RIGHT ARMOR.

Most enemies attack at your time of vulnerability. Robbers strike in the wee hours of the night when it is dark. They break in when you are asleep and incoherent. They may isolate and carefully entangle you in a place of little defense and where you can neither retreat nor call for help. Surprisingly, Satan uses these same tricks in order to defeat you.

However, what do you do when you are suspicious of an attack? You guard yourself. You sleep with your arms in place. You safeguard your house. You secure your doors and every possible entry point. You ensure your security cameras and alarm systems are working. You may have friends, family members, and law enforcement on standby.

Now, translate these preparations into spiritual preparations against Satan, who like a robber, strikes when you least expect him. God wants you to prepare so your enemy does not find you unprepared. Look at God's admonition:

> Finally, my brethren, be strong in the Lord, and in the power of his might. Put on the whole armour of God, that ye may be able to stand against the wiles of the devil. For we wrestle not against flesh and blood, but against principalities, against powers, against the rulers of the darkness of this world, against spiritual wickedness in high places. Wherefore take unto you the whole armour of God, that ye may be able to withstand in the evil day, and having done all, to stand. (Ephesians 6:10–13)

God has provided the right armor for you to successfully fight every day. The armor is not beneficial unless you put it on and take an active role in the wars Satan wages against you. You will only stand and be safe in this battle against the devil's tricks if you put on God's armor.

You need the whole armor to protect yourself fully. Use it to resist and fight back as you hold onto what the enemy is trying to steal and destroy from you.

READ 1 PETER 5:8–9.

GUARD YOUR LIFE WITH TRUTH.

Imagine your nation is in a fierce battle with your worst enemy. Your enemy has studied your troops and he is excited about the battle. He has tricks under his sleeve of which you know nothing about. In pretense, he "hides" in a place that your soldiers can easily blow him up. Your troops fall for the trick. However, as your army aims at the enemy, something weird takes place just before the triggers are pulled and the ammunitions are fired. All your soldiers' clothes, from waist downward, fall to the ground, including their under garments. Perplexed, all soldiers scarily bend to grab their garments but drop their weapons. All this is seen by the entire world on a satellite broadcast. What effect will this have on the war?

I am afraid this is what the enemy does to many of God's children when they try to engage in spiritual battles.

Satan is a liar. He was a liar from the beginning and all he knows is lying. Conversely, God is truth. His Word is truth. Lying is so foreign that He cannot even associate with it. God does not lie. He cannot lie. God Who warns us against lying reveals that one great weapon with which to fight against the wicked schemes of Satan is truth. "Wherefore take unto you the whole armour of God, that ye may be able to withstand in the evil day, and having done all, to stand. Stand therefore, having your loins girt about with truth, and having on the breastplate of righteousness" (Ephesians 6:13–14).

To gird is to fasten and to hold in place. God is challenging us to tie and hold in place the garments that cover us; those that hide our nakedness and privacy, with truth. Meaning, our lying hurts us more than it hurts God. It exposes us and makes us vulnerable to the dangerous attacks of Satan.

Satan works to make converts who can propagate his methods and schemes through lying. The weapon that defeats Satan at his lying game is the weapon of truth. A lying and dishonest Christian has no ground before Satan. A lying heart is a vulnerable target for the devil. A lying heart is a mirror for a conscience that is under attack. Guard your life with truth.

READ JOHN 8:44.

HAVE THE BREASTPLATE OF RIGHTEOUSNESS IN PLACE.

When soldiers get ready for battle, they protect themselves before they can protect the people and the countries for whom they fight. Soldiers do not go to war without ballistic combat or armor shirts and vests as part of the soldier's protection system. This attire protects the soldier's vital organs, especially the heart. It protects the most vulnerable and the most targeted area in combat. God trains Christians to guard the most vulnerable and the most targeted area in spiritual combat too. This is your heart. Look at God's admonition concerning your vital armor of protection today: "Stand therefore, having your loins girt about with truth, and having on the breastplate of righteousness" (Ephesians 6:14).

You fight the enemy by guarding your heart with the breastplate of righteousness. The breastplate of righteousness is the holiness of heart which God instructs that you embrace as you work your salvation with reverential fear and trembling. This is the obedience that God demands of you as you set yourself apart to be undefiled in a sin-sick world. A heart that burns with an honest desire to please God and flees the enslavement of sin is a powerful counterattack to the devil's plans.

A heart whose appetites and lusts are not kept in check is under the constant surveillance and attack of the enemy. Guard your heart with the breastplate of righteousness. Guard it with all diligence. This is the only way you can engage your enemy at close quarters and cause him to flee without fear or hesitation. Develop a true and burning desire to follow God and safeguard your life.

READ PROVERBS 4:23.

SIN WILL COST YOU VICTORY.

God protects His children in many ways. Most of the time, we are oblivious to God's constant presence and protection in our lives. God also teaches and trains His children to stand against the attacks of Satan. Those who embrace God's training and live by His teachings escape most of the snares the enemy sets in their paths of life. This is because they walk with God Who not only directs their hearts and feet but also opens their eyes to the snares by giving them insight and discernment.

Look at God's assurance of His daily commitment to you: "For the eyes of the Lord run to and fro throughout the whole earth, to shew himself strong in the behalf of them whose heart is perfect toward him. Herein thou hast done foolishly: therefore from henceforth thou shalt have wars" (2 Chronicles 16:9).

Sin is the main cause of defeat in the life of a Christian. In Joshua 7, Achan stole garments, silver, and gold against God's orders before Israel faced Ai in battle. Ai's small army struck Israel's large army until the inhabitants melted with fear. Despite God's promise of protection, Achan's sin led to awful defeat and embarrassment.

When you live in sin, you walk in Satan's territory with your heart and life exposed to his flaming darts. God wants to protect and to show Himself strong on your behalf, but you cannot walk without a protective guard of righteousness around your heart. The situations and sins which constantly cause you to fall are known to Satan. They expose you to his attacks. Sin will keep you weak and defeated by the enemy. The remedy for sin is repentance. Repent. Be restored. Be protected.

READ JOSHUA 7.

PREPARE YOUR FEET FOR BATTLE.

When God's presence is absent in any place, you can expect all kinds of wickedness and evil acts. I find it interesting that God includes guarding and preparing our feet for the gospel of peace as part of our armor against the enemy. Why? It is because God is light. The gospel is good news that dispels darkness and shines the light of God in the hearts of men and women and shows itself in the communities where we live.

There is no greater way to fight against the forces of darkness in any society than for men and women to come to the light of the gospel of peace. Look at God's charge for you today: "Stand therefore, having your loins girt about with truth, and having on the breastplate of righteousness; And your feet shod with the preparation of the gospel of peace" (Ephesians 6:15–16).

The Roman soldiers made themselves ready for any terrain of war by guarding their feet with hard, sturdy shoes. They could launch surprised attacks and put their enemy to flight no matter the weather conditions of the time. For you to fight effectively, you will likewise have to follow Christ, to do and testify of Him as He commands.

There is no distinction between secular and sacred for a child of God. When you get saved, God secures the boundary lines of secular life and puts you into His bracket of sacredness. You are sacred and set aside for God at all times. Be His witness light. You are in your position, situation, job, and current place by God's design. God equips and sets His children in strategic places to be witness lights. Keep your shoes on, and keep your light shining. The world is watching.

READ MATTHEW 5:14–16.

September 18

TAKE YOUR SHIELD OF FAITH.

Has God failed you? Have you found God unreliable and untrustworthy? Can you trust God with your life? Can you depend on Him to be there when you need Him?

Many Christians struggle with these practical questions. There are many of God's children who wonder whether they believed a lie or if God is whom He says He is. This struggle is evident during spiritual warfare. It becomes hard to use the recommended shield of faith to fight back the deadly darts with which Satan fights every day. "Faith? When will He come through and how long will I wait and keep hoping?" they wonder. Nevertheless, it is true that faith is a might spiritual weapon that drives the enemy away. "Above all, taking the shield of faith, wherewith ye shall be able to quench all the fiery darts of the wicked" (Ephesians 6:16).

God will not ask for what is humanly impossible without equipping you. He wants you to exercise that very faith which He put in your life upon trusting Him. In battle, you cannot tell from which direction fiery darts may come. You must trust and do as instructed, believing that whoever gave the instructions is a master at war.

Without faith it is impossible to please God. It is this kind of faith that will send you to your knees in obedience as you trust in the living God. It will keep holding and waiting for God to come through as promised. It will not give up until it witnesses the promises of God come true in your life. It will follow God's instructions in moments when there is no human reason for what you are doing. This faith will protect you from Satan's snares because it counts Him who promised to be faithful.

READ ROMANS 4:16–24 AND HEBREWS 11:6.

YOU HAVE THE HELMET OF SALVATION.

Man can live without food and water for many days without dying, and can survive without air for seconds, but no one can live without hope. God has given us eternal hope, which is as real as your spiritual battles. God wants you to use the hope of salvation, which He guarantees every believer, as your helmet during spiritual combat. Hold on to this hope securely like the helmet protecting your head. Look at God's admonition:

- Take the helmet of salvation . . . (Ephesians 6:17a)
- Let us, who are of the day, be sober, putting on the breastplate of faith and love; and for an helmet, the hope of salvation. (1 Thessalonians 5:8)

It is easy to face an enemy when you are well protected. It is even easier to fight your enemy when you are sure of winning. Such an advantage point gives you the zeal and power to fight with boldness. Conversely, you cannot fight your enemy effectively while gripped with intense fear and the reality of losing. Your shots will be off target. Your focus will be diverted from the battle as you will be preoccupied with the shame, the embarrassment, and the humiliation that follow failure and defeat.

Christians fight all spiritual wars from an advantage point. We have hope. We are assured of winning. Our hope extends beyond this world. It is eternal.

If in this life only we have hope in Christ, we are of all men most miserable (1 Corinthians 15:19). God's children have the promise of eternal life. You can look at this promise of eternal hope of salvation and fight your spiritual battles with bravery, patience, and perseverance.

Be courageous as you wage war knowing that there will be an end to your battles. Fight diligently knowing that you will come out victorious in the end.

READ EPHESIANS 6:12–17.

TAKE THE SWORD OF THE SPIRIT.

You must be well armed and well trained to engage skilled gangsters and soldiers in war. This is because they carry dangerous and deadly weapons. They aim and target with precision. Their intention is to kill instantly. Spiritual warfare can be likened to this kind of fight. You have an enemy who is equipped with deadly ammunition. His desire is to kill, to steal, and to destroy. He targets you, your children, your family, and the work of God. God has not left you at the mercy of this dangerous enemy. God has armed His children with the most potent weapons with which to live in this dark and wicked world. God's weapons are deadly. "And take . . . the sword of the Spirit, which is the word of God" (Ephesians 6:17b).

The Word of God has potential like no other known weapon. It is guaranteed to give you victory. See what God says about the weapon which He has given you to fight the enemy. "For the word of God is quick, and powerful, and sharper than any two-edged sword, piercing even to the dividing asunder of soul and spirit, and of the joints and marrow, and is a discerner of the thoughts and intents of the heart" (Hebrews 4:12).

Within your reach is God's Word which will cut, divide, burn, and drive out the enemy without fail. You can carry this deadly weapon anywhere at any time and it is ready to use instantly. Quote it, stand on its principles, and act on its truths as you refuse the seductive voice and attack of the enemy. It will break stony hearts. It will convict, wash, draw, and heal. Soak in the Word of God and arm yourself with this formidable weapon.

READ EPHESIANS 6:12–19.

ARM YOURSELF WITH THE SWORD OF THE SPIRIT.

God works through unconventional ways to give unimagined victories. Those who take Him at His Word, believing that He will do as He promises, see the wonders of God and experience His mighty victories in their daily battles.

When God wanted to defeat Goliath, the great giant, He did not use the well-known and kingly sword of Saul. He chose the "laughable stones and a sling" of a shepherd boy.

God has given you the right weapons for every war you will face in this world. The weapons may not look deadly to your eyes, but they are divine. Your efforts and your manmade weapons may be more appealing, but they will leave you wounded and defeated. "Is not my word like as a fire? saith the LORD; and like a hammer that breaketh the rock in pieces?" (Jeremiah 23:29).

The Word of God is quick and powerful. It is sharper than the sharpest sword ever used. Once it proceeds from your heart and mouth, it will accomplish what no known human weapon can accomplish. It will shutter rocks of impossibilities into pieces. It will reach to the heart of man however calloused. God's Word will give you light, understanding, and discernment as you deal with the enemy (Psalm 119:130). It will warn you of the prowling of the enemy (Psalm 19:11; Proverbs 2).

Speak God's Word when challenged in situations. Speak it to counteract evil thoughts and actions as you stay on God's side. Resist temptation by deciding to go against it with the truth of God's Word. Satan is resisted with the Word of God. God's Word is a divine weapon specifically designed to fight in spiritual warfare. Take it and use it.

READ HEBREWS 4:12 AND PSALM 119:130.

TRAIN FOR SPIRITUAL WARFARE.

We rejoice when our troops return home safely after triumphing in war. We benefit when they deploy their skills with mastery. We share their pride as we feel safe and secure. However, not many of us stop to ask, "Through what kind of training do these soldiers endure in order to protect us?" Armies which do not train well cannot win major wars. The nation, together with its people, suffer the consequences of their lack of training.

Spiritual warfare is no different. Christians who train for spiritual warfare live victorious lives and enjoy close communion with their Master. Christians who do not train for spiritual warfare are under the constant harassment of the enemy. They cannot enjoy a good relationship with their Savior. God wants you to train for spiritual warfare. God wants you to live a victorious Christian life. Allow Him to train you for battle.

> For who is God save the Lord? or who is a rock save our God? It is God that girdeth me with strength, and maketh my way perfect. He maketh my feet like hinds' feet, and setteth me upon my high places. He teacheth my hands to war, so that a bow of steel is broken by mine arms. Thou hast also given me the shield of thy salvation: and thy right hand hath holden me up, and thy gentleness hath made me great. Thou hast enlarged my steps under me, that my feet did not slip. I have pursued mine enemies, and overtaken them: neither did I turn again till they were consumed. (Psalm 18:31–37)

It is God Who recruits and assigns your place in spiritual battle. It is He who trains and prepares you for your spiritual terrain. God knows what it takes to win. He knows when to train you in patience, in faith, or in trust.

Squirming and complaining will make you miss important training lessons. Listen and let God train your hands for war.

READ 2 SAMUEL 22:32–41.

GOD DOES NOT PROMOTE
THE UNQUALIFIED.

Are you going through the same situations repeatedly? Take inventory. Find out whether you are failing God's training sessions. Learn from your mistakes, if any, and grow into spiritual maturity. You will not be promoted if you stay unqualified.

Most people desire positions of prominence. We serve best when we are in the limelight. However, we dislike God's trainings for those who will serve in positions of honor. It is hard for God to use a man or a woman fully whom He has not taken through His threshing floor of thorough winnowing and sieving. To reject such training is to deny those you serve God's blessings and eternal riches. This is where most of us find ourselves. We are overgrown spiritual babies. Allow God's Word to woo your heart into training today.

> Thou therefore endure hardness, as a good soldier of Jesus Christ. No man that warreth entangleth himself with the affairs of this life; that he may please him who hath chosen him to be a soldier. And if a man also strive for masteries, yet is he not crowned, except he strive lawfully. (2 Timothy 2:3–5)

It is easy to opt for the shortest routes and circumvent important lessons in life. Unfortunately, God does not promote unqualified children. He perfects our mastery as He takes us through the same or similar lessons severally. Endure hardship as a soldier of Christ and attain the approval of Him who has chosen you.

Do not remain in spiritual diapers. Let everyday be a learning day. Embrace your training sessions, listen to God, and let Him train your hands and fingers for war. God will not promote you if you remain unqualified.

READ 2 TIMOTHY 2:15.

SOLDIERS DON'T ENGAGE IN CIVILIAN PURSUITS.

It is hard to participate in what credits the devil and still fight from the ranks of God the Almighty. It will hard for you to win spiritual battles. Soldiers don't engage in civilian pursuits.

God does not withhold good things from His children (Psalm 84:11). God is not shrewd. He does not say no to hurt but to protect you from the prowling enemy. Do not allow your heart to covet what you see in Satan's territory. Do not gravitate toward it. You will pay for it with your life. Remain in the safe umbrella of God's provisions and protection. The devil does not have anything that God has not given you. Embrace God's admonition today and stay safe.

> Wherefore seeing we also are compassed about with so great a cloud of witnesses, let us lay aside every weight, and the sin which doth so easily beset us, and let us run with patience the race that is set before us, Looking unto Jesus the author and finisher of our faith; who for the joy that was set before him endured the cross, despising the shame, and is set down at the right hand of the throne of God. For consider him that endured such contradiction of sinners against himself, lest ye be wearied and faint in your minds. (Hebrews 12:1–3)

As a Christian you are in spiritual combat every day. Soldiers of Christ cannot engage and indulge in civilian leisure activities and be safe. Winning calls for maintaining focus and having singleness of purpose. You must be alert and lay aside what distracts you from the race.

READ 1 CORINTHIANS 9:24–27.

RUN WITHIN THE RULES.

Not many people like rules. Most people do not like to be told what to do. However, most of the systems and organization we admire for their smooth running and success have governing rules. The universe operates within God's rules and principles. What happens when you jump off a ten-foot ladder? You do not turn into a bird and enjoy free flying.

God has divine rules for His children. God's rules are for your good. They are not meant to hurt but to protect you.

> Know ye not that they which run in a race run all, but one receiveth the prize? So run, that ye may obtain. And every man that striveth for the mastery is temperate in all things. Now they do it to obtain a corruptible crown; but we an incorruptible. I therefore so run, not as uncertainly; so fight I, not as one that beateth the air: But I keep under my body, and bring it into subjection: lest that by any means, when I have preached to others, I myself should be a castaway. (1 Corinthians 9:24–27)

It is easy to lose focus and get entangled in your race. It is easy to go past God's governing parameters. God has expectations for all who belong to His army. As we stand in His ranks, we strive to please Him.

Your marked race calls for discipline and running according to the rules. Governing rules will keep you active and effective in your expected location. God's guidelines protect and equip us for battle. If you insist on running outside the set rules you will be a spiritual casualty.

READ 1 PETER 5:8–9.

KEEP COMMUNICATION LINES CLEAR.

Armies at war maintain active and clear communication with their commander in chief. This is how they get their orders. This is how they are directed. A good commander in chief understands his enemy and directs his troops accordingly. He knows when and where his army should attack. He knows when to ask his people to take cover too. Armies cannot fight blindly and win. They must be directed by their leaders.

Spiritual warfare is no different. You are in a deadly war, but you have a divine Commander in Chief. He has guidelines and expectations for you. Look at His admonition today: "Praying always with all prayer and supplication in the Spirit, and watching thereunto with all perseverance and supplication for all saints" (Ephesians 6:18).

Always keep communication lines clear while in battle. This is the only way you can follow directions, target the enemy with precision, get reinforcement, or replenish supplies. Prayer is your quick access pathway to the Commander in Chief.

God is a master planner. He has all the instructions you need to go through life successfully. Stop and commune with Him through prayer. He knows what awaits you today and in the future. He desires to show you what to do. His sheep know His voice. They hear and follow Him (John 10:27). You cannot fight an enemy that you cannot see if you cannot receive orders from the army commander who knows Satan well. You are not fighting against flesh and blood but against principalities and rulers of this dark age. You must hear from God if you are to walk in victory.

When did you last hear from heaven? Pray today if you must stand tomorrow.

READ JOHN 10:4–5.

LEARN TO RECEIVE AND OBEY ORDERS.

Having worked with students for many years, I have observed that students who listen keenly not only follow directions better, but they also excel in their studies. Poor listeners spend endless hours teaching themselves and figuring out what they could have learned in class. I find this to be true in Christian living. Good students of the Word of God who follow and obey God's teachings have higher success rates in spiritual warfare than those who barely hear from their heavenly father.

God's admonitions are not complicated. God is clear and precise in His instructions. God wants you to succeed. "This book of the law shall not depart out of thy mouth; but thou shalt meditate therein day and night, that thou mayest observe to do according to all that is written therein: for then thou shalt make thy way prosperous, and then thou shalt have good success" (Joshua 1:8).

God is not silent about what He expects of you. God speaks. He guides as He clearly shows us how to fight every day. We are enlisted in the Lord's battle and our spiritual victory will come when we learn to receive and obey orders.

There are many battles that the best knowledge and scheme will not grant you victory. Listen to God and diligently follow His commands with total obedience. Great men of spiritual warfare are great men of prayer and the Word. This is how they get their orders. Honest, fervent, and sincere prayer coupled with the diligent study of God's Word from a heart commitment to do as God says are guaranteed to win spiritual wars. Cultivate receiving and obeying orders.

READ JOSHUA 1:7.

DON'T FEAR THE BATTLE.

Not many people like war. This is no different for Christians when it comes to spiritual warfare. The most common default is to shy away and or pretend that spiritual warfare does not exist. This is a trick for which Satan, your enemy, desires to see you fall. He works most in places where there is spiritual darkness or where people are oblivious to his deceitful schemes.

You do not have to fear the battle. God does not throw His children in hot battles only to leave them alone to face a fierce enemy. If your own parents cannot do that, why would God dream of such a thing? God is for you. God is on your side. He is fighting for you.

> Fear not: for they that be with us are more than they that be with them. And Elisha prayed, and said, Lord, I pray thee, open his eyes, that he may see. And the Lord opened the eyes of the young man; and he saw: and, behold, the mountain was full of horses and chariots of fire round about Elisha. (2 Kings 6:16–17)

It is easy to see yourself as a grasshopper whose efforts are insignificant when it comes to fighting the devil. The truth is, you can effectively engage the enemy in the battles he brings your way because you never fight alone. If God were to open your spiritual eyes, you too would realize that you are surrounded with heavenly hosts and divine power.

God fights our battles every day. None of the enemy's moves takes Him by surprise. You are God's priority, and He will not leave you to be humiliated by the enemy unless you make the choice. Stay with God. Embrace your training and witness God's presence and power as you stand your ground in battle.

READ 2 KINGS 6:1–23 AND PSALM 125:1–2.

GOD WILL BE FAITHFUL.

If God were to leave us alone to Satan for one day, Satan would crush and sift us like wheat. God does not leave you at the mercy of this dreadful and fierce enemy. God stands with you in battle. Satan, like Goliath, likes to intimidate and prowl as he sends fear and panic. Do not fall for his dirty tricks. You are well able to mastermind his schemes and win because you have divine help. Christ stands at the right hand of God the Father fighting for you every day. Arise and take your place in battle. Fight for the treasures with which God has entrusted you.

> But this man, because he continueth ever, hath an unchangeable priesthood. Wherefore he is able also to save them to the uttermost that come unto God by him, seeing he ever liveth to make intercession for them. For such an high priest became us, who is holy, harmless, undefiled, separate from sinners, and made higher than the heavens. (Hebrews 7:24–26)

Our Commander in Chief will be faithful to you in battle. Christ trains us, allocates our position in battle, fights with us and for us, while He prays for us. He is your advocate. He has been faced with the temptations you are undergoing. He empathizes and steps in to help you strongly.

God knows what is ahead. Let the words of Christ to the apostle Peter encourage you to keep fighting: "And the Lord said, Simon, Simon, behold, Satan hath desired to have you, that he may sift you as wheat: But I have prayed for thee, that thy faith fail not: and when thou art converted, strengthen thy brethren" (Luke 22:31–32).

READ HEBREWS 4:14–15.

YOU HAVE A GREAT INVITATION.

You are special before God. God wants you to live a victorious Christian life. God is not pleased when you are under the constant harassment of an enemy for whom you are equipped to defeat. You must remember that this is the Lord's battle. You are fighting on God's side. God has every provision for you to fight and win. Call on Him. God is ready to hear and answer you. "Ask, and it shall be given you; seek, and ye shall find; knock, and it shall be opened unto you: For every one that asketh receiveth; and he that seeketh findeth; and to him that knocketh it shall be opened" (Matthew 7:7–8).

Do not take a step further on Satan's road of destruction. You have great exhortations from your Master. Heed and live a victorious Christian life.

- God is faithful to cleanse you from all sin when you repent.
- Come boldly to the throne of grace and receive help for your time of need.
- Call and He will hear. Seek and you will find; ask and you shall receive.
- Be strong in the power of God and fight.

Be persistent. Remain within the rules and run toward the finish line. A great price awaits those who fight to the end. You can have victory. You can reclaim what the enemy has stolen, and you can be close to God again. Seek and follow God just for the single day you are alive. Get back into battle.

READ 2 TIMOTHY 4:7.

October

GROWING WITH GOD

Walk hand in hand with God, and experience restoration as you consistently walk with Him.

SEEK THE APPROVAL OF GOD.

We enjoy great love and peace when God is pleased with our work. God is not like man who is constantly looking for something negative for which to chide you. God sees the good in you. He knows the honesty and the sincerity of your heart. Our heavenly Father not only delights in His children but blesses their efforts. There is nothing you do for Him, regardless of size or magnitude, that goes unnoticed. Look at how God deals with His servants:

> And so he that had received five talents came and brought other five talents, saying, Lord, thou deliveredst unto me five talents: behold, I have gained beside them five talents more. His lord said unto him, Well done, thou good and faithful servant: thou hast been faithful over a few things, I will make thee ruler over many things: enter thou into the joy of thy lord. (Matthew 25:20–21)

Not all comments made by people are worth trusting. You will be flattered in life. Hearts are deceitful and desperately wicked. They will say one thing and mean another.

Learn to walk and do everything as one doing it unto God. You will be frustrated when you work to win the approval and favor of man. Not many people are easy to please. As you walk with God it will become more important to receive His approval than that of people. No better words can soothe your heart to restful sleep than to hear the Holy Spirit whisper, "Well done, thou good and faithful servant."

READ REVELATION 16:15.

KEEP YOURSELF PURE.

Before you take a bath after a busy day of outdoor activities, you remain sweaty and stinky. Those around you may be as uncomfortable as yourself. There will be certain things you may not wish to do in that state just as there may be places you may decline to go. However, it is different when you are clean and fresh. Your interactions and associations may be intimate and without second thoughts. I find this to be true in the spiritual world too.

We are sanctified with the Word of God. The truth of God's Word sets us free to live clean in a dirty world. Make it a priority to take a spiritual bath each day by reading the Word of God. It will reveal hidden dirt and point you to the cleansing fountain. It will create in you a desire not only to get it off but to keep away from getting dirty again. God's Word will make you sensitive to what displeases the Lord. "They are not of the world, even as I am not of the world. Sanctify them through thy truth: thy word is truth" (John 17:16–17).

Take a good look at who you are and what you really look like by reading God's Word today. The Word of God is a true mirror. It will reveal the truth in love without any camouflages. It will bring you to closer proximity with God as you follow its leading. Yes, hide God's Word in your heart that you may not sin against Him.

READ PSALM 119:9–11.

EMBRACE GOD.

Our days are filled with activity. The demands of life dictate our actions and drive us in different directions. We run from morning and exhaust every ounce of energy by evening. This leaves us tired and unfulfilled. God is not blind to what faces you. He desires to help you. God wants you to walk closely with Him.

> What man is he that feareth the LORD? him shall he teach in the way that he shall choose. His soul shall dwell at ease; and his seed shall inherit the earth. The secret of the LORD is with them that fear him; and he will shew them his covenant. Mine eyes are ever toward the LORD; for he shall pluck my feet out of the net. (Psalm 25:12–15)

In Christ are all hidden treasures of life. It is easy to run and work so hard day and night without involving God in your endeavors. God knows what you need. He knows the best place and time to find it. Embrace God and let Him guide you. He is interested in the minute details of your life. Don't toil alone and walk away empty.

Those who fear the Lord are taught and guided of God. God's leading is precise and fruitful. It is purposeful and targeted. God entrusts His secrets to those who fear Him. No man has ever walked hand in hand with God and failed in life.

READ PSALM 86:10–11.

LOVE NOT THE WORLD.

I visited family friends who had just moved to a new home recently. The front porch was unusually but beautifully gated. Out of curiosity, I wondered why they made that addition. It was to safeguard their two-year-old granddaughter. They noted that her first actions were to dash out into the road once the front door was opened. I could not help but think about God's protective boundaries of love for His children. When He says don't, stop or wait, it is not for punishment but for our safety. He sees what we cannot see. He knows everything. Look at His admonition today:

> Love not the world, neither the things that are in the world. If any man love the world, the love of the Father is not in him. For all that is in the world, the lust of the flesh, and the lust of the eyes, and the pride of life, is not of the Father, but is of the world. And the world passeth away, and the lust thereof: but he that doeth the will of God abideth for ever. (1 John 2:15–17)

The world has glamour. The world has allure, but do not be deceived. Satan is the prince of this world, and he will not offer you anything for which you will not pay dearly. The enticement of the world has a costly bite. When you embrace it, you walk away from the umbrella of God's love into Satan's snares.

The lust of the flesh, the attraction to what is evil, and the pride that comes from who you are and what you possess are your worst enemies. Do not love the world.

READ 1 JOHN 2:26–29.

October 5

CULTIVATE A CONTRITE SPIRIT.

God takes pleasure in His children. He delights in those whose minds are set on Him. God takes special interest in those who have a contrite spirit. A contrite spirit signifies and heart that is humble and repentant. This means every Christian can enjoy God's closeness. He does not hold our sins against us when we repent. Do not remain estranged from God for fear of calling on Him. He honors that remorseful spirit.

Look at His promise to you today: "For all those things hath mine hand made, and all those things have been, saith the Lord: but to this man will I look, even to him that is poor and of a contrite spirit, and trembleth at my word" (Isaiah 66:2).

The heart is deceitful and desperately wicked. You can be deceived by your own heart. However, God has a cure and a harness for it. His Word can give tenderness and gentleness to your heart.

God's secrets are with those who fear Him. We can join this team as we pray with the psalmist: "Teach me thy way, O Lord; I will walk in thy truth: unite my heart to fear thy name" (Psalm 86:11).

It is God's pleasure to teach and walk with you as He trains your heart to fear His holy name. A heart that is haughty—a know it all—remains weak, unstable, and unreliable; but God will not overlook you when your heart is contrite—remorseful, tender to hear and follow. Cultivate a contrite spirit.

READ PSALM 34:17–22.

FOLLOW GOD IN FAITH.

God honors faith. Those who believe and take Him at His Word witness His hand at work. Their hearts are stilled during uncertainty as they see the manifestation of His great power. Like the men and women of old who followed God wholeheartedly, they see the results of their prayers. They witness the deliverance of those they love from the fires of the enemy and the opening of doors in areas least expected. They go from strength to strength because God holds them to Himself and steadies their feet in response to their faith. Let's learn from Abraham and follow God in unwavering trust today.

> He staggered not at the promise of God through unbelief; but was strong in faith, giving glory to God; And being fully persuaded that, what he had promised, he was able also to perform. And therefore it was imputed to him for righteousness. Now it was not written for his sake alone, that it was imputed to him; But for us also, to whom it shall be imputed, if we believe on him that raised up Jesus our Lord from the dead; Who was delivered for our offences, and was raised again for our justification. (Romans 4:20–25)

Abraham believed God, and it was credited to him as righteousness (see James 2:23). At a hundred years of age, he believed that his wife, Sarah, who was ninety, would bear him a son as God had promised.

God is not looking for you to do the impossible. He just wants you to experience Him as you take Him at His Word and walk with Him to victory in every sector of your life. Is anything too hard for God?

READ HEBREWS 11:1–2.

STAY UNDER GOD'S UMBRELLA.

God protects His children from the snares of the enemy. He does this, most of the time, by placing His holy and divine boundaries of love and protection around us. Those who identify and stay within God's secure borders are spared endless and fierce attacks of the adversary.

However, to live outside God's demarcated walls of safety is to remain under the constant pursuit of this relentless enemy. God does not enjoy seeing you harassed by an enemy He has equipped you to fight and defeat. "But ye, beloved, building up yourselves on your most holy faith, praying in the Holy Ghost, Keep yourselves in the love of God, looking for the mercy of our Lord Jesus Christ unto eternal life" (Jude 20–21).

Stay within the boundaries of God's love. You will find protection and provision as you remain under the umbrella of God's love and boundaries. Outside of this are ravenous wolves seeking opportunity to hurt and drive you from God. Walk within the boundaries of God's commandments and remain secure from the luring snares of Satan. God's precepts are not burdensome. They are meant to nourish and protect and not to harm you.

God is able to keep you from falling. Christ has the power to present you faultless and undefiled before the Father. Build yourself on the most holy faith as you pray and follow God (Jude 20–24). Walking outside God's circumscribed boundary lines will leave you wounded, scarred, and unfulfilled in life. It will rob you of peace and soundness of mind. Stay within the boundaries of God's umbrella.

READ PSALM 46.

October 8

LOVE GOD WHOLEHEARTEDLY.

In life, when two people love one another wholeheartedly and unreservedly, they enjoy each other's company and fellowship. They cherish one other's presence. In fact, they look forward to that. Life is different when two people cannot agree. Halfhearted and reserved love is as good as a pacifier. It leaves either party disgruntled and unfulfilled. This phenomenon can be applied to our relationship with God.

God wants you to love Him with all you've got. God is not a mean and shrewd master. This kind of love will liberate you to experience Him as you live your life to the fullest. You miss out on God because you don't surrender all to Him. Yield to God's love call today.

> And thou shalt love the Lord thy God with all thine heart, and with all thy soul, and with all thy might. And these words, which I command thee this day, shall be in thine heart: And thou shalt teach them diligently unto thy children, and shalt talk of them when thou sittest in thine house, and when thou walkest by the way, and when thou liest down, and when thou risest up. And thou shalt bind them for a sign upon thine hand, and they shall be as frontlets between thine eyes. And thou shalt write them upon the posts of thy house, and on thy gates. (Deuteronomy 6:5–9)

Put God to the test. Love Him wholeheartedly, embrace His Word, and follow Him diligently as you teach it and see the outcome.

READ JOSHUA 1:8.

DELIGHT IN GOD.

God is a Master like no one you have met in your life. He is almighty, all-powerful, self-existing, and self-sufficient, yet He draws us to Himself. He invites us in His presence and delights in us. How many great people have interest in you as a person? How many truly care to know your daily struggles?

God is more than that. He sees the yearnings of your heart. He looks intently into your needs and desires as your heart warms up to Him and purposes to trust and or follow Him. Look at His promises for you today.

> Trust in the Lord, and do good; so shalt thou dwell in the land, and verily thou shalt be fed. Delight thyself also in the Lord: and he shall give thee the desires of thine heart. Commit thy way unto the Lord; trust also in him; and he shall bring it to pass. And he shall bring forth thy righteousness as the light, and thy judgment as the noonday. (Psalm 37:3–6)

Delight yourself in God. Let your drive in life be to please God greatly to the extent that He is deeply satisfied with your pursuit and motives. Pour your love to God and watch His response.

God's promise will stand for you. Your desires will be granted. This is because they will be in line with God's good pleasure for your life. God will fight for you. He will provide and feed you as He watches over you with His righteous eye. He will vindicate you. Those who have learned the true secret to fulfillment in life have tested God and found Him true and trustworthy.

READ PSALM 84:11–12.

CLEAR THE CLUTTER.

God is eager to listen and respond when His children call. God wants to come to your rescue. He is ready to act on your behalf. However, there is one thing that stops His mighty hand from moving. One thing hinders you from experiencing God's move in your life and in the world around you. Sin. Look at God's commentary on sin:

> Behold, the Lord's hand is not shortened, that it cannot save; neither his ear heavy, that it cannot hear: But your iniquities have separated between you and your God, and your sins have hid his face from you, that he will not hear. For your hands are defiled with blood, and your fingers with iniquity; your lips have spoken lies, your tongue hath muttered perverseness. (Isaiah 59:1–3)

God enjoys walking, fellowshipping, and communing with His children. There is no greater fulfillment in life than to hear God's clear voice and to be led by His mighty hand. Nevertheless, it is easy to forfeit such companionship and miss the favor of God.

Sin makes God turn His face from His children. Sin cuts us from God. Those lies, the grumbling, the defilement, and the endeavored scheming to do evil cause God to sniff and turn away in disgust. It robs us from experiencing God and keeps us under the relentless hand of your enemy. Clear the sin clutter and follow God.

READ PSALM 66:18.

October 11

GOD CONVICTS; SATAN CONDEMNS.

God delights in communing with His children. That is why He does not hold our sins against us. When we repent, He wipes them away and keeps them far from us just as the east is from the west. He puts them behind His back where He neither sees nor remembers them.

However, Satan is good at using those very things from which we repent to plague our conscience. He uses them against us and lets us know how useless and unfit for God's service we are. He works to make us believe that God can no longer hear or work with us. That is called condemnation. God does not push us aside when we sin. He woos us to Himself and guides us on the safe road of getting back to Him. Satan is an accuser of God's children.

> And the great dragon was cast out, that old serpent, called the Devil, and Satan, which deceiveth the whole world: he was cast out into the earth, and his angels were cast out with him. And I heard a loud voice saying in heaven, Now is come salvation, and strength, and the kingdom of our God, and the power of his Christ: for the accuser of our brethren is cast down, which accused them before our God day and night. (Revelation 12:9–10)

Be careful to whom you listen. God convicts you and woos your heart to Him. Satan, conversely, condemns and accuses you. He plagues you with criticism as he mocks and beats you to shreds. Satan makes you feel worthless and hopeless. He works to keep you from getting back to God. Remember, he is the accuser of brethren.

You are God's child. You are loved and accepted. God's clear formula for getting back to Him when you miss the mark is repentance. He is faithful to forgive when you repent. Are you under conviction or condemnation?

READ 1 JOHN 3:20–21.

BE MOLDED BY GOD.

You are like a bundle of treasure before God. You possess great potential in the hands of a mighty God. There is no telling what God can make of you let alone do with you as you walk and yield to Him.

Our mistakes hold us back and keep us from the presence of the almighty God, who alone can establish us in life. None of us is perfect. Even at your very best you still make messes. God knows that. However hard we try, He knows that our own righteousness is like filthy rags before Him (Isaiah 64:6; Romans 3:10). He knows our frailty; He remembers that we are dust before Him—a people who are weak, frail, and prone to falling (Psalm 103:14).

Yet, God never leaves us alone to struggle in our weaknesses and failures. Every day presents a new opportunity for us to be molded by God and to be made into something of value that is profitable to God and to the world around us. Look at God's admonition for you today.

> Then I went down to the potter's house, and, behold, he wrought a work on the wheels. And the vessel that he made of clay was marred in the hand of the potter: so he made it again another vessel, as seemed good to the potter to make it. Then the word of the Lord came to me, saying, O house of Israel, cannot I do with you as this potter? saith the Lord. Behold, as the clay is in the potter's hand, so are ye in mine hand, O house of Israel. (Jeremiah 18:3–6)

Those who display the splendor of God are men and women with passions like yours, but they surrender and allow God to prune and shape their lives into what they could never imagine. You are God's candidate for great things.

READ ISAIAH 49:5–6.

SERVE GOD EVEN WHEN YOU ARE THE ONLY ONE.

Many of us fear to stand strong for what we believe. We are easy to sway and quick to follow other people. It is harder to remain firm in your position when what you believe is neither popular nor liked. However, within you is a resilience that can make a difference. God has equipped you with what you need to be a good ambassador regardless of who surrounds you or where you find yourself. Do not abandon what you believe even if you are an alone voice. Do not go against your conscience to gratify other people's desires.

Look at God's admonition: "How long halt ye between two opinions? if the Lord be God, follow him: but if Baal, then follow him. And the people answered him not a word" (1 Kings 18:21).

God is counting on you to serve Him. He is not asking you to serve Him when there are other people to copy and follow. You are God's supreme choice for where you are at this hour. Serve Him. Do not waver or wait to see who else will serve Him. If God is truly God to you, serve Him!

Distance yourself from rebellious crowds and side with Joshua in saying, "But as for me and my house, we will serve the Lord" (Joshua 24:15). God does not make incompetent and wimpy vessels which are unable to serve Him. He has endowed you with what you need to serve Him with all your might. There are many people who are looking and waiting for you to be faithful before they, too, can commit to walking in obedience. Serve God.

READ LUKE 18:27–30.

BUILD A HEAVENLY TREASURY.

As you stay busy on earth, working and providing for your life, be sure to build an eternal treasury in heaven too. Many people will leave treasured possessions when they die only to step into glory and discover how profitless their labors were toward heaven.

> Lay not up for yourselves treasures upon earth, where moth and rust doth corrupt, and where thieves break through and steal: But lay up for yourselves treasures in heaven, where neither moth nor rust doth corrupt, and where thieves do not break through nor steal: For where your treasure is, there will your heart be also. (Matthew 6:19–21)

Invest heavily in the things of God. Make a deliberate choice to serve God each day and build His kingdom. Pray for God's people, serve, witness, and grow into spiritual fruitfulness. Take part in what God is doing and do it wholeheartedly as one serving God and not man. Seek the approval of God and transfer your storehouses from earth to heaven. In heaven, we shall all discover we could have given God much more.

Live as a sojourner. Do not drive your stakes too deep here on earth. Do not hold too tightly to what God gives you. Purpose to be God's conduit; one who channels the blessings He gives to other people. Do not be a hoarder. All that God gives does not belong to you. Have the right perspective and seek His desire as you look at His blessings in your life.

Constantly think of eternity. "What does God expect of me today? Why did He give me this opportunity? What does He require of me? What does He want me to do? What is God saying today?" Build your treasures in heaven.

READ MATTHEW 6:25–34.

SLOW DOWN.

Life is busy. Maintaining a career, a home and going about family activities does not leave many people with down time for relaxation let alone thinking. What effect does this have on one's spiritual growth and stability? It is hard to hear from God when there is hardly any time to stop and listen. This leaves God's children empty and unstable. When times of testing come, we find ourselves fearful, hopeless and with nothing on which to hold or calm our hearts.

Walking and growing with God demand slowing down to tune in and listen. The bottle-neck speed that characterizes our dot.com age will deny you the coveted treasure of knowing God. Modernism not only dictates but sells its lie that makes you believe that you must be first, faster, and not miss any opportunities along the way. God's teachings are different.

> For thus saith the Lord God, the Holy One of Israel; In returning and rest shall ye be saved; in quietness and in confidence shall be your strength: and ye would not. But ye said, No; for we will flee upon horses; therefore shall ye flee: and, We will ride upon the swift; therefore shall they that pursue you be swift. (Isaiah 30:15–16)

God says slow down, calm down, step aside, be alone for some time, stop, retreat, and listen! If you find yourself running nonstop from morning till evening, day in day out, you must guard against physical and spiritual weariness. Your growth will be stunted. Your spiritual senses will be dull and in need of tuning through the sharpening of God's holy Word. Slow down and recharge with God.

READ PROVERBS 21:5.

MEDITATE AND REFLECT ON GOD.

Imagine you have been an active spiritual leader of over two million people for many years. Time has come for you to hand over to a younger head. What advice would you give to ensure the success and well-being of those many people who are dear to your heart?

Moses faced this situation as he handed the children of Israel to a new captain, Joshua. This was Moses's charge: "This book of the law shall not depart out of thy mouth; but thou shalt meditate therein day and night, that thou mayest observe to do according to all that is written therein: for then thou shalt make thy way prosperous, and then thou shalt have good success" (Joshua 1:8).

Taking time to read, understand, and practice God's Word does not look like a formula for great success in our modern day, but God says it is. "Blessed is the man that walketh not in the counsel of the ungodly, nor standeth in the way of sinners, nor sitteth in the seat of the scornful. But his delight is in the law of the Lord; and in his law doth he meditate day and night" (Psalm 1:1–2).

Meditating on God's Word will fill your life with awesome benefits. You will be like a tree which is planted by the riverside. You will yield precious fruit as expected all the time. God promises to proper you in all your endeavors. You shall be established.

Time spent with God is time well spent. Give God His time, and He will help you to accomplish much more with your remaining time. Retreat, step aside, slow down, sit down, and grab your Bible, pen, and paper. Read, reflect, and embrace the truth of God's Word. Soak in it and draw strength for today and courage for tomorrow. Keep your spiritual life aglow with the nourishment that results from meditating on God's holy and divine Word.

READ DEUTERONOMY 11:18–23.

EMBRACE GOD'S GRACE.

God's grace is like no other gift you have received in life. It draws the unlovable to the treasured and merciful arms of our Lord and Savior, Jesus Christ. Grace takes the filthy, whose lives and hearts are plagued with a guilty conscience because of sin, and brings them to the cleansing fountain where their crimson red sins are washed away leaving the sinful heart as white as wool.

Grace is God's gift to help you live a victorious, meaningful, and fulfilled life. Embrace grace. "For by grace are ye saved through faith; and that not of yourselves: it is the gift of God: Not of works, lest any man should boast" (Ephesians 2:8–9).

God extended His mercy and unmerited favor to draw and hold you dear to Himself. You are the beloved of God. He chose you because He wanted you. He wants to walk with you and help you in your everyday life. Do not let God be abstract to you.

I have yet to meet someone who got a treasured gift that never rejoiced or enjoyed it. Enjoy the gift of God. Walk tall as you appreciate what God has done. Enjoy His presence and delight in His protection. Rejoice at the wisdom and knowledge which He gives and use it to the fullest. Giggle in His mercy and shake off the heaviness of spirit with which the enemy enjoys holding you captive. Enjoy your freedom and walk from the shackles of sin to live a fulfilled and victorious life in Christ. Embrace grace and grow.

READ 1 JOHN 3:1–2.

STRIDE PATIENTLY.

It is easy to look at the coveted Bible character Joseph and see him lavished with all the riches and honor of Egypt and forget his long path of loneliness and disappointment along the way. It is hard to envision the prime minister, a man only second to Pharaoh, scrubbing dirty pots and mopping floors in prison. It is also easy to think that men and women who enjoy such accolades had head starts in life and their paths were full of wealthy and significant godfathers. Joseph endured many years of hard labor before getting to that position of power and influence.

With what are you struggling today? Are you misunderstood? Does no one care to understand or are those you know and love quick to pass judgment for lack of spiritual discernment? Stride with patience. Joseph went through similar situations but that did not stop God from accomplishing His will and work as planned. God will come through with His blessings as He has promised. Look at His promise today:

> And we desire that every one of you do shew the same diligence to the full assurance of hope unto the end: That ye be not slothful, but followers of them who through faith and patience inherit the promises. For when God made promise to Abraham, because he could swear by no greater, he sware by himself, Saying, Surely blessing I will bless thee, and multiplying I will multiply thee. And so, after he had patiently endured, he obtained the promise. (Hebrews 6:11–15)

The Christian journey is not a sprint but a marathon. Stride with patience. God will not delay but will come through and do as promised. You, too, like Abraham, can wait and hold onto you promise: "surely blessing I will bless thee, and multiplying I will multiply thee" (Hebrews 6:14).

God is not unfair. Believe His promise in Hebrews 6:10 and keep honoring Him: "For God is not unrighteous to forget your work and labour of love, which ye have shewed toward his name, in that ye have ministered to the saints, and do minister."

READ 2 CORINTHIANS 2:9.

BE TRANSFORMED BY GOD.

What would your answer be if God stopped you amid your endeavors today and asked, "Who are you?" God gives each one of us moments where He confronts us. These moments may be embarrassing, as they reveal hidden truth about ourselves, but God's intention is to draw us to Himself. God does not ask such questions because He does not know us. He knows everything. He is working to save us from the things we hold dear to our hearts without realizing how they hurt and deny us His blessings.

Embrace your encounters with God. Be honest with Him so He can bring healing, victory, and blessings in your life. Look at how He helped Jacob through such an encounter:

> And he said, Let me go, for the day breaketh. And he said, I will not let thee go, except thou bless me. And he said unto him, What is thy name? And he said, Jacob. And he said, Thy name shall be called no more Jacob, but Israel: for as a prince hast thou power with God and with men, and hast prevailed. (Genesis 32:26–28)

Jacob was Esau's brother. He acquired Esau's birthright with the lure of a bowl of lentil soup. He deceived his father, Isaac, by successfully feigning to be Esau and thus inherited his brother's blessings. Jacob was a schemer and a liar. At Elbethel, Jacob encountered God Who confronted him for who he was. God gave Jacob a new name. Israel was no longer a lair but a prince who prevailed with God. He triumphed with God and no longer attained possessions deceitfully. It is this same Jacob from whom the twelve tribes of "Israel" proceeded.

Embrace your defining moments of encountering God and move on to walk in newness of life and live in victory. Who are you? Allow God to change your destiny by transforming you.

READ 2 CORINTHIANS 5:17.

DISPLAY GOD'S SPLENDOR.

It is easy to advocate for a party, a team, a club, or an association to which you belong. However, it is a great privilege to stand in the ranks of God's army to stand for Him and to display His splendor. Many of us underrate the honor God has given by drawing us to Himself and making us sons and coheirs with Christ. In a chaotic world characterized by fear, hate, enmity, and selfishness, God has equipped His children to make a difference by exemplifying His qualities.

Think about eternity as you face each day. Your standing for Him today will be credited to your heavenly treasures. Look at God's exhortation today: "To appoint unto them that mourn in Zion, to give unto them beauty for ashes, the oil of joy for mourning, the garment of praise for the spirit of heaviness; that they might be called trees of righteousness, the planting of the Lord, that he might be glorified" (Isaiah 61:3).

You are living today under God's divine and sovereign plan to display His splendor. You are God's workmanship and coworker to display His splendor and presence to this world. He does not demand more than He has equipped you to do.

Show forth the praises of Him who has called you out of the kingdom of darkness into His marvelous kingdom of light (1 Peter 2:9). Sing praises to Him. Put on your garment of praise and cast your spirit of heaviness and despair to God. Let Him take care of your burdens. Walk free from the bondage of the evil one and let your life glorify God. Allow people to see a reason to believe God through your life. Let His splendor be displayed through you.

READ JEREMIAH 31:16–17.

October 21

LET GOD BE YOUR SHEPHERD.

God's shepherding arms are tender to all His children. He understands what awaits you today. He knows when to fill your heart with courage and when you must take shelter. He understands the fears of your heart because of the uncertainties of the time and that is why He guides you with the skillfulness of His hands.

Let Him turn your heart from the troubles that plague your soul to quiet pastures that will nourish, refresh, and calm your life. Enjoy the comfort of the Shepherd today. "The Lord is my shepherd; I shall not want. He maketh me to lie down in green pastures: he leadeth me beside the still waters. He restoreth my soul: he leadeth me in the paths of righteousness for his name's sake" (Psalm 23:1–3).

Sheep trust and follow their shepherd. They do not question when led to a different pasture or spring of water. They are confident that their owner has their best interest at heart. They eat and drink what is set before them with joy and pleasure.

Growing intimately with God requires your trust and surrender to His sovereignty and leadership. Do not rely on who you are or what you think you are. You do not know what is best for yourself. God knows. Relinquish your stubbornness to God and let Him direct your life. You will never be all God desires of you until you learn to be led of Him. God's choices may seem contrary, but He will lead you to green pastures and satisfy you with peace.

READ JOHN 10:27.

Let God be a Father.

The presence of a good father can make a great difference in our lives. Imagine the tender love, care, protection, provisions, and his presence. Good fathers care for the welfare of their wives and children. They create an atmosphere for growth, stability, and maturity. The family enjoys peace, joy, and fulfillment. God, our heavenly Father, does it better than our good earthly fathers. He wants you to enjoy His presence and love. "A son honoureth his father, and a servant his master: if then I be a father, where is mine honour? and if I be a master, where is my fear? saith the Lord of hosts unto you, O priests, that despise my name. And ye say, Wherein have we despised thy name?" (Malachi 1:6).

We love, honor, and respect our earthly fathers. We live with them until we are of age and enjoy their provisions and care. We trust them and depend on their strength and ability. We formulate and pattern our behavior after their favorable character traits and are happy to be called by their names.

God, your heavenly Father, deserves unmatched respect and honor. Do not struggle in life alone. You are never too old to relate to God as your Father. Get closer and develop deep love. Reverence Him and hold Him in high regard. Be delighted in Him and cultivate a strong relationship. Listen and follow. Failure to relate to God as a Father will lead to significant struggles with burdens and emotions.

Read Matthew 7:9–11.

SEEK GOD.

Life is full of challenges. You cannot navigate the rough terrains of life alone. In fact, you don't have to. God never created you with the intention of punishing or leaving you to carry the heavy burdens of the day alone. He wants to walk with you. Give your burdens to God and allow His hands of grace and mercy to nourish your soul and give you strength to face a new day. "For the Lord searcheth all hearts, and understandeth all the imaginations of the thoughts: if thou seek him, he will be found of thee; but if thou forsake him, he will cast thee off for ever" (1 Chronicles 28:9).

There is nobody who just finds himself close to God. Those who are intimate with God walk and work at developing the relationship.

- When you seek Him early you will find Him (Proverbs 8:17).
- You will find Him when you search for Him wholeheartedly (Jeremiah 29:13).
- When you draw close to God, He draws close to you (James 4:8).
- Let your heart thirst for Him. He will show Himself to you (Psalm 63:1).

There is no one who has monopoly over God. You can have as much of Him as you want and be as close as you desire. You just have to do your part. God is close to those who call on Him out of truth and honesty (Psalm 145:18). Those who do not seek God do not grow spiritually.

READ PSALM 27:8 AND ISAIAH 55:6–7.

LOVE GOD.

It is hard to see or appreciate the goodness of the Lord throughout your life when you only focus on momentary troubles. God loves you. Take a mental tour of the past years and see how He has stood with you and fought your battles. Remember the many times He stepped in tough situations and gave you strength and courage to face the unknown. Look at His unmerited favors as He has lavished you with His blessings. You have more reasons for which to thank God than to complain. Embrace His love but let Him see and know that you love Him, too.

> Ye have seen what I did unto the Egyptians, and how I bare you on eagles' wings, and brought you unto myself. Now therefore, if ye will obey my voice indeed, and keep my covenant, then ye shall be a peculiar treasure unto me above all people: for all the earth is mine: And ye shall be unto me a kingdom of priests, and an holy nation. (Exodus 19:4–6)

True love shines like the sun's rays on a perfect spring day. It penetrates, gives a glow, brings brightness, accentuates beauty, banishes cloudiness of heart, and fills you with joy and optimism. True love is enticing. It is seductive. It demands a response. Once you drink of it, nothing else satisfies.

God loves you. You are peculiar and special. Don't stand aloof! Reciprocate His love and take spiritual strides toward Him. "Taste for yourself and see that the Lord is good" (Psalm 34:8). Love Him unreservedly. Those who leave all and go wholeheartedly for God enjoy the best part of life here on earth.

READ PSALM 34:8–14.

DEPART FROM SIN.

God has washed us with His precious blood and drawn us to Himself out of His great love. God's gift of salvation is like no other gift you have received in life. Salvation takes the filthy sinner, washes him, holds his hand, and makes him to sit at the table with the King of kings and the Lord of lords. Salvation takes the despised and makes them honorable. It takes the beggar and exalts him to prominence in God. It takes the valueless and makes them vessels of honor in the kingdom of God. You are God's treasured possession. Do not allow sin to take away your honor and prestige. Look at God's admonition:

> For if after they have escaped the pollutions of the world through the knowledge of the Lord and Saviour Jesus Christ, they are again entangled therein, and overcome, the latter end is worse with them than the beginning. . . . But it is happened unto them according to the true proverb, The dog is turned to his own vomit again; and the sow that was washed to her wallowing in the mire. (2 Peter 2:20, 22)

Before salvation you were free to live in the filth of sin. Christ has washed you with His blood. You are clean and no longer a smelly outcast. God has filled you with His knowledge and wisdom to help you judge between good and evil. Walk like a child of the light.

Do not return to your mire of sin. The world looks and laughs at you. A lifestyle of sin gives good reasons for people to mock at God. Do not let a sinful pattern cause people to ridicule and despise you. You are far too precious to God for that.

READ 1 CORINTHIANS 6:9–13.

CHERISH THE WORK OF THE CROSS.

Familiarity breeds contempt. This can be true regarding the great and divine work of salvation for believers. It is easy to forget what it took to be called the Son of God. We can take it for granted and live like people who were never redeemed. God, in His great love, left heaven and all its glory and splendor to purchase us with His own blood and to live among sinful and rebellious people. He has given us a place of honor among the beloved and the noble people in the world. This is how God displays His love for us.

> And as Moses lifted up the serpent in the wilderness, even so must the Son of man be lifted up: That whosoever believeth in him should not perish, but have eternal life. For God so loved the world, that he gave his only begotten Son, that whosoever believeth in him should not perish, but have everlasting life. (John 3:14–16)

Make it a point to think back to what Christ accomplished for you on the cross and be thankful. When the heart loses the view of the cross it becomes arrogant and cold to the things of God.

Do not take it for granted that it was the work on the cross that:

- Purchased your redemption and gave you freedom from sin (Ephesians 1:7).
- Triumphed over Satan and gave you power over sin (Colossians 2:13–15).
- Reconciled us to God and now presents us blameless before the Father (Colossians 1:20–22).
- Will deliver you from the presence of sin someday (Galatians 1:4).

Cherish the cross that has made us sons of God, coheirs with Christ, a peculiar people.

READ COLOSSIANS 1:20–22.

CHERISH THE PRESENCE OF GOD.

Who can make war against you when God puts His tender hand of love and care around you? God's presence is a favor that not only thwarts the wicked schemes of enemies but also frustrates their strategies while securing the children of God under the holy umbrella of the Lord God Almighty. What an honor for God to walk and commune with you as He shields you with His abiding presence. There is no greater honor and favor in the world than for God to walk with man.

> And the LORD went before them by day in a pillar of a cloud, to lead them the way; and by night in a pillar of fire, to give them light; to go by day and night: He took not away the pillar of the cloud by day, nor the pillar of fire by night, from before the people. (Exodus 13:21–22)

Two people may preach the same message using the same Scripture, yet one may have a tremendous impact over the other because of the presence of God in his life. Individuals and families can be distinctly different because of the presence or absence of God in their lives.

- God's presence preserved Daniel from the lions which devoured his accusers in the same den (Daniel 6).
- God "blessed the house of Obededom, and all that pertaineth unto him, because of the ark of God" (2 Samuel 6:12).

Seek God's presence; the same that accompanied Israel in the wilderness. His presence is a safeguard, a guide, and a source of blessings. Seek and cherish the presence of God.

READ PSALM 16:11.

CHERISH THE PRESENCE OF GOD (CONTINUED).

When God's presence abides in the life of an individual, a family, a society, or a nation, there is peace, stability, growth, and progress. Conversely, you cannot hide the havoc, the turmoil, and the restlessness that prevail when God withdraws His presence.

Joseph, a slave in a foreign land, was a prosperous man because of the presence of God. His conniving brothers remained to be ordinary people in a free land devoid of God's hand and presence in their lives. "And Joseph was brought down to Egypt; and Potiphar, an officer of Pharaoh, captain of the guard, an Egyptian, bought him of the hands of the Ishmaelites, which had brought him down thither. And the LORD was with Joseph, and he was a prosperous man" (Genesis 39:1–2).

Three Hebrew boys who would not bow to worship King Nebuchadnezzar were bound and thrown into a fiery furnace. God's presence (the fourth man) in the fire preserved them and let them out free and unharmed yet the same flames consumed those who carried the three men.

- Sin will keep the presence of God from your life and family.
- God abides with those who are upright in heart.

Like Joseph, you can honor God even when no one else does. God's presence will set you apart in this world like nothing else will.

READ PSALM 15:1–5.

BE COMMITTED TO THE SAVIOR.

The best way to enjoy life is to be committed to your Lord and Savior, Jesus Christ. There is a worldly notion that propagates halfhearted loyalty that tempts Christians to partially commit to God while loving the world. This is a lie from the enemy to make you miss the treasures of God while leaving your heart plagued with the pleasures of sin and stinging consequences. Those who have learned the secret of true peace, joy, fruitfulness, and fulfillment love the Savior committedly.

> Not as though I had already attained, either were already perfect: but I follow after, if that I may apprehend that for which also I am apprehended of Christ Jesus. Brethren, I count not myself to have apprehended: but this one thing I do, forgetting those things which are behind, and reaching forth unto those things which are before, I press toward the mark for the prize of the high calling of God in Christ Jesus. (Philippians 3:12–14)

Burn the old bridges in your life and be committed to God and leave no room for retreat. Do not allow your mind to dwell on failure, weakness, and the fear of not making it. Christ who has called you is faithful. He gives power to all He saves to become children of God—strong and mighty despite their having been wimpy or weak.

Press on and purpose to be committed to the Savior despite what you may face. Purpose in your heart to finish the race honorably and victoriously.

READ 2 TIMOTHY 4:5–8.

Confess your sin.

There is no one who does not sin. However, those who are redeemed and washed by the blood of the Lord Jesus Christ sin less as they follow God wholeheartedly. God has open access through the power of repentance where we receive forgiveness. It is because of such that God welcomes us into His presence, imploring us to approach His throne of grace with boldness that we may receive mercy and grace to help in our time of need. "If we say that we have no sin, we deceive ourselves, and the truth is not in us. If we confess our sins, he is faithful and just to forgive us our sins, and to cleanse us from all unrighteousness. If we say that we have not sinned, we make him a liar, and his word is not in us" (1 John 1:8–10).

You are saved by grace, but you have a fleshly body which fights against your spirit. When you sin, run back into the arms of God in true repentance as you purpose in your heart and mind to turn from that sin.

Unconfessed sin gives Satan a reason to accuse and torment you. Sin will cause God to hide His face from you. He will not hear when you pray. Sin will keep the presence of God from your life and make you vulnerable to the attack of the enemy. Sin is like rottenness in the body. It will deprive you of good health, rob you of your possessions, and plunge you into worry, anxiety, and despair.

Read James 5:16.

EXCEL IN PRAISE.

Imagine you have two coworkers. One is always grumpy and complains about anything and everything. He is critical and his comments are mean and stinging. His triumph is in putting people down while boasting of his daily achievements. The second is calm, gentle in her approaches, speaks words of encouragement, and seeks ways to lift your spirit. She is thankful even for the smallest things at work and in life. With whom would you desire to associate?

I catch myself wondering what God sees when He looks at His children and how much grumbling and complaining reach His throne of mercy. Look at God's desire:

> Oh that men would praise the LORD for his goodness, and for his wonderful works to the children of men! . . . Oh that men would praise the LORD for his goodness, and for his wonderful works to the children of men! . . . Oh that men would praise the LORD for his goodness, and for his wonderful works to the children of men! (Psalm 107:8, 15, 21, 31)

It is easy to develop a pattern of prayer where asking is your central theme. The truth is, God knows all your requests before you even ask. Cultivate a tradition of praise in your life. Worship and praise God for who He is as you thank Him for what He has done.

Praise will unlock God's power and presence in your life. God inhabits the praises of His people (Psalm 22:3). Praise will soothe, uplift your heart, and drive away depression and hopelessness. Satan's activities will be frustrated and conquered with honest praise to God. Make melody in your heart and praise God as you go about your business and evaluate its effect at the end of each day.

READ PSALMS 8 AND 100.

November

LIVING BY THE PRINCIPLES OF GOD'S WORD

Do you know that God has laid down wonderful principles by which to abide and live a fulfilled life? Let us explore them this month as we grow in our Christian walk.

GOD WATCHES OVER HIS WORD TO PERFORM IT.

Has anybody once made a promise that you depended on, but failed to come through as you had hoped? Dealing with disappointments can be tough, yet this is a familiar road for all of God's children. For the Christian, disappointments do not arise because God does not fulfill His promises, but because He does not tell us when or how He will accomplish His Word to us.

It is hard to wait when your back is pressed against the wall or when you are desperate. However, regardless of where you find yourself today or the tough circumstances that surround you, we can be sure of one thing. God does not lie, and He will come through as He has promised. You may neither know how nor when God will show up, but trust that He will keep His promise and He will stand with you. "For when God made promise to Abraham, because he could swear by no greater, he sware by himself, Saying, Surely blessing I will bless thee, and multiplying I will multiply thee. And so, after he had patiently endured, he obtained the promise" (Hebrews 6:13–15).

God will do as He has promised. None of the good promises He has made to you will fail. God is not like a man who may promise and forget, lie about it, or even lack the ability to do it. You have no reason to fear.

When God promised in Genesis 22:17, saying, "In blessing I will bless thee, and in multiplying I will multiply thy seed as the stars of the heaven . . ." Abraham was faced with a situation that was humanly impossible. But because nothing is impossible with God, Sarah bore a son to Abraham in their old age. Hold onto the consolation that your faith is anchored in a Savior who cannot lie. He will come through for you as promised.

READ NUMBERS 23:19.

November 2

GOD'S WORD WILL PRESERVE YOU.

The world is experiencing unrest and uncertainty. Many people's hearts are filled with despair, hopelessness, and dissatisfaction. There is a deep longing for peace, stability, and fulfillment. Most times, we search for such treasures in people and things that only add to our frustrations.

God, who understands the times in which we live, is here for you. Unlike what surrounds you today, God is dependable and trustworthy. He is sovereign and He knows what is best for you. Anchor your hope and your life in His Word which has clear directions and great strength for every situation. "Man shall not live by bread alone, but by every word that proceedeth out of the mouth of God" (Matthew 4:4).

Embedded within the laws of God's Word are lifelong precepts by which man has to live. Nothing will give you greater freedom, joy, contentment, and ultimate fulfillment in life than living according to God's Word. It is easy to search for answers everywhere else except the Word of God.

God's Word will give you clear direction on what cause of action to take. It will warn you when you are going astray. It will guide you back to the right path and give you knowledge and wisdom with which to operate as you make decisions. His Word will protect you from unseen snares and paths that lead to destruction. It will keep you from sin with its deadly scars and consequences. It will keep your heart tender with mercy and compassion while maintaining a live conscience. It will give you peace in the night and soundness in your body. It will preserve you!

READ PSALM 119:105.

GOD'S EYE IS ON THE RIGHTEOUS.

When you woke up this morning, God's eyes were watching you, and you will remain in His vicinity for the entire day. God will not forsake His people. Regardless of what your surroundings dictate, God stands with those who love Him. Determine in your heart to love and follow God wholeheartedly despite what everyone else does. God stands with individuals, families, and communities that purposefully follow Him, regardless of where they live or what surrounds them. God wants to stand for you today.

Look at your role in this divine deal: "For the eyes of the Lord run to and fro throughout the whole earth, to shew himself strong in the behalf of them whose heart is perfect toward him" (2 Chronicles 16:9).

Every day, God's eyes move and search back and forth throughout the whole world as He looks for people who have hearts turned toward Him so He can show Himself strong on their behalf. The opposite is true. God looks for those whose hearts are haughty and proud before Him so He can frustrate their plans and humiliate them. He disappoints the devices of the crafty so that their hands cannot perform their enterprises and turns the ways of the wicked upside-down (Job 5:2; Psalm 146:9).

There are no regrets for those who align themselves with the living God. God watches over the affairs of the righteous. He shines His face on the upright at heart (Psalm 11:7). Pattern your heart after God, and He will not forsake you. You will enjoy His browsing eye of concern as you become the envy of the wicked.

READ JOB 36:6–7.

GOD DELIVERS HIS CHILDREN.

God hears the cry of His children. God does not keep silent or turn a deaf ear to those who call and cry out to Him. When you have no voice, no place, no status, and even no way out, remember that you have a God Who cares for the least of the people who live on earth today. Look to Him. Talk to Him. Make Him your anchor at all times. This is the same God Who cares for young ravens which cry in the forest for want of food. The One Who feeds the little sparrow that is of insignificant value. He loves you. "The angel of the Lord encampeth round about them that fear him, and delivereth them. . . . The righteous cry, and the Lord heareth, and delivereth them out of all their troubles. The Lord is nigh unto them that are of a broken heart; and saveth such as be of a contrite spirit" (Psalm 34:7, 17–18).

The children of Israel were held in bondage under hard and cruel labor for about four hundred years. God could not keep silent as their cries ascended to Him. He sent Moses to Egypt, saying, "I have surely seen the affliction of my people which are in Egypt, and have heard their cry by reason of their taskmasters; for I know their sorrows; And I am come down to deliver them" (Exodus 3:7–8).

God's angels surround and minister to those who fear the Lord. God knows what you face. He sees the desperation and cannot keep silent as your cries ascend to Him. He knows your sorrow, and He will deliver you. You can count on Him to be faithful.

READ PSALM 37:34–40.

GOD FIGHTS FOR HIS CHILDREN.

God has power to do things that not only perplex you but leave the world marveling. When He decides to fight for a man, who can stop Him? He has power to make a highway in the sea and to hold your hand and lead you through tough situations with victory. Do not focus only on what surrounds you today. Look to God Who has the power to do exceedingly abundantly above what you may ask or think according to His power that works in us.

Look at God's admonition today: "Fear ye not, stand still, and see the salvation of the Lord, which he will shew to you today: for the Egyptians whom ye have seen today, ye shall see them again no more forever. The Lord shall fight for you, and ye shall hold your peace" (Exodus 14:13–14).

The Egyptian army pursed Israel as she journeyed through the wilderness. When she came to the Red Sea, God dried the waters and she passed on dry land. Egypt pursued Israel using the special highway that God had miraculously laid for His children.

It is recorded that "in the morning watch the Lord looked unto the host of the Egyptians through the pillar of fire and of the cloud, and troubled the host of the Egyptians, And took off their chariot wheels, that they drave them heavily: so that the Egyptians said, Let us flee from the face of Israel; for the Lord fighteth for them against the Egyptians" (Exodus 14:24–25). God drowned the Egyptian army. "Fear not. God will fight for you. Be still and know that He is God" (Psalm 46:10).

READ PSALM 23:5.

THE SOUL THAT SINS DIES.

You can be free from familial and even generational sins. God does not hang your parents' sins over your head or use them to determine your eternal destiny unless you make it your choice. God gives everybody a clean slate in life to either emulate what they like, change it, or walk on a totally different road. God offers new life and a new path of life for those whose circumstances could have left them chained and disadvantaged for eternity. "Behold, all souls are mine; as the soul of the father, so also the soul of the son is mine: the soul that sinneth, it shall die" (Ezekiel 18:4).

"The fathers have eaten sour grapes, and the children's teeth are set on edge" was a commonly used proverb in Israel implying that children were punished for their father's sins (Jeremiah 31:29–30). God resounded the truth of His Word as He reassured them that it is only the soul that sins that will die.

God does not hold you responsible for other people's sins. You may be disadvantaged by the wrongs committed by others, but you are held responsible for you own choices and actions. If you chose to walk in the sinful paths of your parents or forefathers, you will be guilty of the same sin and therefore liable to the consequences according to God's order.

You are not obligated to follow a sinful path. It is a choice. You can be different regardless of what lifestyles have been exemplified before you. It's the soul that sins that dies.

READ EZEKIEL 18:20–23.

November 7

GOD PRUNES HIS CHILDREN.

There are many fruit trees in the world. These trees are suited for different climates and geographical locations. Fruit trees found in temperate or tropical climates may not produce fruit if they are planted in cold, wintery climates. God in His wisdom knows how to feed each continent with abundant fruits despite their different climates, and He has Christians in strategic places all over the world too. You are suited for where God has planted you. His desire is for you to produce fruit in abundance as you stand for Him. Look at His formula for producing fruit:

> Every branch in me that beareth not fruit he taketh away: and every branch that beareth fruit, he purgeth it, that it may bring forth more fruit. . . . If ye abide in me, and my words abide in you, ye shall ask what ye will, and it shall be done unto you. Herein is my Father glorified, that ye bear much fruit; so shall ye be my disciples. (John 15:2, 7–8)

Trees do not yield much fruit unless they are groomed, nurtured, and pruned as required. You are a branch on Christ, who is the Vine. God is not only pleased but glorified when His children bear a lot of fruit. That is the whole reason you are still in the world today—to bear fruit that abides.

Pruning calls for cutting and discarding what is undesirable as you make room for what is good and profitable. God uses different means to prune those from whom He desires fruit. Some methods look harsh and are painful. Hang on. He is preparing you for a season of fruitfulness.

READ HEBREWS 12:6–14.

BE MINDFUL OF YOUR MEASURES.

God uses people to meet diverse needs in this world. God knows whom to gift and bless as He looks at prevailing needs. You are a conduit for God's goodness and blessings to others. It is easy to hoard God's blessings for yourself as you overlook His call to help others. Do not close your eyes to the needs surrounding you today. Reach out and make a difference in the lives of others as God nudges your heart and opens your heart to those who need your help. After all, what we have belongs to God and He desires that we use it to His honor and glory.

Let us listen to Him today: "Give, and it shall be given unto you; good measure, pressed down, and shaken together, and running over, shall men give into your bosom. For with the same measure that ye mete withal it shall be measured to you again" (Luke 6:38).

The earth is the Lord's and all that is in it. It is a privilege to serve God with what He gives us to freely enjoy. Be mindful how you do it. God has a way of weighing us in His balances through those He permits to come our way. Serve heartily, doing everything as unto God and not to man.

"Withhold not good from them to whom it is due, when it is in the power of thine hand to do it. Say not unto thy neighbour, Go, and come again, and tomorrow I will give; when thou hast it by thee" (Proverbs 3:27–28). Remember, God loves a cheerful giver. Watch the measure you use. God will reward you. Do it wholeheartedly. He has the power to keep your blessings flowing.

READ 2 CORINTHIANS 9:6–9.

November 9

GOD BLESSES HIS CHILDREN.

It is easy to take credit for the blessings with which God fills our lives. Dedication and hard work pay good dividends. Nevertheless, it is not our great planning and skillful execution of our work that determine the blessings we abundantly enjoy from God. What explanation do you give for those who work harder than yourself but have little or nothing to prove it? Most times, God, who is sovereign and all-knowing, simply choses to bless us abundantly because He has a divine agenda in His heart.

Humanism teaches us to hoard great percentages of what we possess and earn for ourselves. However, this is not a mindset that comes from God. God implores us to share His blessings. Look at His admonition today:

> And God is able to make all grace abound toward you; that ye, always having all sufficiency in all things, may abound to every good work: (As it is written, He hath dispersed abroad; he hath given to the poor: his righteousness remaineth for ever. Now he that ministereth seed to the sower both minister bread for your food, and multiply your seed sown, and increase the fruits of your righteousness;) Being enriched in everything to all bountifulness, which causeth through us thanksgiving to God. (2 Corinthians 9:8–11)

God has blessed you beyond measure. He has given you all you need and much more. Be generous and mindful of the needy. It is God that blesses the work of your hands so you can produce wealth. He gives you health and soundness of spirit and mind to labor wisely. He blesses your efforts and defends your cause so you can be enriched.

You are blessed because God has been on your side. Let your heart overflow with thankfulness.

READ PSALM 29:11.

THE WAGES OF SIN IS DEATH.

"I am sorry, please forgive me," is not a common phrase for most people. We like to look good and make those around us see and acknowledge our goodness. When we sin against God, who knows all things regarding every individual, our first response is to run away. Running does not make things right. God has laid down a clear and sure path for anyone who sins and falls short of His expectations and will. This path is called repentance.

Repentance is being remorseful and honestly sorry for your wrongs and not a mere outward sorrow because you were caught, or your wicked deeds are exposed to others. God has to deal with sin when there is no repentance. "For the wages of sin is death; but the gift of God is eternal life through Jesus Christ our Lord" (Romans 6:23).

It is not God's desire that any man should be estranged from Him. God does not delight in the death of a sinner (Ezekiel 18:23). It is His desire that all come to the saving power of His Son, Jesus Christ. From creation, God has always given man a choice. Choices have consequences.

To choose the path of sin is to choose death. Sin, as it has been commonly said, will keep you longer than you desire, cost more than you want to pay, and take you further than you intend. Sin will scar you more than any whip will and injure you more than any wound. Sin will wound you spiritually, physically, and emotionally. The ultimate cost of sin is death.

You don't have to choose the way of sin. You can be made clean. You can live free from condemnation and the fear of tomorrow. Christ gives eternal life. Choose Him and live.

READ JOHN 3:17–21.

THERE IS SALVATION FOR WHOSOEVER BELIEVES.

We live in a world of inclusion and exclusion. You cannot belong or participate in everything your heart desires. You may not feel welcome or comfortable in certain places and groups for obvious reasons. You will feel comfortable with some people and not others. However, all of us have an unbiased invitation from God. God, who does not respect or elevate one individual over the other, disseminates His love equally. When you say yes to Him, you may feel like He loves you above all His children, but all who belong to Him feel this way. No one is an outcast before God. You are important.

God has a place in His house for you. Heaven is for you too. Look at God's promise. It includes you. "For God so loved the world, that he gave his only begotten Son, that whosoever believeth in him should not perish, but have everlasting life" (John 3:16).

Man is born a sinner. You are not a sinner because you sin, but you sin because you are a born sinner. There is no one who is born sinless. We are all descendants of Adam and Eve, patterned after their fallen sinful nature which is enmity with God. God has a laid-out plan to reconcile us to Himself through Christ Jesus. "He that believeth on him is not condemned: but he that believeth not is condemned already, because he hath not believed in the name of the only begotten Son of God" (John 3:18).

It is not God's will for any to perish. That is why He has opened His redemptive plan to everybody. Whosoever believes in Him shall not perish but will have everlasting life. God loves you. There are many distorted teachings regarding the paths that get people to heaven. Tithing or giving offerings and alms do not guarantee a passage to God. Good works, baptism, catechism, and even prayer and fasting do not get you to heaven either. Despite what you may have learned, know that salvation only comes by Jesus Christ. Believe in Him.

READ ROMANS 10:8–11.

GOD WILL NOT WITHHOLD GOOD.

Tough situations can make one question and doubt the love of God. God cares for you. God understands what surrounds you and He knows how to respond to your needs. God is not stingy. He is not mean, and neither does He delight in your sorrow and affliction. Contrary to what you may believe, God rejoices when you rejoice and hurts when you hurt. God is quick to bless and to stand with His children.

Look at His promise to you: "For the Lord God is a sun and shield: the Lord will give grace and glory: no good thing will he withhold from them that walk uprightly. O Lord of hosts, blessed is the man that trusteth in thee" (Psalm 84:11–12).

God is a light and a protector to His children. He is gracious and deals kindly as He sheds His mercy and glory on us. God does not withhold anything good from those whose walk is upright.

There is no reason for you to wander away from God or loiter in the camp of the enemy. There are no greener pastures outside the gates of God's boundaries. Beware, what glitters may not be gold. What looks like denial may be a loving gesture of grace and protection from God. Accept it and wait on God. "The young lions do lack, and suffer hunger: but they that seek the Lord shall not want any good thing" (Psalm 34:10). God will not withhold good from you.

READ LUKE 11:9–13.

WE HAVE A PART IN TEMPTATION.

Every Christian is tempted. There is a false notion that makes us think and believe that only weak Christians face temptation. We all face seductions regardless of our spiritual standing, position, and rank in God's service. Temptations also come in different magnitudes. You will face what you may consider small or big temptations. How we handle those everyday provocations, regardless of their magnitude, determines how well we stand with God and content for the faith. Temptations test and reveal the character of a Christian. It is good to know that God does not leave His children to gamble with temptation alone.

> Blessed is the man that endureth temptation: for when he is tried, he shall receive the crown of life, which the Lord hath promised to them that love him. Let no man say when he is tempted, I am tempted of God: for God cannot be tempted with evil, neither tempteth he any man: But every man is tempted, when he is drawn away of his own lust, and enticed. Then when lust hath conceived, it bringeth forth sin: and sin, when it is finished, bringeth forth death. Do not err, my beloved brethren. (James 1:12–16)

When the serpent presented his temptation to Eve in the garden of Eden, he did not force her. He enticed. All of Eve's senses were functional and she could have chosen to run, call for help, turn away, or say no. And yet, she yielded (Genesis 3).

The devil does not make you sin. You have a role to play in your temptations. Satan entices as he focuses on areas where you are most vulnerable. Remember, you have other choices. You don't have to yield to temptation.

READ 1 JOHN 2:14–17.

November 14

YOUR TEMPTATIONS ARE WEIGHED.

God, who created you, understands you very well. He knows the fabrics He used to weave you with intricacy. This means that He knows what you can and cannot handle. He also knows the best times for you to face temptations. This is because temptations are not meant to crumble and destroy, but to build, shape, grow, and draw us closer to Him. Look at God's expectations for His children in times of temptation:

> Wherefore let him that thinketh he standeth take heed lest he fall. There hath no temptation taken you but such as is common to man: but God is faithful, who will not suffer you to be tempted above that ye are able; but will with the temptation also make a way to escape, that ye may be able to bear it. (1 Corinthians 10:12–13)

Your temptations are weighed. God will not permit you to be tempted above what you can withstand. You will not face anything that nobody else has not faced before. The deep desires and appetites which gnaw at your heart have and will always be.

There is no temptation that is irresistible. Be sober! Be vigilant! Look around, there is a way out. Within you, too, is God-given strength to help you overcome. Don't be quick to yield to your temptation. Instead, be quick to call on God, who will not only show the way out but will help you master each temptation that you may help others effectively.

READ JAMES 1:2–4.

BE SPIRITUALLY MINDED.

It is easy to be carnal, indifferent, or spiritually dull. Our adversary, the devil, desires to see many of God's children in this state. It is easy for him to steal, kill, and destroy when we are spiritually docile. He can camouflage easily and use his characteristic deception when our spiritual senses are dull and insensitive. Do not leave the treasures with which God has blessed you to chance. Engage in spiritual exercises that will get you back in the safe umbrella of God's presence.

You will have great spiritual influence in people's lives if you are spiritually minded. The world is full of carnally minded people. Can a Christian be different? Look at what God says about spirituality and carnality:

> That the righteousness of the law might be fulfilled in us, who walk not after the flesh, but after the Spirit. For they that are after the flesh do mind the things of the flesh; but they that are after the Spirit the things of the Spirit. For to be carnally minded is death; but to be spiritually minded is life and peace. (Romans 8:4–6)

The world is full of people who will benefit from those who are spiritually minded. The many who are suffering are longing for real answers to their problems. Those under the chains of sin are looking for real freedom. Lonely and desperate hearts are desirous of lasting solutions in life.

Be spiritually minded. Walk with God and have the touch of God on your life. Let God give you the tongue of the learned that you may have His timely Word for the many who are weary (Isaiah 50:4). Walk in God's power, that you may effectively help the many desperate hearts with whom you interact every day.

READ 1 JOHN 1:5–7.

DON'T RUN AHEAD OF GOD.

Does God seem silent, indifferent, and ultimately late in certain areas of your life today? Do you feel like taking action to initiate or speed up progress?

Step back and wait on God. God is not late. Don't run ahead of Him. God works at His own pace and in His own fashion, and He understands the times because He sees the beginning from the end. When we run ahead of God, not only do we ruin His perfect plan and will for us, but we settle for God's second best as we forfeit the ultimate good purposed and prepared for our lives. Sometimes, we miss His plan and blessings altogether. Look at your situations through the eyes of God today:

> To everything there is a season, and a time to every purpose under the heaven: A time to be born, and a time to die; a time to plant, and a time to pluck up that which is planted. . . . He hath made everything beautiful in his time: also he hath set the world in their heart, so that no man can find out the work that God maketh from the beginning to the end. (Ecclesiastes 3:1–2, 11)

God has your life under His control. He knows the right time for you to be on earth, go to school, get married, and rear a godly family as you serve Him.

God is a master planner. Look at how orderly His creation is despite the billions who engage it every day. God knows what is best for you at every stage of your life. He will not fail you. Be patient and watch out for His boundaries in your life. Those are God's arms of protective grace, mercy, and love. Wait on the Lord. I say again, wait.

READ PSALM 27:13–14.

HAS GOD DEPARTED?

What happens when God decides enough is enough and withdraws His abiding presence from an individual, home, community, or nation? What are obvious signs of God's departure? What consequences follow such a move or action from God? Look at what happened to the children of Israel when God took such a stand against His beloved people:

> And the ark of God was taken; and the two sons of Eli, Hophni and Phinehas, were slain. . . . Phinehas' wife, was with child, near to be delivered: and when she heard the tidings that the ark of God was taken, and that her father in law and her husband were dead, she bowed herself and travailed; for her pains came upon her. . . . And she named the child Ichabod, saying, The glory is departed from Israel: because the ark of God was taken . . . (1 Samuel 4:11, 19, 21)

Very sad but sobering words are recorded in Judges 16:20 concerning God's choice servant, Samson, who was in a strange woman's lap: "And he awoke out of his sleep, and said, I will go out as at other times before, and shake myself. And he wist not that the Lord was departed from him."

You are faced with an enemy whose aim is to drive you from God. Be careful how you live. Israel lost the glory of God. Samson did not realize that God had departed. Where is God in your life?

God's presence is your greatest protection in life. It is more effective than the best army a land can possess and the fiercest guard you will ever post for your home. Do not gamble with what will drive the presence of God from your life. You cannot do life without Him.

READ 1 CORINTHIANS 15:33–34.

FIRE BURNS.

God, in His sovereign will, created us with the liberty to make choices. However, every choice has consequences. Good choices often have pleasant and desirable consequences unlike the bad ones. As you may realize, we are free to make choices but not the resultant consequences. God chooses the repercussions.

You are faced with an enemy whose aim is to drive you from God. Be careful how you live today. Think about your choices. Evaluate your possibilities and options today. Involve God in what you do, and listen to His wise counsel.

> Lust not after her beauty in thine heart; neither let her take thee with her eyelids. For by means of a whorish woman a man is brought to a piece of bread: and the adultress will hunt for the precious life. Can a man take fire in his bosom, and his clothes not be burned? Can one go upon hot coals, and his feet not be burned? So he that goeth in to his neighbour's wife; whosoever toucheth her shall not be innocent. (Proverbs 6:25–29)

Stop and analyze your steps today. To where are your thoughts and feet leading you? Be sober, be vigilant; because "your adversary the devil, as a roaring lion, walketh about, seeking whom he may devour" (1 Peter 5:8). Contrary to popular belief, Satan does not just target the weak and frail. He is looking for God's precious children, both the weak and the strong. He desires to conquer the most influential.

No Christian is too strong for Satan. Guard your heart. Guard your feet. Don't play with fire; it will burn.

READ JAMES 1:12.

GOD WILL MEET YOUR NEEDS.

There is no one who can charge God with neglect. God maintains the earth and the universe with His great power and wisdom. He takes care of all creation. God is more than able to meet all your needs. From creation, God had an eternal plan for sustaining the world. There are no needs that take Him by surprise. Have you talked to Him about your needs today? God is dependable and He has the power to meet all our needs. "And the Lord God said, It is not good that the man should be alone; I will make him an help meet for him" (Genesis 2:18).

When God created Adam, He took it upon Himself to meet Adam's need. Despite the impeccable beauty with which Adam was surrounded, God saw that it was not good for man to be alone. God put Adam to sleep and with His own hand, created Eve whom He took to Adam.

When Israel journeyed from Egypt to Canaan, God took it upon Himself to provide for the millions He had delivered from bondage. When Christ was surrounded with crowds as He taught in different places, He fed and met their needs.

You are God's business. God will take care of you. There is no need too great for God to meet. Numbers have never been a problem to God. You will not be faced with any situation for which He will not have a solution. Don't be afraid. Just believe. God will meet your needs.

READ MATTHEW 6:25–34.

GOD DOESN'T SHOW PARTIALITY.

God does not show favoritism, but He has favorites. Everyone can be God's favorite. God does not have a pool of first- and second-class children. All His children are special. You are special and you can be God's favorite. Look at God's testimony and admonition on this matter: "Then Peter opened his mouth, and said, Of a truth I perceive that God is no respecter of persons: But in every nation he that feareth him, and worketh righteousness, is accepted with him" (Acts 10:34–35).

God does not show partiality. He is not a respecter of persons. He is dear to all who decide to walk in His fear and righteousness. There is no second-class citizen before God. Your status, gender, power, color, age, influence, or nationality does not determine your standing before God. You can enjoy as close a relationship with God as you desire. The Lord is righteous in all his ways, and holy in all his works. The Lord is nigh unto all them that call upon him, to all that call upon him in truth. He will fulfil the desire of them that fear him: he also will hear their cry, and will save them (Psalm 145:17–19),

God's arms of love and care are open unto all, and this includes you. You, too, can be God's favorite.

READ PSALM 145:9–21.

GOD FAVORS THE RIGHTEOUS.

Do you feel unimportant today? Does it feel like you do not belong to the "meaningful" circles of people's lives? Do you feel cut out and left to chance with no eye of compassion, heart of mercy, or act of kindness? That may be true. Nevertheless, there is a greater truth. God loves and favors you; you matter before Him.

God has better things to say about you. Before you believe what everybody thinks about you, listen to God. Before you step out with fear, worry, and anxiety, think about who you are as a child of God. "But let all those that put their trust in thee rejoice: let them ever shout for joy, because thou defendest them: let them also that love thy name be joyful in thee. For thou, Lord, wilt bless the righteous; with favour wilt thou compass him as with a shield" (Psalm 5:11–12).

God favors His children. He makes those who put their trust in Him to rejoice. This is because He defends them. He makes those who love and delight in Him to be joyful in life. He takes it upon Himself to defend those who walk uprightly like one who is keeping vigilant watch against an enemy to ensure they are protected.

Those who find God find favor with Him (Proverbs 8:35). Those who diligently seek for good find God's favor (Proverbs 11:27). "A good man obtaineth favour of the Lord: but a man of wicked devices will he condemn" (Proverbs 12:2).

You have many reasons to rejoice and go about your business with joy and gladness. Don't go by people's opinions. Believe God.

READ PSALM 30:1–7.

GOD GIVES GRACE.

Our daily walk with God can be likened to the natural terrain of life. Some days we are on flat planes; other times we are either descending or ascending a mountain. In all those times, God is faithful. He does not leave us in the valleys of life only to surface again on the mountaintops. Look at the testimony of one of God's choice servants who was faced with uncertainty and wonder:

> For this thing I besought the Lord thrice, that it might depart from me. And he said unto me, My grace is sufficient for thee: for my strength is made perfect in weakness. Most gladly therefore will I rather glory in my infirmities, that the power of Christ may rest upon me. Therefore I take pleasure in infirmities, in reproaches, in necessities, in persecutions, in distresses for Christ's sake: for when I am weak, then am I strong. (2 Corinthians 12:8–10)

Has your life been characterized with numerous challenges in the past months? Have things been painful and even unbearable? Do you feel like God remained silent when He should have spoken out loudly for you? Are you still perplexed with what is going on in your life? You are not alone. All of God's children go through times of trial and challenges. God does not leave any of His children alone in those moments.

Every Christian, like Paul, has a thorn that keeps him close and dependent on God. Learn to graciously live with your infirmities, insults, and difficulties because God's grace will be abundantly available for you and He shall manifest His strength in your weaknesses.

READ PHILIPPIANS 4:11–13.

GOD GIVES GRACE TO THE HUMBLE.

The ways of God are higher than our ways, and so are His thoughts. He sees what our eyes cannot see even when it is well hidden, disguised or camouflaged. God does not see as man sees. God looks at the heart and dissects the intentions and motives behind what we see and believe. This is the same God Who humbles pride and stands against arrogance.

Remain true to yourself and look unto God when confronted with proud and arrogant people. God knows how to help His children. He knows how to fight for you. He will gird you with strength and do what man cannot do for you. Watch and see God at work. "But he giveth more grace. Wherefore he saith, God resisteth the proud, but giveth grace unto the humble" (James 4:6).

God is a rock of offense; a stumbling block to those who will neither hear nor follow Him. He is the rock that the builders rejected that has become the cornerstone. He is gracious to the humble.

Hannah came to this knowledge and left us a testimony from which to learn, saying,

> There is none holy as the Lord: for there is none beside thee: neither is there any rock like our God. Talk no more so exceeding proudly; let not arrogancy come out of your mouth: for the Lord is a God of knowledge, and by him actions are weighed. The bows of the mighty men are broken, and they that stumbled are girded with strength. They that were full have hired out themselves for bread; and they that were hungry ceased: so that the barren hath born seven; and she that hath many children is waxed feeble. (1 Samuel 2:2–5)

READ 1 SAMUEL 2:6–10.

November 24

GOD GIVES POWER TO BE WEALTHY.

It is God Who fills you with strength each day. He protects you. He makes your feet steady, prepares you for your battles and fights with and for you to give you victory. With His gentle care, He supports and makes you great. He ensures that His boundary lines fall for you in pleasant places. It is God Who gives you health and skill to prosper. He fills you with will power, knowledge, wisdom, and understanding. Let us heed God's caution today as we evaluate the blessings with which He has filled our lives: "And thou say in thine heart, My power and the might of mine hand hath gotten me this wealth. But thou shalt remember the Lord thy God: for it is he that giveth thee power to get wealth, that he may establish his covenant which he sware unto thy fathers, as it is this day" (Deuteronomy 8:17–18).

Are you living in abundance of goods and substances? Have you been prosperous this year? Are you enjoying the comforts of a warm place to live, good food, and pleasant means of traveling? Remember, this did not come to you because of your wonderful abilities.

It is not by your own power or might that you have prospered. Don't be tempted to think that your intellect, good thinking, planning, or even investments have gotten you where you are today. Let us get off our high horses and express our gratitude. Bow before your Maker and give God thanks.

READ JAMES 4:13–17.

GOD FILLS US WITH BOUNTY.

God has been with you this year. Many were His personal visits that you may have assumed to be normal, if not deserved, occurrences. His focus was to see that you were well cared for. As He saw your need, He walked by and watered the land richly. He monitored, safeguarded, and prospered that for which you labored.

Take a moment and reflect on how God has blessed you this far.

> Thou visitest the earth, and waterest it: thou greatly enrichest it with the river of God, which is full of water: thou preparest them corn, when thou hast so provided for it. Thou waterest the ridges thereof abundantly: thou settlest the furrows thereof: thou makest it soft with showers: thou blessest the springing thereof. Thou crownest the year with thy goodness; and thy paths drop fatness. (Psalm 65:9–11)

In moments of doubt and fear, His rays of hope and courage filled your heart and He steadied you again. In moments of hopelessness and despair, He carried you. It is God Who has surrounded your life with blessings and crowned the year with goodness and plenty. Acknowledge and thank Him.

If God were to take away His eyes from us for a moment, our lives would turn in the wildest direction you could imagine. If He were to withdraw His hand of grace and protection, we would lose everything almost in an instant. God has been good to us. God loves you. He cares for you. Take time and bless Him for His goodness, kindness, and mercy.

READ JEREMIAH 31:15.

YOU ARE BLESSED OF THE LORD.

When you stop to count your blessings, your heart will be astounded by how much God has blessed you. God has not poured His blessings on you because you are better than other people. God lavishes us with His bounty because He has a divine agenda for us to fulfill. God blesses us because He is good. He loves you. That is His nature and He cannot walk away from it. Look at His promise today and see the pure love behind it:

> Ye that fear the Lord, trust in the Lord: he is their help and their shield. The Lord hath been mindful of us: he will bless us; he will bless the house of Israel; he will bless the house of Aaron. He will bless them that fear the Lord, both small and great. The Lord shall increase you more and more, you and your children. Ye are blessed of the Lord which made heaven and earth. (Psalm 115:11–15)

You are blessed beyond measure. God delights in you. You have no reason not to trust Him. He is your help and shield, ensuring your comfort and safety. God has been mindful of you (Psalm 28:7).

God is not done yet. He is constantly thinking about you. He will see to it that He blesses you personally. Just honor and reverence His name. God will increase you more and more together with your children. Yes, you are blessed of the Lord who made heaven and earth. Take time and thank Him.

READ PSALM 115:17–18 AND ROMANS 8:18.

HAVE YOU THANKED GOD?

November 27

God has been your help this year. He has stood with you and carried you under His wings when times were tough. He has preserved your life and protected you in many ways. He has comforted and directed you by His grace and love. God loves you. God has not treated us as our sins deserve but He has been merciful and mindful of us. Let us confess His goodness as we acknowledge His mighty hand at work in our situations.

> If it had not been the Lord who was on our side, now may Israel say; If it had not been the Lord who was on our side, when men rose up against us: Then they had swallowed us up quick, when their wrath was kindled against us: Then the waters had overwhelmed us, the stream had gone over our soul. (Psalm 124:1–4)

If it had not been for the Lord who was on your side, you would not have made it this far. The torrents of the world would have engulfed and drowned you in despair. If it had not been of the Lord, you would have crumbled at the accusations of Satan and man and lost hope. The devil would have sifted you like wheat (Luke 22:31). If it had not been for the Lord, you would not have emerged victorious from all the things you faced this year.

You have escaped the evil snares at the Lord's doing. You are alive to testify of God's grace. You are a testimony of God's faithfulness. Will you take time to thank God for His goodness and kindness?

READ PSALM 136.

November 28

TAKE TIME AND THANK GOD TODAY.

The password to God's presence is thanksgiving. The password to fulfillment and contentment is thanksgiving. The only thing you can give God is true praise, worship, and thanksgiving. Everything else belongs to Him. Today, take at least fifteen minutes to be in His presence with only thanksgiving and praise.

> Oh that men would praise the Lord for his goodness, and for his wonderful works to the children of men! For he satisfieth the longing soul, and filleth the hungry soul with goodness. . . . Then they cried unto the Lord in their trouble, and he saved them out of their distresses. . . . For he hath broken the gates of brass, and cut the bars of iron in sunder. (Psalm 107:8–9, 13, 16)

You have no reason to reserve your praise. Give God the honor due His name. Praise Him for His goodness. Did you thank Him for satisfying the longings of your heart and filling your soul with His goodness? Did you thank Him for defending and getting you out of trouble? How about for breaking those chains, swinging the doors, and setting you free?

It is God Who sends the sun to charm your heart to gladness and fruitfulness. He watered and nourished the land, and ensured that what was planted germinated and multiplied. His presence gave soundness of mind, life, and vitality. Take time and thank Him!

READ PSALMS 106:1–2 AND 136.

IS YOUR HEART THANKFUL?

Take a mental trip around your life and assess the many ways in which God has blessed you. Take time and thank Him for each one of His blessings. A thankful heart will unlock doors that prayer and petition alone will not. A grateful heart will usher you into God's presence and will subdue forces of evil around you. Let us learn from King David today. His was the most adorned family ever known to live on earth, yet he excelled in praise and gratitude. "Search me, O God, and know my heart: try me, and know my thoughts: And see if there be any wicked way in me, and lead me in the way everlasting" (Psalm 139:23-24).

Christ passed through Samaria on His way to Jerusalem. Ten lepers, desiring to be healed, approached Him and shouted, saying, "Jesus, Master, have mercy on us" (Luke 17:13). He asked that they present themselves before the priest and as they went, they were healed.

> And one of them, when he saw that he was healed, turned back, and with a loud voice glorified God, And fell down on his face at his feet, giving him thanks: and he was a Samaritan. And Jesus answering said, Were there not ten cleansed? but where are the nine? There are not found that returned to give glory to God, save this stranger. (Luke 17:15–18)

It is easy to grumble and complain. It is easy to focus on what is wrong and what you do not have. A thankful heart will open stores of God's blessings in your life. How is your heart?

READ PSALM 100.

HONOR GOD WITH YOUR SUBSTANCE.

God's formulas for blessings, success, and fulfillment are trustworthy and sure. They yield expected fruits. Make them principles on which to operate in your life. The firstfruits belong to God. A tenth of every blessing is His too. When this is done in honor of God and not for show, it opens windows of God's blessings and fills your stores ensuring that you always have sufficiency. I am not talking about endless wants but needs. God will supply all your needs according to His riches in Christ Jesus. Honor God with whatever He gives. "Honour the Lord with thy substance, and with the first fruits of all thine increase: So shall thy barns be filled with plenty, and thy presses shall burst out with new wine" (Proverbs 3:9–10).

When God blesses you abundantly, He also brings those you are to bless. He will open your eyes to the needs of the hour. Honor Him. Do it as unto God and not to man. Don't be tempted to hoard it for yourself. God uses man to accomplish many tasks in the world. Do not close the windows of your blessings by being selfish. You never go wrong honoring God with your substance.

An easy way to see this is to look at yourself as a conduit for God's blessings. God, who is sovereign, has eternal purposes for the gifts and blessings with which He enriches your life. Seek Him and let Him direct your heart, eyes, and hands that you may honor Him with your substance.

READ PROVERBS 11:24.

Living a Fulfilled Christian Life of Fruitfulness

God wants you to enjoy your Christian walk with Him. He wants you to be fulfilled in life. Let us walk toward fruitfulness.

Taste and enjoy God.

God wants you to enjoy your Christian walk with Him. When the children of Israel traveled from Egypt to the Promised Land, they faced the great unknown with uncertainty. The wilderness stretched vastly before them, and their fears were many. There were times when they forgot that God Who delivered them with an outstretched great arm of power was with them.

Our Christian walk today is no different. Challenges are many and so are uncertainties. It is easy to focus on the surrounding troubles that overshadow the great Savior until you miss God's desired victory for your life. God has not changed. God wants you to enjoy your journey with Him.

> O taste and see that the Lord is good: blessed is the man that trusteth in him. O fear the Lord, ye his saints: for there is no want to them that fear him. The young lions do lack, and suffer hunger: but they that seek the Lord shall not want any good thing. Come, ye children, hearken unto me: I will teach you the fear of the Lord. What man is he that desireth life, and loveth many days, that he may see good? (Psalm 34:8–12)

Taste and see for yourself that God is good. Trust and hold Him in reverence and witness for yourself that God takes care of His own. He will not withhold anything good when you seek and delight in Him. Those who endeavor to follow His teachings enjoy life to the fullest.

God watches intently for the righteous. His ears are attentive to their cry. He satisfies them. He is close when you are brokenhearted. He cares and carries you when the journey gets rough and tiring. Taste and see that God is good. Enjoy your relationship with the almighty God.

Read Psalm 34.

GOD IS MINDFUL OF HIS CHILDREN.

Has someone once covered your back when you did not expect it? Has anyone gone to great lengths to remember and look out for you in bizarre circumstances, to your pleasant surprise? God does that for His children all the time. There is not a moment you are not on His mind. He looks out for you more than you can think or imagine. He guides your heart and thoughts because He sees the future you can neither see nor comprehend. He holds your hand and guides your steps with tomorrow in mind.

> Ye that fear the Lord, trust in the Lord: he is their help and their shield. The Lord hath been mindful of us: he will bless us; he will bless the house of Israel; he will bless the house of Aaron. He will bless them that fear the Lord, both small and great. The Lord shall increase you more and more, you and your children. Ye are blessed of the Lord which made heaven and earth. (Psalm 115:11–15)

Even though God is in heaven, He is mindful of His children. Do you fear and trust in God? Does your heart tremble at His commandments? He shall be a shield to you. This is His promises to those who fear Him whether they be small or great. He will come through for you in ways that are best known to Him. He will prosper you and your children.

He will pour His blessings of knowledge and wisdom on you and your children. Even those around will see that you are blessed of God.

READ ISAIAH 44:2–5.

PUT YOUR TRUST IN GOD.

It is easy to put our trust in people and to go through life leaning on others. Nevertheless, what happens when such people are no longer near or available to help? Where is our help? Is God trustworthy, and can He stand with His children in tangible and meaningful ways for them to live fulfilled lives? How do we view God in the midnight hours when life is tough, and heartaches are deeply painful?

God is faithful. God is dependable. He is an anchor; the unchanging and stable Savior who will help you.

> Thus saith the Lord; Cursed be the man that trusteth in man, and maketh flesh his arm, and whose heart departeth from the Lord. For he shall be like the heath in the desert, and shall not see when good cometh; but shall inhabit the parched places in the wilderness, in a salt land and not inhabited. (Jeremiah 17:5–6)

Do not be deceived. Man, however strong and promising, will let you down. Those who put their trust in the help of human beings get frustrated by God. God stops their schemes and brings their plans to ruin. They cannot prosper.

> Blessed is the man that trusteth in the Lord, and whose hope the Lord is. For he shall be as a tree planted by the waters, and that spreadeth out her roots by the river, and shall not see when heat cometh, but her leaf shall be green; and shall not be careful in the year of drought, neither shall cease from yielding fruit. (Jeremiah 17:7–8)

Put your trust in God and watch Him prosper your plans.

READ PSALM 33:16–21.

KEEP YOUR HEART FOCUSED ON GOD.

Life has many challenges that can throw you off track if you do not keep God in His rightful place. God gives peace to those whose mind is always meditating on His Word and trusting in Him. Make God your strength and watch Him stand to keep your heart calm and at rest. Look at His promise of peace and repose: "Thou wilt keep him in perfect peace, whose mind is stayed on thee: because he trusteth in thee. Trust ye in the Lord for ever: for in the Lord Jehovah is everlasting strength" (Isaiah 26:3-4).

Challenge your heart to focus on God every day and watch the effect it will have in every area of your life. Listen to Him. Pray, and involve Him in all you do. Nothing will give you quietness of spirit and trust than hearing from God and feeling His strong arms of love and protection around you. It is when His blessed Word sinks deep into your soul and falls on an anticipating heart while speaking directly to the needs of the hour that the heart holds dear to God's assurance. Such a heart will weather any storm and remain quiet and secure in God the Rock—the tower of protection.

God humbles the proud and brings the arrogant to dust. He takes what is theirs and gives it to the poor. God favors those whose hearts are stayed on Him. He carries them under His wings when their path is rough and treacherous. He smoothens the rough paths and lifts those who love to do His will. Let your heart's desire be to glorify God's name. Earnestly seek Him. Peace of heart and favor come from the Lord. Trust in the Lord always.

READ PSALM 91:14–16.

BE GOVERNED BY GOD'S WORD.

When an individual, family, or nation is faced with uncertainty and difficulty, it helps to have God's clear voice. When you look at the chronicles of the kings who ruled over God's people in Bible times, those who surrounded themselves with God's servants not only heard but received clear counsel and direction from God. It is easy to be led astray when our hearts deviate from God's Word and counsel. There are many orators and schemers in the world who are good at speaking to the hearts of people and leading them away from God without revealing their hidden motives.

Do you need guidance, clear direction, and preciseness in your decision-making? Do you desire practical solutions for your daily encounters? Try the first line of defense and operation for all spiritual endeavors: God's Word. "All scripture is given by inspiration of God, and is profitable for doctrine, for reproof, for correction, for instruction in righteousness: That the man of God may be perfect, thoroughly furnished unto all good works" (2 Timothy 3:16–17).

God's Word is divinely inspired to help you go through life successfully. It is God's heavenly formula for man's earthly problems. Make it a point not to go through a day without the guidance of God's Word. Listen to God as He teaches what He expects of you. Pay attention to His correction so you do not continue on a wrong and misleading path for a long time. Be attentive as He reveals His chosen way. It is your daily walk, and your intentional tuning in to hear what God has each day, that will lead to your being thoroughly equipped to stand and to do what He desires.

God's Word is our compass in life. It is our spiritual thermometer that alerts us when we are plagued with worldly fevers and soul sickness. Stay in the Word.

READ PSALM 119:78–82, 92–94.

THERE IS STABILITY IN GOD.

It is common to align ourselves with leaders and friends who speak our language while representing our thoughts, beliefs, and actions. When they speak, we find our place in their lines as we duck under their protective wings. However, God Who is interested in our personal relationship with Him and our living good quality life, has a way of taking such people away from our lives. God does this because of His deep love for us. He sees how anchoring ourselves on such sandy and shaky foundations leave us unstable in Him.

Our unstable hearts become a threat to our peace, health, and fulfillment in life, let alone serving God. "They that trust in the Lord shall be as mount Zion, which cannot be removed, but abideth for ever. As the mountains are round about Jerusalem, so the Lord is round about his people from henceforth even forever" (Psalm 125:1–2).

There is stability in God. God puts His hedge of protection around those who trust in Him. God promises to surround and fortify you, thus making it hard for your enemies to get to you if you trust in Him. He will not allow the wicked to overtake and harass you. He has power to frustrate and overthrow their plans while sheltering and preserving you.

God will watch over you as you go and come back each day. Your safety is a priority to Him. It is God Who cares for you. He defends you every day. You are no match for the devil with his schemes. Left on your own, you would never make it successfully any single day. Together with the psalmist, you, too, can say, "My help cometh from the Lord, which made heaven and earth" (Psalm 121:2). You are safe in God.

READ PSALM 121.

GOD WILL STAND WITH YOU.

Is your heart fearful and anxious today? Are you afraid of unknown outcomes? Is your heart wondering what to do and what to expect? Do not fret. God will stand with you.

God takes full responsibility for His children.

When He delivered His chosen race from their land of bondage—Egypt, into the place allocated for their rest—Canaan, He stood with them. He led them through the dark wilderness where they were faced with numerous troubles and uncertainty. God's children had every reason not just to fear but to despair. Nevertheless, God neither left them at the mercy of their enemies nor to the seeming fate of their circumstances. He walked with them and encompassed them with His holy presence and mighty hand of power. God is doing the same for you today.

> But now thus saith the Lord that created thee, O Jacob, and he that formed thee, O Israel, Fear not: for I have redeemed thee, I have called thee by thy name; thou art mine. When thou passest through the waters, I will be with thee; and through the rivers, they shall not overflow thee: when thou walkest through the fire, thou shalt not be burned; neither shall the flame kindle upon thee. (Isaiah 43:1–2)

True, challenges are many, and there is every reason why you would fear, but that is not God's choice for you. Each reason only increases your fear. Fight against your fears and side with God. Just as you trust to see the night usher in day every morning, you can trust God to stand with you faithfully.

It is God Who has redeemed you from the bondage of fear. He has called you by name unto Himself. He will be with you when you pass through deep waters and diverse troubles. He will be present to protect you through the fires of life.

READ ISAIAH 43:3–5.

December 8

GOD USES THE ORDINARY.

When God chose to subdue the enemies of Israel and to give unsurpassed victory to a nation subdued by the Philistines, He did not use the mighty, well-known personalities of the time. He used a young shepherd boy whom He trained in unconventional ways.

When God wanted to rescue His children, who lived in subjection and intimidation in Babylon after being captured from Jerusalem, He dethroned a well-known favored queen and handpicked Esther—an orphan and a nobody—for the job.

Do you know that you are God's vessel of choice for this generation? Do you understand that God is depending on you today? You belong to the company of those who can leave a godly legacy for this generation.

> Because the foolishness of God is wiser than men; and the weakness of God is stronger than men. For ye see your calling, brethren, how that not many wise men after the flesh, not many mighty, not many noble, are called. But God hath chosen the foolish things of the world to confound the wise; and God hath chosen the weak things of the world to confound the things which are mighty; And base things of the world, and things which are despised, hath God chosen, yea, and things which are not, to bring to nought things that are: That no flesh should glory in his presence. (1 Corinthians 1:25–29)

God uses ordinary, willing vessels to accomplish His work. His view of you is different from everybody else's. If He were to look for the wise, the noble, and the mighty, you could take a lifetime and still never make His list.

God has chosen the foolish things of the world to confound the wise. He has chosen the weak things of the world to confound the things which are mighty. He uses what is neglected, rejected, despised, and most unlikely to bring Him glory so that no flesh may glory or boast in his presence. Let Him who has any reason to boast only boast in God.

Do not disqualify yourself. You are a powerful candidate in the hands of a mighty God. Obey and do as He instructs.

READ 1 CORINTHIANS 6:9–11.

THE MIGHTY GOD IS IN YOU.

Heaven will have many surprises. One of the perplexing things to all Christians, I believe, will be the realization that we endured and suffered many things here on earth because we could neither trust nor depend on God fully. God loves His children. God has power to stand, walk and fight battles with and for those washed in His precious blood.

He desires to not only share but to carry us in our troubles. There is a reason why blood pressure rises when we are stressed beyond measure. Our bodies have breaking points. It is no surprise that God choses to live inside the believer. "Ye are of God, little children, and have overcome them: because greater is he that is in you, than he that is in the world. They are of the world: therefore speak they of the world, and the world heareth them. We are of God: he that knoweth God heareth us" (1 John 4:4–6).

There is not a single moment when a child of God is on His own. The great and mighty God lives in you. Do not go through life like one who is forsaken. God fights for you. He has promised never to leave nor forsake you (Hebrews 15:5). Regardless of how you feel today, let your heart know that God is on your side. Despite the battles that rage in your life, let your heart remember that you belong to God. He will not let go of your hand.

If God is on our side, who can be against us (Romans 8:31)? Do not be deceived by the acting of the enemy. His shouts may be loud and intimidating but His power is subject to God Who lives in you. Let God help you carry the cares that bring weariness to your heart. Give them to Him. Trust His Word and watch Him do as He has promised. Remember, He lives in you, and He is only a prayer away.

READ 1 JOHN 2:12–14.

December 10

WALK IN GOD'S FAVOR.

If you were to survey a cross section of the world's population for their dreams and aspirations in life, you will not miss a large percentage desiring a long, prosperous, fulfilling life. Truthfully speaking, not only do we desire these things, but we labor for them in life. These are the reasons for which we wake up early and work all day. But how does one get to enjoy such a dream life of length of days filled with peace and satisfaction of heart? Is this a myth for which we chase, like the vapors and the mists of the atmosphere, only to die without ever catching them? What does God say concerning these things?

> My son, forget not my law; but let thine heart keep my commandments:
> For length of days, and long life, and peace, shall they add to thee. Let not
> mercy and truth forsake thee: bind them about thy neck; write them upon
> the table of thine heart: So shalt thou find favour and good understanding
> in the sight of God and man. (Proverbs 3:1–4)

Embedded within God's Word are treasures of life. The holy Scriptures is a road map to what God considers satisfaction, fulfillment, and prosperity in life. God's law is meant to be a safeguard for our lives. Obedience to God's Word channels us into the circle of the favored. It yields longer, peaceful, and fruitful life. You find favor with God.

One of the greatest blessings you can acquire is to have the touch of God on your life. God's favor will cause you to be treated with goodness and kindness. It will enable you to serve Him with greater joy and fulfillment as He makes others to be inclined toward you. Don't forsake God's law; among the righteous there is favor. Cease not to pray; God is favorable to those who seek His face. No good thing does He withhold from those who walk uprightly with Him.

READ PROVERBS 11:27.

ALLOW GOD TO WORK THROUGH YOU.

Whose help would you seek if you had an opportunity to reach the entire world with a special message? Let me take a guess! Your top ten list may include the CEO of Apple, Microsoft, Google, Amazon, Facebook, Snapchat, and YouTube. Why do I think so? Our inclination is often to seek and align ourselves with the well-known, the influential, and the most successful.

I have not met many people who happily or proudly associate with those plagued with failure or the grossly insignificant. Nevertheless, this is not how God operates to accomplish His eternal plans and purposes on earth. God's ways are higher than our ways, just as His thoughts are higher than ours. God works in ways that are incomprehensible to the human heart and mind. "Now when they saw the boldness of Peter and John, and perceived that they were unlearned and ignorant men, they marvelled; and they took knowledge of them, that they had been with Jesus" (Acts 4:13).

Do not limit God. There is no telling what God can do with a man He decides to favor. When God favors His child, only the sky is the limit. God is not limited with your inabilities and even what looks like misfortunes in life.

Christ handpicked common men engraved in their fishing trade and transformed them into mighty disciples to spread the good news of the gospel to the world. When His hand rested upon them, there was no doubt that they were special vessels set aside for God's worthy course. The world was astonished. Those who had treated them with contempt as ordinary, unlearned, and ignorant men marveled at their knowledge, wisdom, and understanding as they took notice that they had been with Jesus.

Allow God to mold and train you into His vessel for noble use. Do not be hardheaded. Allow Him to bless you with favor and to compass you as with a shield. Yield to His mighty hand as you obey and follow. You are a potential candidate for God's great use.

READ PSALM 32:9.

YOU ARE FAVORED FOR A REASON.

Words have power to build, nurture, and lead to success. Words can also break, cripple, and lead to failure. God's Words guide, grow, bless, and give life. Unfortunately, most of us believe and follow the powerless words of secular godfathers and heroes more than God. This leaves us dejected and too dull for our spirits to hear and believe God. Every child of God is highly favored of God. You are special. God, in His sovereignty has created you for special work for which He has not only prepared but anointed you. "I will sing of the mercies of the Lord for ever: with my mouth will I make known thy faithfulness to all generations. . . . For thou art the glory of their strength: and in thy favour our horn shall be exalted" (Psalm 89:1, 17).

Don't waste God's favor. You are favored for a reason. Joseph, Jacob's favorite son, was sold by his jealous brothers to Egypt. God's favor turned Joseph's misfortunes and difficult situations into divine opportunities for His work. God favored Joseph in Potiphar's house. The pagan Pharaoh, too, realized that the young Hebrew slave boy was not an ordinary man. Joseph prospered (Genesis 17:37).

It is such favor that took an ordinary shepherd boy and turned him into a mighty king. David testified of this favor as he faced the giant Goliath. God Who had protected him from the bear and the lion would hand the uncircumcised Philistine into his hand.

God's favor in your life will enable you to accomplish special tasks assigned to you.

Walk with Him and be what He desires of you. To help you avoid fear, review what God has done for you.

READ PSALM 5:11–12.

YOU HAVE BEEN STRATEGICALLY PLACED.

God draws and demarcates boundary lines for all His children. He knows when and where to bring us into the world in order to fulfill His holy purposes. He orchestrates events to rightfully shape and conform us to desired vessels. It is not surprising that God refers to His children as clay in the hands of the Potter (Jeremiah 18; Isaiah 64:8). Pliable clay in the hands of the great Maker acknowledges the power of the Molder and yields to His training and conditioning. It comes off the Potter's wheel shining like a precious jewel ready to execute God's purposes with eternal power and anointing.

> Bless the Lord, O my soul: and all that is within me, bless his holy name. Bless the Lord, O my soul, and forget not all his benefits: Who forgiveth all thine iniquities; who healeth all thy diseases; Who redeemeth thy life from destruction; who crowneth thee with lovingkindness and tender mercies; Who satisfieth thy mouth with good things; so that thy youth is renewed like the eagle's. (Psalm 103:1–5)

A young orphan girl was raised and strategically placed where an entire race could be saved in the history of the Jews. Esther, the Bible says, obtained favor in the sight of all those that looked upon her (Esther 2:15b). She was chosen to be queen in place of Queen Vashti, who had disgraced the king. Mordecai, Esther's uncle, challenged her at the opportune time, saying, "And who knoweth whether thou art come to the kingdom for such a time as this?" (Esther 4:14).

Has God lavished His love, mercy, and kindness on you in exceptional ways? He is sovereign. Your being where you are at this point is divinely appointed. Remember, no misfortune is too unfortunate for the great and powerful molding hands of God. Serve Him.

READ PSALM 8:4.

Embrace the Holy Spirit.

Our daily lives can be likened to a journey you take early in the morning that ends late in the evening. You do not start off anticipating traffic delays, roadblocks, unexpected eventualities, or even missing the mark. However, all these are characteristic and realistic marks of a normal journey. Knowing how uncertain our futures are, God has given His children the Holy Spirit to live within our hearts.

When God announced the coming of the Messiah, this is what He said of Christ, who would live in the hearts of the believers: "And his name shall be called Wonderful, Counsellor, The mighty God, The everlasting Father, The Prince of Peace" (Isaiah 9:6b). God knew how desperate we would require the functions of these offices in our daily walk with Him. "These things have I spoken unto you, being yet present with you. But the Comforter, which is the Holy Ghost, whom the Father will send in my name, he shall teach you all things, and bring all things to your remembrance, whatsoever I have said unto you" (John 14:25–26).

Do not neglect the work of the Holy Spirit in your life:

> For they that are after the flesh do mind the things of the flesh; but they that are after the Spirit the things of the Spirit. For to be carnally minded is death; but to be spiritually minded is life and peace. Because the carnal mind is enmity against God: for it is not subject to the law of God, neither indeed can be. So then they that are in the flesh cannot please God. (Romans 8:5–8)

The Holy Spirit helps you in your daily infirmities. He helps you pray even in moments when you do not know how to do it (Romans 8:26). He communes with you, teaches, and reminds you of Scripture (John 14:26).

Read Romans 8:26–27.

December 5

REACH OUT AND TOUCH HIM.

Life has many challenges, and its sting is real and painful. Look around and see the suffering of many and the numerous minds plagued with infirmities. It is easy to put on a smile to camouflage the inner aches of the heart, but a smile can only go so far. As pressure mounts, smiles have a way of breaking into bleeding wounds, subjecting us to unfathomable agony. God is neither blind to the plight of His people nor to the heartaches of this generation. God is moved with your sorrows. God wants to help you. Reach out today and call on Him. Touch Him.

> And, behold, a woman, which was diseased with an issue of blood twelve years, came behind him, and touched the hem of his garment: For she said within herself, If I may but touch his garment, I shall be whole. But Jesus turned him about, and when he saw her, he said, Daughter, be of good comfort; thy faith hath made thee whole. And the woman was made whole from that hour. (Matthew 9:20–22)

Each day presents you with opportunities to either get closer or further away from Christ. You are surrounded with crowds and intimidating personalities who not only obscure your view of the Master but hinder your getting to Him.

The unnamed woman with an issue of blood had to overcome the crowds before she could get her healing. Christ stops to listen to you every day. God is never too busy for His children. Step out in faith and go for God. He has your answer. Follow the yearnings of your heart in faith, reach out and touch the Master.

READ JOHN 6:37.

GOD HAS A REMNANT.

Regardless of how bad things look around you and in the world, God has a holy remnant on whom He can count to accomplish His work. God can neither be overtaken nor overcome with evil. Nothing takes Him unawares just as nothing occurs to Him. God is not only sovereign but omnipotent. He is in control and that is why He alone can be God. Do you know that God is counting on you to stand out for Him? You can be God's faithful remnant in this century.

> And he said, I have been very jealous for the Lord God of hosts: because the children of Israel have forsaken thy covenant, thrown down thine altars, and slain thy prophets with the sword; and I, even I only, am left; and they seek my life, to take it away. And the Lord said unto him . . . Yet I have left me seven thousand in Israel, all the knees which have not bowed unto Baal, and every mouth which hath not kissed him. (1 Kings 19:14–15, 18)

Life has many challenges. Life is also full of Christians who have wandered away from the faith to engage in worldly pleasures which disgrace God. Like the prophet Elijah, there are discouraging moments when you feel like you are the only one striving to live for God. However, this is not true.

In every generation, God has a remnant that does not bow to the "Baals" of the time. God has faithful Christians spread throughout the world who honor Him and shine their lights beautifully and clearly. Stand with the remnant. God delights in you. You do not have to be a well-known influential figure. Your heart just needs to burn with the fire of God as you listen and follow Him as He guides your steps. You are God's chosen vessel for such times.

READ ROMANS 11:1–5.

WALK IN FAITH.

One great surprise in heaven, I believe, will be knowing how much God spoke to our specific situations without our stopping to either hear Him or act on His spoken Word. God did not design the Christian walk to be a life of mystical mysteries of ever groping in darkness and never hearing God or finding His direction. God promises to guide us: "I will instruct thee and teach thee in the way which thou shalt go: I will guide thee with mine eye. Be ye not as the horse, or as the mule, which have no understanding: whose mouth must be held in with bit and bridle, lest they come near unto thee" (Psalm 32:8–9).

God speaks. He guides. Nevertheless, this cannot help us unless we listen, hear, believe, and act accordingly. "And the Lord spake unto Moses, saying, Send thou men, that they may search the land of Canaan, which I give unto the children of Israel: of every tribe of their fathers shall ye send a man, everyone a ruler among them" (Numbers 13:1–2).

The eyes of faith make us see things as God sees them and believe God to do as promised. The whole reason why Israel was walking through the wilderness was because God was taking them to the promised land. When He asked Moses to send people to search the land, there were those who forgot that Canaan was their land of promise. They saw the land for what it was, a land flowing with milk and honey and plenteous in fruit, but they were terrified by the size of the inhabitants.

Caleb and Joshua took God at His Word and stilled the Israelites saying, "Let us go up at once, and possess it; for we are well able to overcome it" (Numbers 13:30). Believe God for what He has said and walk in faith.

What is God saying to you? Take time to seek, hear and follow Him without being distracted by fear or the critics of our times. The eyes of faith will lead you to God's purposeful paths in life.

READ ROMANS 4:16–25.

BELIEVE GOD.

Is God real? Can someone follow God wholeheartedly in this century? Is there a place for faith in modern times?

Most people do not like challenges. However, I have not met or read of many people whom God used greatly who did not fight through numerous obstacles. Most times, God's blessings come camouflaged in problems. To avoid or to hate difficulties is to miss God altogether in our daily encounters. Remember, God only allows what He weighs and permits to come our way.

> For thus saith the Lord God of Israel, The barrel of meal shall not waste, neither shall the cruse of oil fail, until the day that the Lord sendeth rain upon the earth. And she went and did according to the saying of Elijah: and she, and he, and her house, did eat many days. And the barrel of meal wasted not, neither did the cruse of oil fail, according to the word of the Lord, which he spake by Elijah. (1 Kings 17:14–16)

You will not witness your miracle or the full working of God in life until you step out in faith to believe God. Elijah was sent to the widow of Zeraphath when the land was plagued with famine and drought. Elijah could have discredited the possibility of having his needs met by an old poor widow. The widow could have disregarded the prophet's words and continued in her usual lifestyle.

Believe God and do as His Word directs. His ways are higher than your ways even when they don't make sense.

READ NUMBERS 23:19.

YOU HAVE DIVINE PROTECTION.

One of the greatest tools Satan uses to defeat and undermine Christians is fear. The enemy works to make us believe we are incapable, helpless, and even useless. He paints the picture of being very powerful while Christians are weak, vulnerable, and at his constant mercy. The truth is that God has impeccable protection for His children. No one protects like God. Do not underrate and underestimate God Who used Pharaoh to not only protect but to educate and meet all life's needs for the very child—Moses—he wanted to kill.

> And when the servant of the man of God was risen early, and gone forth, behold, an host compassed the city both with horses and chariots. And his servant said unto him, Alas, my master! how shall we do? And he answered, Fear not: for they that be with us are more than they that be with them. And Elisha prayed, and said, Lord, I pray thee, open his eyes, that he may see. And the Lord opened the eyes of the young man; and he saw: and, behold, the mountain was full of horses and chariots of fire round about Elisha. (2 Kings 6:15–17)

If our protection were to be left entirely to us, none of us would survive beyond a day. God protects His children in more ways than we can imagine. He surrounds us with His heavenly armies and weighs what must come our way. He holds off the forces of evil and takes fear and anxiety from us.

Don't be afraid. Only believe. You have divine protection from God.

READ PSALM 91.

Do business with God.

Halfhearted devotion to God is dangerous and fruitless. God purposed to spit the church of Laodicea out of His mouth for lukewarmness. He warned and cautioned them to be either hot or remain cold like ice. Unfortunately, most of us remain in the box of noncommittal, lukewarm fellowship and service to God. We hurt ourselves as we can neither know nor enjoy God. We miss His voice and direction. We stagger with one leg in the devil's camp while hopping to please and follow God. God cannot use us mightily in such a state. "And such as do wickedly against the covenant shall he corrupt by flatteries: but the people that do know their God shall be strong, and do exploits. And they that understand among the people shall instruct many" (Daniel 11:32).

When you remain in the shallow waters of Christianity, you can do nothing but endure your Christian walk. Often, life will seem unfair and its burdens too numerous to bear. You will carry the weight of your burdens and maintain a defeated disposition and attitude. This will discourage your heart and make you walk in unbelief. You will follow reluctantly, at a distance, and miss the intended joy for your journey.

Those who walk close and maintain fellowship with God witness His works and power. They acquire understanding and do exploits for God. They become teachers of what they have seen and heard (1 John 1:3). Don't be satisfied with lukewarmness. God would rather you were either hot or cold (Revelation 3:15–16). Halfhearted commitments and service are counterproductive. The devil likes nominal commitment. This way he can target, entice, and defeat you easily. Do business with God.

Read Psalm 107:23–25.

PAY YOUR DUES.

The man who manufactured the larger earth-moving machinery testified of how he began tithing ten percent just because his father told him to. After a few months of tithing, he still had too much left over. He promised to give God twenty percent. His business blossomed and he decided to give God thirty percent. He increased to fifty percent, reasoning that an equal split was still perfect, since it was God Who gave the ideas that resulted in his making millions of dollars.

> Will a man rob God? Yet ye have robbed me. But ye say, Wherein have we robbed thee? In tithes and offerings. Ye are cursed with a curse: for ye have robbed me, even this whole nation. Bring ye all the tithes into the storehouse, that there may be meat in mine house, and prove me now herewith, saith the Lord of hosts, if I will not open you the windows of heaven, and pour you out a blessing, that there shall not be room enough to receive it. (Malachi 3:8–10)

Pay your tithe. It will unlock great blessings. Don't be afraid of living on the ninety percent that remains. It is blessed of God and will accomplish more than one hundred percent. Don't give tithe with a secret eye tracking the anticipated blessings. Obey God by giving what is His without twisting His hands for blessings.

God opens His windows of heaven and pours overflowing blessings to those who tithe. He rebukes what destroys and steals your blessings. Pay your dues. God will ensure that you are blessed. To fail to tithe is to miss God's favor.

READ MALACHI 3:8–12.

KNOW THE TRUTH.

We live in an era of lies. The saddest thing about these unprecedented times is that most people, including Christians, are quick to believe a lie. Look back at what we have believed and followed with concern and passion. Look at the individuals in whom we placed our hopes and trust. How truthful are they? If you were to weigh them in God's holy balances, would you find them honest and full of integrity? To stand and perpetuate a theater of lies is to set up a platform for the deceptive schemes of Satan and the antichrist without knowing. "Then said Jesus to those Jews which believed on him, If ye continue in my word, then are ye my disciples indeed; And ye shall know the truth, and the truth shall make you free" (John 8:31–32).

There is a price to be paid by those who desire to know God intimately. Those who believe on Him must continue in Him. They have to stay with the Word. Truth if found by digging treasure from God's Word. Truth once found liberates and sets you free.

There are many false teachers who target the flock of God. They present distorted truths with adequate hooks to deceive the elect of God. For what are you passionate? What does God's Word say about it? Is it fundamental Bible truth or traditional fables mixed with fallacies?

Christ knowing what would befall the church in latter days prayed saying, "They are not of the world, even as I am not of the world. Sanctify them through thy truth: thy word is truth" (John 17:16–17). Devote time to study God's Word to know the truth.

READ 2 TIMOTHY 2:15–19.

December 23

WHEN AFRAID, TRUST GOD.

As you look back on this year, you will not miss many moments when fear gripped your heart. Much of what you held dear to your heart was carefully tucked away, as those in whom you put your hope and trust faded from active stages of life. There have been many challenges. However, God has not changed with the changing times. He remains a rock and a sure foundation for all who will look to Him and trust in His care. Neither His power nor ability have dwindled because of the tough times we face. You can still trust God. "What time I am afraid, I will trust in thee. In God I will praise his word, in God I have put my trust; I will not fear what flesh can do unto me" (Psalm 56:3–4).

There will be many moments in your life when you will have reasons to be afraid. Turn your eyes to heaven and let God speak courage and strength to your heart. This is part of what Jesus Christ came to do. See the words that were used to pronounce His birth as the shepherds trembled with fear: "And the angel said unto them, Fear not: for, behold, I bring you good tidings of great joy, which shall be to all people. For unto you is born this day in the city of David a Saviour, which is Christ the Lord" (Luke 2:10–11).

Trials will come and burdens will grow. You may be tempted to grow weary but don't be afraid. Just believe. God cares. Given unto us is a Savior who has power to help you. He invites the weary to Himself.

READ MATTHEW 11:28–30.

December 24

HAVE YOU TRIED JESUS?

This year has left many people disappointed and feeling lost. There are those who do not know where to turn or whom to trust. Allow me to introduce you to One Who cares and knows about all your hurts. His name is Jesus. He loves you and seeks to save your soul as He gives you meaning for which to live while culminating in eternal life.

Many people will let you down, but Jesus does not disappoint. He is truthful and honest. He is real. Those who find Him find life. Since He has faced the challenges you face, not only does He understand but He knows how to help you? Try Jesus before you give up. "For God sent not his Son into the world to condemn the world; but that the world through him might be saved" (John 3:17).

Don't let the celebrations and merchandise of the season obscure your heart from seeing God's plan. It is for you that the Savior is born. He has come to light the way that you may walk in the newness of life without groping and stumbling in the dark. "For unto us a child is born, unto us a son is given: and the government shall be upon his shoulder: and his name shall be called Wonderful, Counsellor, The mighty God, The everlasting Father, The Prince of Peace" (Isaiah 9:6).

There is no life outside of Jesus Christ. It is Christ who gives meaning to life. Without Him, burdens are unbearable. God has come to carry your burdens. The mighty God is a great counselor. Led Him bear your load. Let the Prince of Peace give you peace which surpasses all human understanding. Get into His arms that He may be your everlasting Father. Have you tried Jesus?

READ PSALM 23.

RESPOND TO GOD'S LOVE.

God loves you. God cares for you. God has been working behind the scenes of your life and helping you in ways you will neither know nor understand. God's love for you is unconditional. He is not like your friends or other people in your life whose love is depended on who you are, what you have or what you do. God has nothing to gain from you. He loves you for who you are. He knows your beginning from the end and understands your road of life. He just wants to help you. "For God so loved the world, that he gave his only begotten Son, that whosoever believeth in him should not perish, but have everlasting life" (John 3:16).

The coming of Jesus Christ to the world was an act of love toward you from God. God still stands with His arms stretched out to you today. Listen to His call, "Ho, every one that thirsteth, come ye to the waters, and he that hath no money; come ye, buy, and eat; yea, come, buy wine and milk without money and without price" (Isaiah 55:1). In Christ is true living water. Those who drink of Him never thirst again.

His invitation is for you. He says, "Come unto me, all ye that labour and are heavy laden, and I will give you rest. Take my yoke upon you, and learn of me; for I am meek and lowly in heart: and ye shall find rest unto your souls. For my yoke is easy, and my burden is light" (Matthew 11:28–30). Respond to God's love today.

READ ROMANS 10:8–11.

CHRIST IS HERE FOR YOU.

Heaven is real and God has a place for you in that wonderful place. However, there is only one way to that blessed city. Those who get there go by the way of the cross through the Son of God Who loved us and gave His life to redeem and to reconcile us back to God the Father. Man born of a woman is a sinner. Sin does not get to heaven. But when we confess our sin and believe in the Lord Jesus Christ, who shed His blood to atone for our sins, we die in Him as He births in us a spiritual seed that lives in newness of life following our rebirth.

> But when the fulness of the time was come, God sent forth his Son, made of a woman, made under the law, To redeem them that were under the law, that we might receive the adoption of sons. And because ye are sons, God hath sent forth the Spirit of his Son into your hearts, crying, Abba, Father. (Galatians 4:4–6)

Christ has come that you may have life and have it more abundantly (John 10:10). God sent his only begotten Son into the world, that we might live through him (1 John 4:9). He who has the Son has life. He who has not the Son has not life (1 John 5:12). Man who is born a sinner is spiritually dead are corrupted with sin. Sin has no entry to heaven. A person cannot enter the kingdom of God without the spiritual rebirth.

Christ regenerates the heart calloused with sin by washing it with His shed blood on the cross. He gives you spiritual life when you turn to Him. This is what quickens man from being spiritually dead to being spiritually alive.

READ 1 JOHN 5:12.

GOD REVEALS HIMSELF.

As this year comes to an end, it is needful that you establish clear and tangible truths about God.

- It is not God's desire that any should perish. Salvation is free to all. You are invited to eternal life.

- God does not want you to live a defeated life. There is power, deliverance, and victory in Jesus.

- God desires fellowship and a deep father-son relationship with you.

- God hears when you call. He desires to show you great and mighty things which you do not know.

- God loves you. He cares for you. He is touched with your sorrows and the travails of life.

- Every day, God's eyes move to and fro over the whole world to see those whose hearts are steadfast in Him so He can show Himself strong on their behalf.

None of us should remain the way we were a year ago. God is the Potter and we are clay in His holy hands. He molds us into vessels and people of honor for noble use as we yield to His chiseling. He does not hold our sins over our heads. He is a forgiving Father ready to see you take the next step in life. "Call unto me, and I will answer thee, and show thee great and mighty things, which thou knowest not" (Jeremiah 33:3).

You will seek God and find Him when you seek Him with all your heart. For every stride you take toward God, He takes a leap in your direction. In fact, it is God Who woos you to Himself as He works in your both to will and do of His good pleasure (Philippians 2:13).

God loves those who love Him. Those who seek Him early find Him.

READ PROVERBS 8:17 AND JEREMIAH 29:13.

GOD FULFILLS YOUR LIFE.

Nobody can take care of you like God does. No one will fulfill your life like God can. God does not leave His children destitute in this world. We may opt to feed with the pigs like the prodigal son, but that is our choice and not God's plan for us. "O taste and see that the LORD is good: blessed is the man that trusteth in him. O fear the LORD, ye his saints: for there is no want to them that fear him. The young lions do lack, and suffer hunger: but they that seek the LORD shall not want any good thing" (Psalm 34:8–10).

God will meet your needs according to His riches in Christ Jesus. He will walk with you. He will protect and fight for you. His presence will accompany you. The Holy Spirit will counsel and commune with you. He will comfort and help you pray.

It is a privilege to be a child of God. He takes pride in His own and delights in you as He sees to it that you are fulfilled.

The most blessed people on the face of the earth are God's children— Christians who have put their faith and truth in the Lord Jesus Christ. Those who depart from sin to walk with God in righteousness find God to be a Father who cares and meets their needs.

Look at God's testimony for those who love and follow Him. "For the Lord God is a sun and shield: the Lord will give grace and glory: no good thing will he withhold from them that walk uprightly" (Psalm 84:11). God does not leave His children destitute in wild and dangerous world. You cannot charge God with neglect. God will fulfill your life.

READ PSALM 23:5–6.

GOD IS ENOUGH.

It is cool to know and follow God. It is even cooler to love and follow God wholeheartedly as you display His love and splendor to many who are seeking truth and an honest path of life. There is no shame in knowing God. Stand strong and let the world see God for who He is. The world is searching for truth and honest people who wear the coat of Christ with integrity. We have a golden opportunity to show and tell God's goodness and His sufficiency.

> That their hearts might be comforted, being knit together in love, and unto all riches of the full assurance of understanding, to the acknowledgment of the mystery of God, and of the Father, and of Christ; In whom are hid all the treasures of wisdom and knowledge. . . . For in him dwelleth all the fulness of the Godhead bodily. And ye are complete in him, which is the head of all principality and power. (Colossians 2:2–3, 10)

You are complete in God and God is enough. God has equipped you with what you need to make it in life. He has put you in the right place and surrounded you with the right people. He has made His knowledge and wisdom abundantly available to you. You are surrounded with His presence, and you have access to Him at any moment.

There is no reason for you to be envious or jealous. God has promised to meet all your needs. There is no reason for you to loiter of get lured into Satan's camp. God is the best caretaker you will ever have.

READ HEBREWS 13:5.

YOU ARE THE APPLE OF GOD'S EYE.

God loves you. God guards you jealously. You are God's treasured possession. Look at His promise to you today:

> Shew thy marvellous lovingkindness, O thou that savest by thy right hand them which put their trust in thee from those that rise up against them. Keep me as the apple of the eye, hide me under the shadow of thy wings, From the wicked that oppress me, from my deadly enemies, who compass me about. (Psalm 17:7–9)

Have you believed on the Lord Jesus Christ? If yes, then you need not fear. Step out in faith and courage knowing that God has gone ahead of you. God's promise is sure. He will hover over you as He shows you His strong and marvelous love.

You are dear to God. He will keep and protect you like one would protect the pupil of his eye from the slightest hurt. God will hide you in the shadow of His wings. Look back and see the many ways in which He has stood for you and protected you. You are the apple of God's eye and He will show you His wonderful lovingkindness.

READ PSALM 91:1–16.

GOD HAS GOOD PLANS FOR YOU.

God loves you. God's desire is for you to walk with Him. Don't follow at a distance or straddle the fence. You hurt yourself and miss what God has for you as you expose yourself to the fierce and relentless attacks of Satan. God does not withhold any good thing from those whose walk is upright. Walk with God. Get back to Him with your whole heart. Your joy, healing, happiness, fulfillment, and total satisfaction in life are in God. Look at His Word for you today:

> The Spirit of the Lord God is upon me; because the Lord hath anointed me to preach good tidings unto the meek; he hath sent me to bind up the brokenhearted, to proclaim liberty to the captives, and the opening of the prison to them that are bound . . . To appoint unto them that mourn in Zion, to give unto them beauty for ashes, the oil of joy for mourning, the garment of praise for the spirit of heaviness; that they might be called trees of righteousness, the planting of the Lord, that he might be glorified. (Isaiah 61:1, 3)

God has good plans for your future. He has plans of peace and not for harm. They are plans to prosper and fill you with hope (Jeremiah 29:11–12).

God is sovereign. He has plans to stand with you; to comfort and to set you free from the bondage of the enemy. He has plans to give you beauty instead of ashes and joy in place of mourning. God wants to plant you as an oak of righteousness for the display of His splendor.

READ ISAIAH 30:15.

Conclusion

When we surrender our lives to God in faith and repent of our sins to believe in the Lord Jesus Christ and follow Him as His disciples, we start off as newborn spiritual babies. Just like little babies require nourishment and tender care to grow into steady children, spiritual growth demands the same.

How do Christians grow spiritually? The psalmist offers us clear direction:

> Blessed is the man that walketh not in the counsel of the ungodly, nor standeth in the way of sinners, nor sitteth in the seat of the scornful. But his delight is in the law of the Lord; and in his law doth he meditate day and night. And he shall be like a tree planted by the rivers of water, that bringeth forth his fruit in his season; his leaf also shall not wither; and whatsoever he doeth shall prosper. (Psalm 1:1–3)

Your spiritual growth will take a deliberate act of your will. You will have to:

- Do as God tells you.
- Do what you are supposed to do.
- Study, meditate, and obey God's Word.
- Show yourself a servant approved by God Who rightly divides the Word of truth.

Your spiritual growth demands that you:

- Follow God out of love and reverence.
- Make wise choices.
- Resist temptation.
- Feed the inner man and starve your outward man.
- Have a teachable spirit.

Endeavor to grow spiritually and continue to find hope and strength from the pages of God's Word and in sweet fellowship with the Father.

Don't Hoard the Bread

Samaria was under severe famine to the extent that people sold a donkey's head and dove's droppings for a fortune, according to 2 Kings 6–7. Four lepers who presumed they had nothing to lose either in death or life went down to the Syrian camp to look for food. God made their footsteps sound like a mighty army. The Assyrians fled. The lepers ate to their fill but remembered their countrymen who were dying of hunger. God used this act to save Samaria . . .

- Have you benefited from these devotionals? Tell someone about them.
- Did you find strength and hope in these readings? Share the message. Buy it for a friend.
- Do you know a family member, a friend, or an organization that can benefit from this content? Recommend it, share it, or bless them with copies. **Don't hoard the bread.**

For more information about
Amilliah Kenya
and
Finding Hope and Strength in God
please visit:

www.amilliahkenya.org

More from Amilliah Kenya

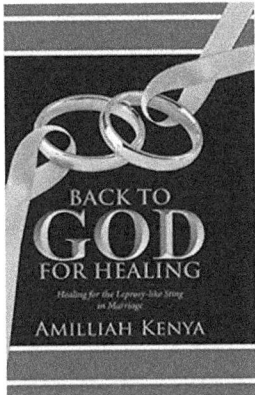

BACK TO
GOD
FOR HEALING
Healing for the Leprosy-like Sting in Marriage
AMILLIAH KENYA

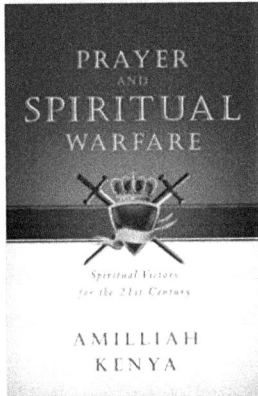

PRAYER
AND
SPIRITUAL
WARFARE
Spiritual Victory for the 21st Century
AMILLIAH
KENYA

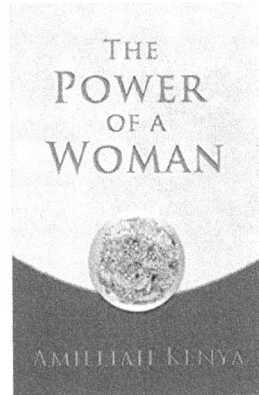

THE
POWER
OF A
WOMAN
AMILLIAH KENYA

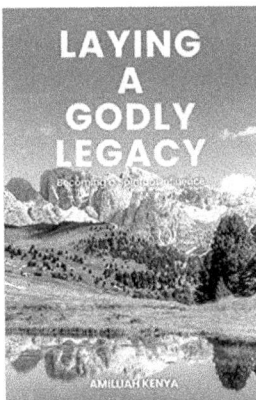

LAYING
A
GODLY
LEGACY
AMILLIAH KENYA

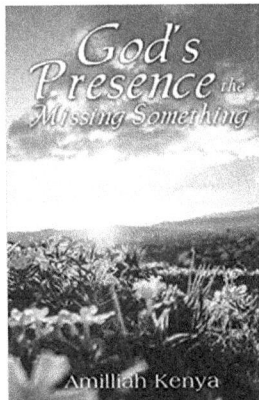

God's
Presence *the*
Missing Something
Amilliah Kenya

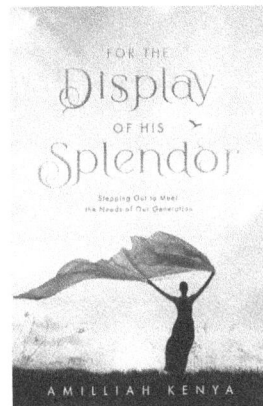

FOR THE
DISPLAY
OF HIS
Splendor
Stepping Out to Meet the Needs of Our Generation
AMILLIAH KENYA

More from Ambassador International

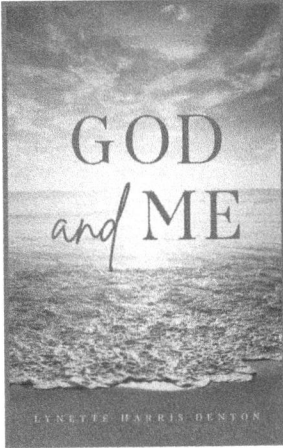

GOD and ME

We all struggle with the every day trials of this life, whether we are dealing with sickness, finances, relationships, or just drudgery. While we may feel hopeless, we can have confidence that God is always walking alongside us to help us and guide us along the way. But we must lean on Him and meditate on His Word every day. In *God and Me*, Lynette Harris Denton offers brief devotionals to help you start your day and draw you closer to God.

How do you think God feels about you? Don't tell yourself the answer you know you're supposed to say. Don't recite lines from children's church or your grandmother's house that never sank beneath the surface of your heart. Tell yourself the real answer. What God really feels for you is love, and He's done specific, personal things for you so you'll know it. As you read *Always Been Loved*, you'll finally discover God's true feelings for you—the feelings He's had for you since before you were born and that you can never lose. He's ready to show you: you've always been loved.

ALWAYS BEEN LOVED
Celeste Hawkins

Psalms is widely considered the most-loved book in the Bible. Its intensely personal passages picture our own struggles, defeats, and victories; its instruction includes numerous principles and practices for godly worship, service, and day-to-day living. *The LORD My Shepherd* captures these and many more pertinent subjects in a devotional topical format. It's for understanding and applying the Psalms in your own life and worship.

www.ingramcontent.com/pod-product-compliance
Lightning Source LLC
Chambersburg PA
CBHW062358090426
42740CB00010B/1320